Iraqi Kurdistan in Middle Eastern Politics

The changes brought by the Arab Spring and ensuing developments in the Middle East have made the Kurds an important force in the region. Tel-Aviv and Washington place high hopes on Erbil to facilitate their dealings with Baghdad, Damascus, Teheran and Ankara. Kurds living in Turkey, Syria and Iran have been inspired by the successes of their brethren in Iraq who managed to gain significant independence and make remarkable achievements in state building. The idea of a greater Kurdistan is in the air.

This book focuses on how the Kurds have become a new and significant force in Middle Eastern politics. International expert contributors conceptualize current developments putting them into theoretical perspective, helping us to better understand the potential role the Kurds could play in the Middle East.

Alex Danilovich lectures in Comparative Politics at the University of Kurdistan-Hawler in Iraq. He is the author of *Russian-Belarusian Integration: Playing Games Behind the Kremlin Walls* (Ashgate 2006), *Iraqi Federalism and the Kurds: Learning to Live Together* (Ashgate 2014) and is co-author of *Kazakhstan: Contemporary Politics* (EastBridge 2009).

'This book brings together the analyses of a group of scholars intimately familiar with the Kurdish issue, international relations, federalism and U.S. foreign policy towards the Kurds. Together they objectively pose a series of hard and extremely timely questions regarding the past, present and future of the Kurds in Iraq. Academics, policy makers and general readers alike will all find plenty of food for thought in this fine volume'.

Professor David Romano, Thomas G. Strong Chair in Middle East Politics, Missouri State University, USA, author of *The Kurdish Nationalist Movement* and co-editor of *Conflict, Democratization and the Kurds in the Middle East*

'This work provides a remarkable, if not unique, analysis of Iraqi Kurdistan. Despite all the problems it faces – some of them stemming from tribal traditions – this autonomous entity has become a significant force in Middle Eastern politics. A team of excellent specialists covers the overall spectrum of a region, which might become independent. An achievement which helps the understanding of a complex reality'.

Professor Gerard Chaliand, Nanyang University, Singapore and expert on non-conventional warfare

'This book is a must read for anyone who wishes to understand Iraqi Kurdistan, which has become a kind of microcosm for the turbulent Middle East. The contributors to the book shed light on the complex and controversial issue of Kurdistan's independence, analyzing it from different historical, geographical, economic and political perspectives. As such it should interest laymen, scholars and students of the history of the Middle East. Kurdish intellectuals and politicians who are engaged in drawing the future of this entity may also gain insight from the discussion in the different chapters which raise a lot of question marks regarding the understanding of the dynamics in Iraqi Kurdistan and has far reaching effects on the Kurds in a Greater Kurdistan as well'.

Professor Ofra Bengio, Tel Aviv University, Israel, author of *The Kurds of Iraq: Building a State within a State* and editor of *Kurdish Awakening: Nation Building in a Fragmented Homeland*

Iraqi Kurdistan in Middle Eastern Politics

Edited by Alex Danilovich

LONDON AND NEW YORK

First published 2017 by Routledge

2 Park Square, Milton Park, Abingdon, Oxfordshire OX14 4RN
711 Third Avenue, New York, NY 10017

Routledge is an imprint of the Taylor & Francis Group, an informa business

First issued in paperback 2018

Copyright © 2017 selection and editorial matter, Alex Danilovich; individual chapters, the contributors

The right of Alex Danilovich to be identified as the author of the editorial material, and of the authors for their individual chapters, has been asserted in accordance with sections 77 and 78 of the Copyright, Designs and Patents Act 1988.

All rights reserved. No part of this book may be reprinted or reproduced or utilised in any form or by any electronic, mechanical, or other means, now known or hereafter invented, including photocopying and recording, or in any information storage or retrieval system, without permission in writing from the publishers.

Notice:
Product or corporate names may be trademarks or registered trademarks, and are used only for identification and explanation without intent to infringe.

British Library Cataloguing in Publication Data
A catalogue record for this book is available from the British Library

Library of Congress Cataloguing in Publication Data
A catalog record for this book is available from the Library of Congress

ISBN: 978-1-138-20447-8 (hbk)
ISBN: 978-1-138-36143-0 (pbk)

Typeset in Times New Roman
by Out of House Publishing

Contents

List of figures ix
List of contributors x
Preface xi
List of abbreviations xiii

Introduction 1
New opportunities for the Kurds 2
Part I: Soul searching 4
Part II: Iraqi Kurdistan in Middle Eastern politics 5

PART I
Soul searching 9

1 Learning from history: Kurdish nationalism and state-building efforts 11
   ANWAR ANAID

   The historical background of Kurdish nationalism 11
   The onset of Kurdish nationalism 14
   The Kurds in Iraq 16
   Attempts at statehood and causes for failure 20
   The Kurdistan region in the context of the post-1991 regional and global changes 25
   Prospect for independence and the KRG's current socio-economic policies 28
   Conclusion 31

2　New horizons: Iraqi federalism　　　　　　　　　　　　　　35
　ALEX DANILOVICH

　　Federalism: A technological solution to human problems　36
　　Iraqi federalism: Constitutional design and reality　39
　　Conclusion　51

3　Rebels without a cause? A historicist analysis of Iraqi
　Kurdistan's current political and economic development
　and prospects for independence　　　　　　　　　　　　　　57
　NIGEL M. GREAVES

　　Kurdish nationalism and difference　59
　　Kurdish nationalism and Islam　61
　　Modernity and ideology　62
　　Kurdish political parties and political culture　64
　　Gorran and tradition　67
　　Governmental elitism　68
　　Economy and orientalism　69
　　Dubai-ification　71
　　Conclusion　73

4　Erecting buildings, erecting a state: public perception
　of Kurdish statehood　　　　　　　　　　　　　　　　　　　78
　UMUT KURUUZUM

　　Modern buildings in Erbil　79
　　Narratives of modern buildings　84
　　Conclusion　92

PART II
Iraqi Kurdistan in Middle Eastern politics　　　　　　　　　　　97

5　Oil, the Kurds, and the drive for independence: an ace
　in the hole or joker in the pack?　　　　　　　　　　　　　　99
　FRANCIS OWTRAM

　　Introduction: Oil, independence and the divisive
　　　lines of Sykes-Picot　99
　　Analytical aims, theoretical framework and structure
　　　of the chapter　100
　　Oil, the Kurds and the creation of the modern Middle East state
　　　system　104

*The Kurds and western intervention, 1991–2001: From no-fly zones
to regime change   107
From 9/11 to US withdrawal from Iraq   108
Iraq, the Kurds and oil resources since the Arab Spring   109
Conclusion   116*

6   Kurdistan's independence and the international system
    of sovereign states   120
    RYAN D. GRIFFITHS

   *The sovereignty club   121
   The evolving recognition regime   122
   Iraqi Kurdistan and independence   128
   Conclusion   131*

7   Turkey and the Iraqi Kurdistan Federal Region:
    Bonds of friendship   135
    SARA SALAHADDIN MUSTAFA AND SARDAR AZIZ

   *Literature on oligarchy capitalism   136
   Turkey-KRG relations: Origins and recent developments   138
   Turkey's new thinking   139
   The KRG, an active non-state actor   140
   The delicate context of the Turkey-KRG relationship   141
   KRG benefits of friendship with Turkey   141
   An asymmetric relationship   142
   An anonymous friendship: Introducing the main players   143
   Turkey eyes Iraqi Kurdistan   146
   The Turkey–KRG–Iran triangle   149
   Turkey and the idea of KRG independence   151
   Conclusion   152*

8   The Kurdish issue on the USA foreign policy agenda   158
    PAULA PINEDA

   *Introduction   158
   The US and the Kurds   159
   Analytical framework   160
   Instrumental motivations   163
   The dominance of instrumental considerations in past US Policy   163
   Affective motivations   165
   Current US protection of the Kurdistan region   167
   Perception of Kurds as integral to aims in Iraq   169
   Kurdish mobilization in Iraq and US policy   171*

viii *Contents*

Kurdish disappointment with US policy 173
Possibility of Iraq's disintegration 175
Conclusion 176

Conclusion 187

Index 192

Figures

4.1	The west side of Erbil	81
4.2	Downtown Erbil project by Emaar Properties in the west side of Erbil	82
4.3	New Park View residence compound	83
4.4	Billboards depicting the future life of a residential complex	88
4.5	Billboards depicting the future life of a residential complex	89
4.6	Refugees living at a hotel construction site near the Dream City	90
6.1	Kurdistan and Independence	130

Contributors

Editor

Alex Danilovich lectures in comparative politics at the University of Kurdistan-Hawler in Iraq. He is the author of *Russian-Belarusian integration: Playing games behind the Kremlin walls* (Ashgate 2006), *Iraqi federalism and the Kurds: Learning to live together* (Ashgate 2014) and is co-author of *Kazakhstan: Contemporary politics* (EastBridge 2009).

Contributors

Dr Anwar Anaid, PhD, University of Sydney

Dr Sardar Azeez, PhD, University College Cork and Sara Salahaddin Mustafa

Dr Nigel M. Greaves, PhD, University of Northampton

Dr Ryan D. Griffiths, PhD, Columbia University

Umut Kuruuzum, PhD Candidate in Anthropology, London School of Economics and Political Science

Dr Francis Owtram, PhD, London School of Economics

Dr Paula Pineda, PhD, Houston University

Preface

Daily news from the Middle East grows scarier by the day, unavoidably tied to terrorism, morbid executions aired on social networks, and masses of refugees fleeing the region. In response to this uproar, two international coalitions have been formed and have intervened militarily, further complicating the turbulent situation with their own geostrategic goals. Under the circumstances, it is impossible to discern reasonable patterns, find a way out or even make some sense of the situation. There is one mounting force in the region that acquires the potential to seriously influence military and political developments there and whose actions can be reasonably explained and interpreted. This force is the Kurds, the world's largest stateless nation divided among four countries; they see an opportunity in the deepening security and political bedlam. They hope to fix the historic injustice done to them during the dismantlement of the Ottoman Empire. By denying the Kurds their statehood at the time of Sykes-Picot, a massively destabilizing force was built into state structures and forcibly contained over a century in the Middle East.

The book focuses on this particular issue in an attempt to conceptualize the current developments and reflect on whether the mischief can be undone now, one hundred years later. Eight international scholars, with unparalleled knowledge of the region and fascinated by the ongoing events decided to put their heads together in an attempt to understand what may await the Kurds in the Middle East. We contemplated an ambitious scope and our initial title was *The Kurdish card in the Middle East*, but finally agreed to downplay our ambitions and focus mostly on the Southern Kurds, the Kurds of Iraq, who already have a sort of polity with governmental structures and a decades-long experience of taking care of their own destiny within the loose Iraqi federation. Each contributor looks into one significant aspect of Iraqi Kurdistan's domestic situation, action and plans. We did not try to achieve unanimity in our interpretations, but all were driven by a sincere desire to understand and explain things to an outside reader overwhelmed by the scope and intensity of changes in the Middle East.

All the contributors have close relations to the Kurds one way or another: several authors are ethnic Kurds, while others have worked in Kurdistan and have been moved by the Kurdish cause. All are scholars who sincerely wish the Kurdish people every success while seeking to improve understanding of the current developments. Each is convinced that the Kurdish question in the Middle East can be put off no longer and offers theory informed interpretations.

Alex Danilovich

Abbreviations

AKP	Justice and Development Party (Turkey)
Bbl	Barrels of oil
CHP	Republican People's Party (Turkey)
CPA	Coalition Provisional Authority
DAESH	Arabic Abbreviation for Isis
DGA	dynamic global advisors
EU	European Union
FPDM	foreign policy decision making
ICG	International Crisis Group
IDEA	Institute For Democracy and Electoral Assistance
IGC	Iraqi Governing Council
IKP	Iraqi Kurdistan Parliament
IOC	international oil companies
IS	Islamic State
ISCI	Islamic Supreme Council Of Iraq
ISG	Iraqi Study Group
ISIS	Islamic State of Iraq and Syria
ITF	Iraqi Turkmen Front
KDP	Kurdistan Democratic Party
KIG	Kurdish Islamic Group
KIU	Kurdistan Islamic Union
KNA	Kurdistan National Assembly
KR	Kurdistan region
KRG	Kurdistan Regional Government
KRI	Kurdistan region of Iraq
MHP	Nationalist Movement Party (Turkey)
MP	Motherland Party
NSA	Non-state actor
PKK	Kurdistan Workers Party
PUK	Patriotic Union of Kurdistan
RAF	Royal Air Force (British)
R2P	Responsibilitiy to protect

SDP	Socialist Democratic Party
TAL	Transitional administrative law
TNA	Transitional national assembly
Tcf	Trillion cubic feet
UN	United Nations
UNAMI	United Nations Assistance Mission for Iraq
YPJ	Kurdish Women's Protection Units
WMD	Weapons of mass distruction

Introduction

The serial democratic revolutions that have swept across the Middle East over the last few years have left a significantly changed political landscape. As luck would have it, they have niether established democracy, improved domestic governance, nor brought stability and optimism about the future of the region.

Kaddafi's orderly Libya is no more. The country's picturesque dictator, who understood his countrymen well and managed to take account of all tribal interests through a delicate balancing act, was killed in the most horrific way. The country has been plunged into a state of nature, a war of all against all.

Egypt, the most powerful regional country, elected the Muslim Brothers to power, but the popular choice did not prove sustainable for long; the democratically victorious Muslim Brothers were ousted by a military coup. The new government evinces signs of Egypt's return in force to regional politics.

Syria's civil war and the massive international support for regime change and democratization have ultimately added to the current upheaval. The radical opponents to Bashar Assad's government went further than expected and set their own agenda – the creation of a caliphate in the entire Middle East and beyond. The implementation of their plans has been significantly facilitated by the situation in Iraq, the country whose transition to democracy was assisted in 2003 by *Shock and Awe*.

Iraq's Shia numeric majority elected representatives of their sect to power in the most democratic way, putting an end to the domination of the Sunni minority under Saddam. The Shia democratic majority, led by Prime Minister al-Malaki, totally ignored Sunni interests and antagonized the Sunni Muslims who have become the powerbase of the Islamic radicals.[1] The Iraqi Sunni and Syrian rebels joined their efforts and established the Islamic State of Iraq and al-Sham (ISIS) that covers large swathes of the Iraqi and Syrian territories.

The emergence of the State of Iraq and the Levant in the Sunni areas of Syria and Iraq signifies, in a sense, the abolition of the artificially created borders during the partition of the Ottoman Empire, first under the Sykes-Picot agreement, then under the Treaties of Severs and Lausanne. The artificial nature of the resulting states of Syria and Iraq is particularly obvious when one looks at how the national border cuts into the area inhabited by Sunnis, making part of them Syrian, the other Iraqi. The Kurds were totally ignored by the Western powers after World War I and ended up living in four different countries.

The ISIS terrorists have been successful because they have, restored some form of justice and united the divided Sunnis in a caliphate. That is likely to entail a drastic reshuffle of the political geography of the region to the point that the name of Iraq might soon become a historical–cultural concept rather than a reality, as with Syria. These ongoing changes have made Kurds important players throughout the region. And that is just the beginning. Tel-Aviv and Washington have high hopes for Erbil in their dealings with Baghdad, Damascus, Teheran and Ankara. *Nolens volens*, Iran supports the Syrian Kurds in their fight against ISIS out of its geopolitical considerations, although an independent Kurdistan would constitute an obvious threat because of Iran's own substantial Kurdish population. Turkey has always opposed any Kurdish nationalist movements, be it at home or abroad. Now with the Syrian crisis, Turkey dreams of establishing a buffer zone in Northern Syria (Kurdish areas), allegedly to create a safe haven for Syrian refugees, but more probably to prevent the Syrian Kurds from forming an autonomy. The USA and NATO as a whole seemed to support the idea of a safe haven in Northern Syria, but the unexpected Russian military intervention in Syria has severely changed the dynamics of regional events and planning. The outcome of these new developments in the Middle East is hard to foresee. It is certain, though, that open global rivalry is only likely to compound the situation.

The Middle East today is characterized by several new features: (1) failed or failing states in Iraq, Syria, and also Libya and Yemen; (2) fragile states in Lebanon, Jordan; (3) the upsurge of terrorism all over the region; (4) sectarian tensions between Shiites and Sunnis; and (5) the emergence of new strong actors such as the Kurds in Iraq, Syria but also Turkey. Another noticeable feature in the new Middle East is the increasing role of external powers and their influence despite some unsubstantiated beliefs to the contrary.

New opportunities for the Kurds

The dismantlement of the Iraqi state after the invasion in 2003 can be compared to the demolition of one of the load-carrying beams of the contemporary Arab world. The imminent collapse of the Syrian state is likely to completely bring down the edifice barely holding onto Arab nationalism, which in turn is severely weakened by sectarianism. At the same time, current chaos offers opportunities to others. The Kurds constitute the largest stateless ethnic group in the world. Split between four sovereign countries, it has never managed to receive its own nation-state. The Kurds' belated but increasing desire to create a nation-state at any price is humanely understandable. Historically unrealized statehood makes them strive for the implementation of the highly normative concept of statehood, in which nation and state coincide. Today only Southern Kurds (Iraq) have a sort of polity within the loose Iraqi federation. The Kurdish region has all the attributes of statehood, such as a legislature, an executive with extended bureaucracy, a judiciary and even their own ethnic armed forces. The Southern Kurds are tempted to declare independence and become, they hope, a sovereign state.

The idea is so popular that the leadership of the Kurdish federal region often invokes it to boost political support. The most recent appeal was made in December 2015 by Masoud Barzani, the regional president. These appeals do not seem to be meant to effect independence in earnest, as the Kurdish leaders understand the magnitude of challenges this move would entail, but they garner some popular support when needed. Curious enough in this respect is an interview given by the late Evgeni Primakov, a former Russian Foreign Minister and a close friend of the Barzani family, to a Russian TV channel. He recounted his last meeting with Masoud Barzani and said that when asked about the seriousness of his intent to break away from Iraq, Barzani allegedly expressed some doubts about the realization of such plans. Today with the controversies surrounding Masoud Barzani's presidency, which put the legitimacy of his new term in office into question, his Kurdish Democratic Party may launch an independence campaign hoping to turn Masoud Barzani into the Gandhi of Kurdistan and the father of the Kurdish nation.

Obviously, Kurdish national aspirations have been caught in the geopolitics of the region. In the recent past, Iran often positioned itself as friends of the Kurds in an attempt to exert pressure on the government in Baghdad. Syria has used Kurdish nationalism against its regional rivals, notably supporting the PKK in its fight against Turkey. During the twentieth century 'the Kurds have been used repeatedly by the USA, Israel and Iran to destabilize the state of Iraq, then left to their fate once immediate strategic goals have been achieved' (Anderson and Stansfield 2009: 180). This situation has hardly changed.

Kurdistan hit the headlines during the 'no-fly zone' established in 1991. This provoked global sympathy for the plight of the Kurdish people and their cause. Now Kurds have come into the international spotlight again in relation to the cataclysm caused by ISIS in 2014, when terrorists came as close as 29 miles to the capital city of Erbil. The horrific theatrical executions carried out by ISIS and aired on world TV channels and social networks, as well as the military success of the KRG in the fight against ISIS terrorists, have brought the Kurdish cause back to prominence.

The Kurds living in Syria, Turkey and Iran have been inspired by the successes of Iraqi Kurdistan; the idea of a greater Kurdistan is in the air despite almost universal international disproval. Today only Israel openly encourages Iraqi Kurds to break away from the Iraqi federation. The secession of Kurdistan from Iraq will immediately affect Turkey, and to a lesser degree Iran, while the Syrian Kurds would also welcome the move and try to emulate the example at home given the weakness of the Syrian government.[2] In sum,

4 *Introduction*

the Kurds have emerged as a new and significant force in Middle Eastern politics. Regional media news headlines, like *Assad Plays the Kurdish Card* (Al Arabiya News), Iraqi Kurdistan – *Western Fifth Column in the Middle East* (CounterPunch), *Will Russia Play the Kurdish Card?* (Al-Monitor), and *The Kurds: Expendable Pawns in Middle Eastern Machinations* (The Kurdish Tribune), all point in the same direction.

This book focuses on this particular issue in an attempt to conceptualize the current developments and put things into theoretical perspective. All the contributors to this volume are scholars sincerely wishing the Kurdish people every success while seeking to improve the understanding of current developments. Each is convinced that the Kurdish question in the Middle East can be put off no longer and offer theory-informed interpretations.

The book is comprised of two parts: I. Soul searching and II. Iraqi Kurdistan in Middle Eastern politics.

Part I: Soul searching

Chapter 1, 'Learning from history: Kurdish nationalism and state-building efforts', is written by Dr Anwar Anaid, an international scholar of Kurdish descent. He sets out to explain the origins and nature of Kurdish nationalism and why attempts at statehood have failed in the past. Taking cues from theories of modern nation state emergence and adopting the modernist approach to nationalism, he argues that throughout history, the Kurds have missed several good opportunities in their nationalist project. The belated, slow and ineffective actions of Kurdish nationalizing elites, combined with adverse external circumstances, led to the failure of Kurdish statehood efforts in the twentieth century. In the author's view, the deep political changes that have been taking place in Iraq since the 1991 uprising, combined with the current structural makeover of the Middle East in the wake of the Arab Spring, have created favorable conditions for a new statehood project.

In Chapter 2, 'New horizons: Iraqi federalism', I introduce the main features of the Iraqi federal system. My main argument is that federalism provides the Kurds with a golden opportunity to realize their statehood dreams within a loose Iraqi federation without making a big splash in regional and international politics. For the first time in many generations, Kurds living in Iraq are pretty much in charge of their own destiny. It is obvious that sovereign nation-states seem solid constructions well tested by time, but federalism today has proved a very promising arrangement to address the world's many problems. It is based on the European principles of a statehood that protects minorities by decentralizing state administration. Iraqi federalism has already stopped the logic of zero-sum violence between Arabs and Kurds and has more potential.

Chapter 3, 'Rebels without a cause? A historicist analysis of Iraqi Kurdistan's political and economic development and prospects for independence', is written by Dr Nigel Greaves, a scholar who has spent many years in Kurdistan and who is unparalleled in his knowledge of the local realities which he conceptualizes and explains. He tackles the idea of Kurdish statehood guided by Gramsci's neo-Marxist insights. His main argument well reflected in the chapter's title, questions the rationality of Kurdish plans to acquire an ethnic state in the twenty-firstt century, as Kurdistan's politics is rooted in pre-modern traditional practices where they appear to remain today. Kurdish political parties do not seem to have any association with the socio-economic class drivers that have brought other nations to modernity. The main Kurdish political parties remain tied to a fundamental regional schism, which is rather feudal in origin. The deep regional division in Kurdistan is not mitigated by the cross-cutting cleavages that modernity has produced elsewhere. A tentative cross-party national consensus is not easy to achieve by an elite governing caste that has become somewhat detached from the largely passive mass of Kurdish society. The idea of an independent sovereign Kurdistan may help to find such a consensus, engage the people, and thereby attempt to legitimize the essentially pre-modern political system.

Chapter 4, 'Erecting buildings, erecting a state: Public perception of Kurdish statehood', by Umut Kuruuzum echoes the previous chapter and provides, in a sense, empirical support for the argument voiced by several contributors that the Kurds have no clear vision of the contours of their would-be state. This chapter results from an anthropological field study conducted in Erbil in 2015. The author takes the reader right to where the action unfolds, introduces his interlocutors and engages in casual conversations with ordinary citizens in the streets of Erbil. As a result, the reader has a sense of physical presence in the city. The author juxtaposes the construction boom in Erbil and the pervasive plans of building an independent Kurdish state through ordinary people's understanding and interpretation. The two topics appear quite intertwined. The author looks into the specific meanings attributed to various aspects of newly built luxurious high-rises and illustrates the insights they convey to ordinary people's perceptions about Kurdish statehood. Although the population sample in this study is restricted to urban areas, in fact the dwellers of the capital city of Erbil, the inferences made are interesting and cogent.

Part II: Iraqi Kurdistan in Middle Eastern politics

Chapter 5, 'Oil and the drive for independence: An ace in the hole or joker in the pack', is written by Dr Francis Owtram who has also spent many years in Kurdistan. The title of this chapter is self-explanatory. The wealth of energy resources makes the Kurds of Iraq think that they can easily achieve independence, build their state and live happily ever after. Abundant Kurdish oil reserves seem to make many heads spin. Indeed, oil has allowed the region to raise its international profile, strengthen security and military capabilities, and achieve relative material prosperity vis-à-vis the rest of Iraq. However, is this enough to create a viable state accepted by its neighbors and the international community in general? This chapter explores the role that oil resources have played in Iraqi Kurdistan's putative quest for state independence. The author sets two main analytical tasks: to answer the question as to whether the oil resources help or a hinder the achievement of state independence for the Kurds of Iraq. In other words, it analyzes the role that oil has played in the contemporary political trajectory of the Kurdistan Region of Iraq, blending firstly the conceptual and analytical framework offered by Harvey and Stansfield with Fred Halliday's analytical notion of post-colonial sequestration, on the role of changes in the international system facilitating or inhibiting the movement towards the recognized independence of ethnic groups.

Is the presence of abundant hydrocarbon resources in the Kurdistan Region of Iraq a help or a hindrance for the realization of aspirations for independence? Can we say that the possession of hydrocarbons is an 'ace in the hole' or 'a joker in the pack'[3]?

Chapter 6, 'Kurdistan and the international system of sovereign states', is written by Dr Ryan D. Griffiths of the University of Sydney. His main research question is under what conditions the international community grants a secessionist movement sovereign recognition. The author attempts to offer a systematic explanation of the dynamics of recognition over various historical periods and how they have varied regionally, projecting his reflections onto the case of Iraqi Kurdistan.

The author offers to theorize the set of sovereign states as a club – one whose membership has varied across time and space; he also discusses the manner in which admittance to the club has been managed through history and geography. Throughout this discussion, he shows how each configuration has balanced the competing demands of the sovereign and liberal traditions, and highlights the strengths and weaknesses of each international order. The author repeatedly draws on Iraqi Kurdistan as an example case, discussing how Kurdistan's statehood aspirations would have fared during each of these periods and how a Kurdish nation-state would have a hard time to achieve admission to the club of sovereign states historically. He finishes by considering the future of Kurdistan's bid for independence.

In Chapter 7, 'Turkey and the Iraqi Kurdistan Federal Region: Bonds of friendship', is written by Sara Salahaddin Mustafa and Dr Sardar Azeez who examine the striking change in the official Turkish position on Iraqi Kurdistan during the last decade. In 2003, Turkey's foreign minister stated that Turkey would intervene militarily to 'guarantee Iraq's territorial integrity' in order to prevent the Kurds from breaking away or achieving too much independence. Today, Turkey has established the most cordial bilateral relationship with Iraqi Kurdistan; this contrasts sharply with the way Turkey treats Kurds both at home and in Syria. President Erdogan has set a red line regarding the Kurds in Syria: 'We will never allow the establishment of [Kurdish] state in Syria's north and our south. We will continue our fight in this regard no matter what it costs.' Ankara is afraid that Kurdish trans-border solidarity could indeed increase the claim for autonomy in Syria and in particular in Turkey.

As for the Iraqi Kurds, Turkey seems to be the single most significant contributor to the very idea of Iraqi Kurdistan's independence by strengthening the region's economy. The Turks and Kurds in Iraq seem to have found some common ground, putting aside their ideological differences and traditional hard feelings. The authors claim that the oligarchic capitalist systems on both sides of the Turkey–Iraq border create fertile soil for this rather unnatural friendship when businessmen, politicians and their cronies are increasingly hijacking state institutions and policies.

Chapter 8, 'The Kurdish issue on the US foreign policy agenda', is our final contribution by Paula Pineda, a US-based scholar. The claim of some analysts that the American era in the Middle East has come to an end does not seem to sit well with reality. The U.S. is not only omnipresent in the Middle East, it pretty much controls the region. To keep and strengthen its domination, the U.S. needs loyal allies. The faithfulness of Turkey and the Saudis proves, at times, rather doubtful, their behavior quite capricious. The nature of the relationship between the USA and the Kurds of Iraq (Southern Kurds) is difficult to grasp and explain. On the one hand, thanks to the 2003 U.S. invasion of Iraq, the Kurdish *de facto* autonomy within Iraq was constitutionalized and consolidated through federal design and US support. The very survival of the currently broad Kurdish autonomy within the Iraqi federation depends on the US. We still remember the US emergency bombing of the advancing ISIS forces that prevented the fall of the Kurdistan capital city of Erbil late in summer 2014. Today the Kurds seem upset and disillusioned by the official US position on the idea of independence. Yet they remain cognizant, in their dreams of a nation-state at any price that they depend on US support, not only on the mountains. Paula Pineda thoroughly researches this issue in an attempt to explain the determinants of the 'inconsistent' US policy towards the Kurds.

Notes

1 ISIS now controls almost all of Iraq's Sunni territories ranging from the Syrian border to the outskirts of Baghdad.
2 Syria's Kurdish region of Rojava has been *de facto* autonomous in the country's north since 2013. The Kurds have this safe and stable autonomous region ... the cities are protected by the Kurdish security (Asayish) and the frontline by the People's Protection Units (YPG). Schools and markets run as if there is no war just a few miles down the road ('Syrian Kurds don't Need the Geneva Talks'. Rudaw, January 28).
3 In a card game, an ace in the hole is a card placed face down which, once turned over, will have the certain effect of winning the game. In contrast a 'joker in the pack' is a card which could lead to different unexpected and unpredictable outcomes.

Reference

Anderson, Liam and Gareth Stansfield. 2009. Kurds in Iraqi: The Struggle between Baghdad and Erbil. *Middle East Policy* 16 (1).

Part I
Soul searching

1 Learning from history

Kurdish nationalism and state-building efforts

Anwar Anaid

The first aim of this chapter is to provide a brief historical background to Kurdish nationalist movements that mainly emerged during the First World War and after the demise of the Ottoman Empire. The second is to provide a broad-based analysis of the causes behind the failure of post-Ottoman Kurdish nationalists to establish a nation state. The third aim is exploring the dynamic changes that occurred in the Iraqi Kurdistan region since the 1991 popular uprising and the potential for the establishment of an independent state in the region.

Informed by a modernist approach to nationalism and the emergence of modern nation states, I argue that the Kurds failed to adapt to the socio-political changes required for a successful implementation of a nationalist project in a timely manner. The belated, slow and ineffective nationalist movements, combined with several other factors, led to the failure of Kurdish statehood efforts early in the twentieth century and the ancient Kurdish *ethnie* was not transformed into a unified Kurdish nation.

The factors that are likely to influence the developmental trajectory of Kurdish nationalism in the early twenty-first century are assessed in this chapter. It is argued that the political changes which have happened since the 1991 uprising by the Kurds in Iraq are relatively integrated. This, combined with the post-Arab Spring structural changes in the Middle East, have created more favorable conditions for the establishment of an independent Kurdish state in the Kurdistan region.

The historical background of Kurdish nationalism

A relatively large volume of literature is now available on the Kurdish national movements. Scholars such as Wadie (1960), Edmonds (1971), McDowell (1997), and Van Bruinissen (1991) have focused on different aspects of Kurdish history and Kurdish nationalism. More recently, Gunter (2004 and 2005) and O'Leary (2002) have written extensively about the latest developments in Kurdistan. There is also a large volume of literature written by the Kurds in Kurdish and other languages on the subject.

From time immemorial, the Kurdish people have inhabited the land of Kurdistan[1] situated in the mainly mountainous regions that – as a unified entity – includes parts of Iraq, Turkey, Iran, Syria and the former Soviet Republic of Armenia. A record of the Kurds' '... interaction with Europeans appears in Xenophon's Anabasis when the Greek army retreating from Mesopotamia to the Black Sea had to cope with the depredations of people called the karduchoi'[2] (Ghasimlow 2007: 38–39). Toward the end of the tenth century:

> Shaddadids ... and the other two major Kurdish dynasties – the Marwanids and Rawwadids – collectively dominat[ed] much of the huge region between the Caucasus range and northern Mesopotamia and Persia.
> (Blaum 2006: 3–4)

Kurdistan was the battlefield of numerous wars between successive Persian Empires on one side and Greeks, Romans and Byzantines on the other. Consequently, parts of Kurdistan changed hands many times. In more recent history, the Battle of Chaldiran between the Ottoman and Safavid Empires in 1514 is often mentioned as an historical event that divided Kurdistan, a division that was formalized in a treaty between the two empires in 1639 (Hassanpur 1992: 53).

Early experience of self-rule

Looking at the history of Kurdistan through a viewpoint corrupted by modern prejudices and informed by the characteristics of modern nation-states has led to the popular but misleading argument that the Kurds have never had a state of their own. The Kurdish principalities that existed in the seventeenth to nineteenth centuries were largely 'autonomous' in running their affairs and only pledged loyalty to Ottoman or Safavid rulers based on the requirements of time and circumstance (see Dunn 1995: 75 and Fawcett 2001: 111). These Kurdish quasi-states were not ruled under the banner of a unified Kurdish entity that included all parts of Kurdistan, but they enjoyed relative freedom and independence. When these autonomous emirates' liberties were endangered, or when they saw an opportunity for expansion of their domain of influence, these Kurdish principalities would rise against Ottoman rule. In 1820, for example, the famous Emirate of Soran, under the rule of Mohammad Pasha (1763–1846) or *Pashai Kora* (the Blind King as he is known in Kurdish), challenged Sultan Mahmud and established a Kurdish quasi-state based in Rawanduz.[3] Mohammad Pasha gradually expanded his domain to include Mosul, Bahdinan and most of the Ottoman Kurdistan. According to Eppel (2008: 250):

> ... the Soran Emirate under Muhammad 'Kor' [4] became the strongest force in southern Kurdistan ... within the confines of the Ottoman

Empire, with the exception of the Bohtan emirate under the Emir Badr Khan, who had his own ambitions toward bolstering his status and expanding the territory under his rule.

The Ottoman centralization campaign

From the second half of the nineteenth century onwards, the situation changed as the Ottomans pursued centralization policies, in response to the weakening status of the empire relative to its European counterparts (Gunter and Yavuz 2005: 2). As part of a broader defensive modernization strategy, the Ottoman Empire gradually reduced the regional self-rule of the Kurdish emirates and 'the autonomous life of Kurdistan came to an end' (1995: 5).

The Ottoman centralization policies gradually weakened the empire's power base. On the one hand, the concentration of power antagonized the Kurds who 'jealously' protected their independence and liberties (Pasha 2001: 130).[5] On the other hand, the modernization process weakened the religious foundation of the empire which was fundamental to the legitimacy of the Ottoman rulers. The Ottoman reforms planted the seeds of a gradual internal disintegration of the empire and its ultimate collapse.

The declining Qajar dynasty in Iran also suffered from structural weaknesses. Simko Agha Shikak used the opportunity provided by both Qajar's feebleness and the chaos of the Great War. Simko managed to successfully reign in a large part of Kurdistan that crossed the boundaries of Iran and the Ottoman Empire.

Following the collapse of the Ottoman Empire, as enshrined in the Treaty of Sèvres (1920), the allies agreed to establish an independent Kurdish homeland. However, due to the changing geopolitics of the region, the subsequent Treaty of Lausanne (1923) ignored these promises, and Kurdish self-rule did not materialize. The situation worsened when the Kurdish territories of the Ottoman Empire were divided among the three emerging states of Turkey, Iraq and Syria. For the following decades, the last two countries remained under the influence of Britain and France, respectively.

The Kurds reacted to the imposition of artificial boundaries that divided Kurdistan along colonial lines of interest. Kurdish discontent with the new territorial arrangements manifested in numerous revolts. Sheikh Sa'id rose against the newly emerged Turkish state in 1925 and shook its foundation (see Olson 2006). Ghasimlow quotes Frooghi, the Iranian ambassador to Turkey at the time: 'the uprising was so important that it threatened the existence of Turkey as a state' (2007: 59).

The post-Ottoman socio-political changes were profound. The religious nature of Ottoman citizenship largely incorporated the Kurds into the empire. The Kurds and the Turks had a shared religion and faced the common threat of the Russian-Armenian cooperation. Such a religiously inspired alliance significantly delayed and lowered the intensity of a unified Kurdish demand for a nation state in the declining days of the Empire.

The Kurdish allegiance to the Ottoman rulers was a pragmatic strategy in an age of faith-based empires. The misfortune started when the Kurdish masses failed to grasp that the nature of global politics had radically shifted toward secular ethnonationalism. Centuries of shared historical experience was not enough to keep the otherwise diverse Ottoman ethnic groups together in a context when the formation of nation states with clear ethnic boundaries became a globally prevalent political ideology.

In the post-Ottoman period, the secular, ethnocentric and exclusive nationalist ideologies of the emerging states that incorporated Kurdistan (Turkey, Iraq and Syria) alienated the Kurds. Iran experienced similar changes after the collapse of the Qajar Dynasty, and the emergence of a nationalist state under Reza Shah Pahlavi. The often discriminative policies of the newly established states meant that the emergence of further Kurdish nationalist movements in the later years was inevitable.

The onset of Kurdish nationalism

Modernist theoreticians of nationalism, such as Benedict Anderson, Ernest Gellner, and Eric Hobsbawm, suggest that nationalism is a recent and modern development in human political history. In explaining the factors behind the emergence of nationalism and modern nation states, they often referred to modernization and the rise of capitalism as the underlying dynamics. The development and expansion of capitalist markets on a national scale needed nationalism as a supportive and complementary political ideology for the state to be able to mobilize the masses. In this phase of capitalist evolution, nationalism encouraged the standardization of all factors that helped in strengthening countrywide markets, including a wide-ranging legal system, a uniform state bureaucracy, and a national language. Nationalist ideologies also filled in the ideological vacuum created by the rise of secularism and weakening religious identities (see Anaid 2014).

Smith (2002: 7–16) agrees that 'nationalism' is a modern occurrence but he argues that 'nation' has an ancient core called *ethnie*, which includes:

> … a self-designated collective proper name, myths of origin, migration, and election, an ethno-history including memories of sages, heroes, and golden ages, one or more elements of shared culture, including perhaps a link with a particular ancestral terrain, and a measure of social solidarity among, at least, the elites.
>
> (2002: 25)

If we adapt a Smithian perspective on what constitutes an *ethnie*, a Kurdish *ethnie* had existed since time immemorial. The historical evidence suggests that the emergence of Kurdish national consciousness, at an elite level, dates backs several centuries. The classical Kurdish poet, Ahmad-e-Khani of Botan (1650–1706), undoubtedly demonstrates nationalistic aspirations (Edmonds

1971, Hassanpour 1992). For centuries, outsiders have referred to the Kurds as a nation. For example, the *Oxford English Dictionary* quotes from T. Roe (1899: 310) that 'in 1616 the [Mogul] King ... tooke occasion to take in by force a reuolted Nation to the East of Babilon. The People are Called Coords' (OED 2008). While in modern times, as Yavuz and Gunter argue '... the major difference between Turkish, Iranian, Iraqi ... and Kurdish nationalism is the presence of the state [in the case of non-Kurdish ethnic groups]' (2001: 33).

Most of the modern states emerged after the First World War and transformed Smith's *ethnies* into modern nations animated by the ideology of nationalism. These states worked on internal homogenization, including the standardization of language, bureaucracy, economy and other factors that are the foundation of a modern nation state. If we take language as an example, the presence of many regional dialects was/is common among other languages and is not unique to Kurdish. However, these linguistic differences are less visible in established national languages because of deliberate state policies that – among other things – had promoted a standard print language or what Anderson (2006) refers to as 'print capitalism.' According to Erikson:

> At the identity level, nationhood is a matter of belief. The nation ... is a product of nationalist ideology; it is not the other way around. A nation exists from the moment a handful of influential people decide that it should be so, and it starts, in most cases, as an urban elite phenomenon. In order to be an efficient political tool, it must nevertheless eventually achieve mass appeal.
>
> (1993)

While Kurdish nationalism flourished among the Kurdish elites at the beginning of the last century (for example, see Bedr Khan 2004), the nationalizing elite failed to establish a modern Kurdish state which could have supported the task of nation building, the main reason being the failure of Kurdish nationalism to achieve the necessary mass appeal that Erikson refers to above.

The disintegration of the Ottoman Empire and subsequent partition of Kurdistan denied the Kurds an historic opportunity to strengthen the binding principles of their nation through the systematic efforts of a Kurdish state. While the established nation states after the First World War such as Turkey and Iran, underwent a process of nation building and the modernization of their respective languages, these processes were often reversed in Kurdistan due to the deliberate anti-Kurdish policies of these states.

Different historical experiences and subjection to different socio-economic organizations imposed by the boundaries of the new states further increased the diversion from a unified nationalistic project.[6] It is surprising that despite systematic policies for the subversion and assimilation of their ethnic identity, the Kurdish people have been able to keep the core aspects of their national uniqueness intact.

The Kurds in Iraq

Following the establishment of the Iraqi state under the British imperial mandate, Arab forces that had supported British war efforts against the Ottomans were placed in charge of ruling the newly emerged Iraq. 'Emir Faysal ... – Sharif of Mecca – was made [the] King of Iraq by the British High Commissioner' in 1921 (Fatah 2006: 6). A major factor behind promoting Arab nationalism and the subsequent establishment of Arab states was the British and French imperial interests in using Arab patriotism against the Turkish-dominated Ottoman Empire. To undermine the Ottomans, British officers in Mesopotamia encouraged the Arab tribes to think in nationalist terms rather than use prevailing religious and tribal identities. British officers like T. E. Lawrence 'idealized Bedouin life' and fostered the idea of an Arab national identity as the strategy to weaken the Ottoman Turks and promote British interests in the Middle East (Martin 2003: 545).

Britain envisaged, though hesitantly, the creation of an autonomous Kurdish state in the predominantly Kurdish Ottoman province of Mosul in the early years of the occupation of Mesopotamia (in 1920s) and considered Sheikh Mahmud as its King (Eskandar 2000, Fatah 2006). However, in the following years it withdrew from its early position on supporting Kurdish self-rule, which was also mandated by the League of Nations. Instead, the United Kingdom limited the Kurdish rights to a vague form of local autonomy. The reasons for this change in British policies are disputed. Some of the British colonial officers at the time suggested that the Kurds were not ready for the task of nation building nor could they economically support any emerging Kurdish state (Eskandar 2001: 154). While to some extent it is true that Kurds were not ready for the radical changes that were occurring at the time, the economic argument is incorrect. On the contrary, the predominantly Kurdish *vilayet* of Mosul was attached to the Arab Ottoman provinces of Bagdad and Basra for its economic superiority. According to Eskandar (2001):

> Wilson[7] always represented, as a justification for his attempt to incorporate the Kurdish area into British-administered Mesopotamia ... the economic riches of Southern Kurdistan in comparison with Arab Mesopotamia ... [and] referred to the Kurdish region as having a considerable surplus in wheat production, lumber, fruits, tobacco and most importantly oil wealth.
>
> (2001: 154)

More convincing explanations lay in the changing geopolitics of the region and the shifting balance of power between the major players, caused by many factors including the rise of an assertive Turkey under Mustafa Kamal. The withdrawal of Russian forces after the October revolution, and the consequent power vacuum and radical shifts in Russian foreign policy, also played a significant role. Moreover, while Britain strongly promoted Arab nationalism to foster its geopolitical goals, it did not do so for Kurdish nationalism with the same vigor. This may have contributed to less mobilized and coherent Kurdish nationalist movements. The overall weakness of the Kurdish national consciousness did not help either.

Britain and the Iraqi kingdom did not change their approach to the Kurdish question after Iraq's formal independence from Britain in 1932. According to Rayburn:

> in the spring of 1931, as the formal handover of sovereignty to the Iraqis approached, the British 'roused themselves to pacify the Kurds for good. For over a month, the RAF [Royal British Air Force] bombed Kurdish villages, finally forcing the rebels to capitulate'. [The] 'new Anglo–Iraqi treaty that spelled out British rights in Iraq ... contained no language protecting Iraq's minorities'.
>
> (2006: 34–36)

The Allies' failure to facilitate the establishment of a Kurdish state led to many Kurdish revolts in the following decades. The Kurdish unrest was initially led by Sheikh Mahmud (Eskandar 2001, Fatah 2006) and continued mainly under the leadership of the famous Kurdish leader Mustafa Barzani. Barzani did not limit the Kurdish aspiration for statehood to Kurdistan-Iraq; with his Pehsmarga forces, he supported the establishment of the Kurdish Republic of Mehabad in Iran in 1946 (Sajadi 2005).

From the 1950s onward the Kurds saw the firm commitment of the major powers to the state system that had emerged following the two World Wars. As evident in the formal position of the Kurdistan Democratic Party in Iraq, the Kurdish demand was gradually reduced to the request for regional autonomy for Kurdistan and a democratic political system for Iraq.

The post-monarchy and the Kurdish question

The Iraqi state temporarily changed its policies toward the Kurds when General Abdul Karim Qasim came to power in a coup that overthrew the Iraqi monarchy in 1958. Qasim encouraged 'the participation of the Kurds in the new government until his power was consolidated' (O'Leary 2002: 9). During this period, the Kurdish nationalist leader, Mustafa Barzani, returned from the Soviet Union where he had been in exile since the collapse of the Mehabad Republic in 1946. A few years later, the Kurdish achievements under Qasim's rule followed the familiar historical pattern that characterizes Kurdish national movements in Iraq. Kurds were able to attain temporary concessions from the new and weak central Iraqi governments, but these concessions would be withdrawn as soon as they consolidated their power. Consequently – as far as the Kurds were concerned – Qasim, the hero who recognized some Kurdish rights in 1958

(Sajadi 2005: 345), became the villain in 1963 when he did not honor his early promises.[8]

The Ba'ath party that came into power subsequent to a series of military coups made similar promises, leading an agreement with the Kurds known as 'the Proclamation of March 11th 1970.' The agreement recognized Kurdish autonomy in Iraq, pending a solution to the territorial dispute over Kirkuk in a four-year period. Following a treaty between the Shah of Iran and Saddam Hussein in Algeria, Iran withdrew its tactical support for the Kurdish national movement; in return, Iraq 'traded ... total control over the Shatt al Arab waterway' to Iranians (Cowell 1988). These events led to the failure of yet another Kurdish nationalist revolt in 1975.

Mahmud Othman,[9] a prominent Kurdish politician and representative at the time, rightly identifies the lack of solid basis that underlies the Kurdish national movements. In a handwritten letter to General Mustafa Barzani penned on the March 8, 1975, Othman, who was in Tehran waiting to meet the Shah of Iran, writes:

> ... it is really sad, but it is the reality on the ground. It looks like the Algeria agreement is a great loss to our people ... indeed, none of us expected this,... if there were no political foundation and effective measures (*Iltezami malmoos*), sooner or later, such issues would arise.
> (Mustafa 2007: 434).[10]

Arabization and ethnic cleansing

As O'Leary writes, 'the ethnic cleansing and Arabization began when the Ba'ath party first came to power in 1963 [...] to reduce the predominantly Kurdish population in areas deemed of strategic economic and political importance to Iraq' (2002: 9). The Ba'athist had no sincere interest in a genuine settlement that could help in finding a lasting solution to Iraq's Kurdish question. In the following years the 'Ba'athist ideology [which] leaves little room for ethnic plurality' led to genocide (Rubin 2003: 4). After the end of the Iraq–Iran war, the Iraqi army destroyed almost all of Kurdistan's villages:

> 182,000 Kurdish civilians were taken away from their homes to disappear forever. In this period, the Iraqi Army routinely used chemical weapons against the Kurds. The best-known chemical attack occurred at Halabja in March 1988 [in which] ... at least 5,000 people died immediately ... and it is estimated that up to 12,000 people died during ... three years.
> (O'Leary 2002: 2)

After its humiliating defeat in the 1991 Gulf war, the Iraqi army turned against the Shias and the Kurds who had risen against Saddam Hussein. The massacres committed by the Iraqi army led to a mass exodus and the displacement of Kurds on an unprecedented scale. International public opinion, touched by the gravity of the situation, forced the allies to create a safe haven to protect the Kurds from the criminal policies of the Iraqi regime. A no-fly zone that was introduced in parts of Kurdistan-Iraq led to the creation of a de facto Kurdish entity. General elections were held in 1992 and the two main Kurdish political parties, the Kurdistan Democratic Party (KDP) and the Patriotic Union of Kurdistan (PUK), came to power. However, the Kurdish experiment with democracy was disrupted by infighting between these two parties in 1994. Competition for supremacy and limited revenues in the region, as well as the usual meddling of the regional countries in Kurdish affairs, were the primary reasons for the internal conflict. The infighting led to the establishment of two governments: one based in Hewler (Erbil) and administrated by the KDP, and the other based in Sulaymaniah and administrated by the PUK.

From 1998 onward, the rival parties gradually reconciled and formed a unity government in the Kurdistan region. The KDP and PUK formed a unified front in Iraqi national elections held after the 2003 Iraq war. The Kurdistan Regional Government (KRG) was formally recognized in the 2005 Iraqi constitution. Since then, the major parties have made several power-sharing arrangements, both in the Kurdistan region and the Iraqi Federal government.

From 2004 onward, Kurdistan witnessed rapid economic development, its democracy gradually improved, and a third political force – the *Gorran* movement (meaning 'change' in Kurdish) – emerged in the political landscape. The decade from 2004–2014 was arguably a golden age in the history of the Kurdistan region. Per capita income radically increased, in an unprecedented period of political stability.

With the emergence of ISIS forces in Syria and Iraq, which attacked the Kurdistan region in August 2014, everything came to a sudden halt and Kurdistan faced an existential threat. Parts of the Kurdistan region came under the control of *Daesh* (the Arabic name for ISIS). Ezidi Kurds were massacred; their women and children enslaved and sold on the ISIS markets. The Kurds became victims of one of the most brutal criminal forces that had emerged in modern human history.

In the following months, the Kurdish military force reorganized. Helped by Western countries, it recovered most of the territories from ISIS forces. In Kurdish Syria, Kobani, an unknown town of little significance, became the symbol for heroic Kurdish resistance. The Kurdish fighters are now considered one of the few viable forces that can effectively fight Daesh. *Peshmarga*, the traditional Kurdish name for Kurdistan's armed forces, has become an internationally recognized term.

Relations with Baghdad after 2003

After the 2003 Iraq war, Erbil and Baghdad gradually reconciled and their political and economic relationships significantly improved. KRG received its budget from the federal government of Iraq. Kurdish politicians held senior positions in Baghdad, including the Foreign Ministry, one of two Vice Prime Minister positions, and the largely ceremonial post of the Presidency. Despite gradual reintegration, the familiar historical pattern of Baghdad's tendency of dishonoring its earlier agreements re-emerged. The Arab-Iraq resorted to classical tactics; this time in the form of the Maliki government's bid for Shia domination of Iraq. The rules of Bagdad's game were the same: keeping the Kurdistan region dependent on the center, underplay its achievements and confine its autonomy – whether economic, military or political.

Consequently, in the period after 2011–12, the relationship between Erbil and Baghdad deteriorated considerably. The Kurdistan region accused Al Malki's government of moving toward authoritarianism. In the final years of his rule, Al Malki refused to send the Kurdish share of the Iraqi budget and ignored Kurdistan's warnings about the threat of ISIS. Mosul, the second-largest Iraqi city, fell into the hands of ISIS on June 10, 2014. This had dire consequences for the security of the Kurdistan region, which had to depend on its limited resources for self-defense. On one hand, the federal government had refused to arm and pay the Peshmarga forces in earlier years. On the other hand, ISIS captured a large amount of American heavy weapons from the Iraqi army, which had fled the city of Mosul without a fight. The captured weapons, combined with ISIS brutality and criminal war tactics, made them potent fighting forces.

After the ISIS attack on Kurdistan, some international support followed, but Baghdad continued its budget sanction while, ironically, sending salaries to the public employees working in territories under ISIS control. The federal government provided little or no assistance to Kurdistan's war effort.

After the 2014 national elections, a political marathon led to the appointment of Al-Abadi as Iraqi Prime Minister. The Kurdish politicians joined his cabinet but, for whatever reason, Al-Abadi is yet to fix the damage that his predecessor had done to Erbil-Bagdad relations, as most of the disputes have not yet been resolved.

At the time of writing this chapter, the KRG's relations with Bagdad are strained and the Kurdistan regional government is under multiple pressures, including the need to support and service more than 1,000 kilometers of battlefield with ISIS, the burden of around 1.5 to 2 million refugees, budget cuts, and the historically low price of oil – the KRG's main source of income.

Attempts at statehood and causes for failure

There are different arguments for the failure of Kurdish national liberation movements to establish an independent Kurdish state. In Fawcett's view 'the Kurds' lack of unity of purpose, leadership, and organization ... [as] ... key factors behind the failure of any Kurdish state to emerge' (2001: 118). This is also perhaps the most popular explanation given by ordinary Kurds of their failure to establish their own state. Dunn (1995: 72) sees 'many divisions – linguistic, religious, tribal and feudal – [within Kurdish society]' and that 'the tactics of the states with large Kurdish populations have prevented the Kurds from building a nation state of their own'. Elsewhere Gunter (2004) refers to a Kurdish 'tendency to infighting' which allows the 'neighboring states to use divide-and-rule tactics against them' (2004: 107). Ghasimlow (2007: 87) underlines the tribal character of the leadership and tribal mentality in general as the fundamental reasons; while Sajadi (2005: 700) points to the role that Islam and the simplicity of the Kurdish mentality has played in subjugating the Kurds to other dominant Muslim ethnic groups.

While it could be argued that a combination of all these factors played a role in the failure of Kurdish nationalist movements to achieve their goals, these arguments are only partially correct and are inadequate if taken in isolation. There are numerous independent Islamic states where religion has not become an obstacle to independence. An historical review suggests that many other nations have started from tribalism and engaged in infighting as well. The Kurds have also not been short of strong and committed leaders. But great leaders achieve great goals only when they have the right material to build with and under the right circumstances (to borrow a Machiavellian argument). Unfortunately, the pronounced Kurdish leaders of the twentieth century were unable to establish a Kurdish state, because they did not have ripe socio-political materials to work with, nor were the regional or global circumstances working in their favor.

Nationalist political ideology suggests that a comprehensive analysis of the causes behind the failure of Kurdish national liberation movements should focus on how well the Kurds were influenced by the waves of nationalism that shaped the regional and global politics of the time. Moreover, how well-timed, adequate and effective were the Kurdish masses' and leadership's response to the demands of their time and circumstances?

Based on such an approach, the pattern that emerges from the study of historical Kurdish national movements presents several characteristics.

The inability to capture contemporary socio-political dynamics

Broadly speaking, Kurdish society was caught unprepared for the changes that were reshaping the region at the age of nationalism and nation-state building. The lack of historical readiness for adopting nationalism on a grand scale led to a delayed and ineffective Kurdish response. The fact that the Kurdish masses failed to foresee that the emerging nationalist Turkish state would be ideologically incapable of incorporating the Kurdish nationalist aspiration points to the religiosity and simplicity of Kurdish society at the time. In fairness, it can be argued that Kurdish trust in the emerging Turkish state was informed by the historically dominant notion of religious brotherhood that characterized the Ottoman period. In a similar vein, and during the same period, the Russians and British used their common religion to influence the

Armenians and other Christian populations in the region. Russians supported Armenians in their fight against the Ottoman forces, while Britain had an Assyrian levy fighting on its behalf. But the predominance and continuation of a religious alliance with the Turks indicates that the Kurds failed to consider the structural changes that had occurred in the power base of the emerging Turkish state, which made it qualitatively different from that of the Ottoman Empire.

On the whole, the Kurds hoped for peaceful coexistence with their Turkish religious brothers, even after the collapse of the Ottoman Empire. The mostly religious background of Kurdish leadership is another factor that points to the secondary nature of the Kurdish nationalist sentiment at the time. The Kurdish nationalist elites were either religious or ineffective in neutralizing the impact of religion. This meant that these leaders had to attenuate their nationalist goals because of religion. Olson sees the use of religion 'as a strategy and tactics necessary for carrying out successful revolution' (1989: 1). This is what the Ottoman Turks did before the establishment of the modern Turkish state. They used religion as long as it was strategically useful against the invading 'Christian' armies, but abolished the Islamic Caliphate as soon as it was no longer needed.

While the Turkish national movement had effectively gone beyond the Ottoman Islamic identity and promoted a Turkish nationalist agenda, the Kurds, lagging behind in accommodating the ideological changes, appealed to religion while promoting a nationalist agenda. The religious background of the principal Kurdish leaders, versus the strongly secular Turkish and Iranian rulers at the time, suggests that Kurdish society was not prepared for the increasingly secular form of socio-political organization that nationalism required.

Consequently, the Kurdish nationalist movement failed to foresee and adjust to the consequences of nationalist politics for the Kurds in Turkey. They realized that only when the Turkish state had established itself well enough to defeat any threat that came from the Kurds. Ghasimlow quotes from an Englishman named Harold Nilsson, who says 'when we told the Kurds to establish a state, they did not try hard to get it. While all of a sudden they demanded 14 points in 1922. However, it was really too late' (2007: 82).

Underdevelopment and not seriously being affected by the process of secularism and modernization could well be among the main reasons for the failure of the Kurdish masses to adapt their Kurdish nationalism.

The inability to solidify opportunities and achievements

The Kurds often managed to capitalize on opportunities, but they were unable to solidify the foundation of their achievements and turn opportunities into concrete gains. When Abdul Karim Qasim came to power in 1958, he acknowledged some Kurdish national rights that were withdrawn in 1963. The Ba'athists gave several concessions to the Kurds including a limited self-rule in 1970 but withdrew them in 1975. The Kurdish inability to consolidate their achievements can be explained by the failure of Kurdistan's underlying social, economic and political structures to support and sustain their nationalist ambitions. In other words, the Kurdish leadership lacked the socio-economic infrastructure and a supportive international alliance system that could help them achieve their goals and deny their enemy the 'recovery time' or what Kissinger calls 'the most precious commodity' (1979: 63).

The current Kurdish autonomy in the Kurdistan region follows a similar pattern, as it was achieved by filling the power vacuum that occurred after 1991 and therefore was not built on a solid foundation. In a similar argument Stansfield writes:

> Within the parameters of external economic controls, political and military intervention and internal rivalry, the KDP and PUK [the two main ruling parties in the Kurdistan region], possibly by accident more than design, succeeded in heading an independent entity [Kurdistan-Iraq].
>
> (2003: 131)

In fact, in a striking resemblance, the Kurds have provided the Shia-dominated Iraqi state with considerable time to reassert its power, without finalizing central issues between Erbil and Bagdad. Examples of such issues include the disputed lands and the failure to implement Article 140 of Iraq's constitution to settle territorial disputes. While the 2005 constitution guaranteed many of the Kurdish rights in Iraq, these rights were delayed, disputed or denied altogether in the later years. During Prime Minister Al Maliki's government, many radical Shi'a and Sunni politicians hoped to reverse the Kurdish constitutional achievements and were publicly calling for a review of the constitution. Despite such historical similarities, there are differences between the short-lived Kurdish gains of the twentieth century and the Kurdistan region's achievements in the twenty-first century. These differences are addressed in detail in the next section.

Insufficient strategic weight

The weak strategic weight of the Kurds, relative to other regional actors and within the context of the strategic interests of the great powers, has played a significant role in the failure of Kurdish nationalist movements since the establishment of post-First World War states in the region. During the First World War, British interests briefly encouraged Kurdish nationalism and the establishment of a Kurdish state, perhaps as a buffer zone against the expansion of Russian influence in the region. The Soviet Union also showed some half-hearted interest in Kurdish affairs during the Mahabad Republic. But these attempts were hesitant and short-lived. It was more convenient for the leading powers at the time to deal with other more organized ethnic groups than to try unifying the Kurds to promote their agenda in the period after the Great War. When Kurdistan came under the control of non-Kurdish ethnic groups, it increased their international leverage at the expense of the Kurds. The slower nationalistic evolution of Kurdish society translated to a less-coherent and unified voice that failed to assert itself at the right time, something that haunted the Kurds for decades.

Apart from few instances where world powers showed an interest in the establishment of a Kurdish state, there is not much evidence for the strategic importance of such a state in the eyes of the main powers in the twentieth century. Interestingly, the regional states have sporadically provided support to the Kurds in their neighboring countries to promote their immediate strategic goals. Examples include Iranian support for the Kurdish revolt in Iraq in the early to mid-1970s and the Syrian support for Turkish and Iraqi Kurdish opposition groups.

Unfavorable regional balance of power

After the establishment of modern states in the post-First World War period, the creation of a Kurdish state does not seem to be in the interests of the balance of power in the region. Additionally, the global powers do not want to upset their traditional allies by supporting an independent Kurdish state.

Despite the advantages of a divided Iraq that would be at the mercy of bigger regional powers such as Turkey and Iran, these countries have so far resisted its disintegration as this is likely to lead to the emergence of a Kurdish state with all its perceived implications for their own Kurdish issues.

Furthermore, from the perspective of the global powers, manipulation of the Kurdish minorities was a winning card in their hand. These powers could use the Kurdish question when any of these states threaten their interests in the region by fostering Kurdish nationalist revolts. Iranian and American support for the Kurdish movements in the 1970s against an increasingly pro-Soviet Iraqi state constitutes a good example. Therefore, as Fuller argues about the established state system in the Middle East, post-First World War,

> ... If the Kurds are to achieve statehood anywhere, the region will then undergo a dramatic change in the borders and geopolitics of Iraq, Turkey, and Iran, thus transforming the traditional balance of power in the region.
>
> (1993: 119)

Ineffective international public relations

A factor that could break the unfriendly geopolitical setting of the Middle East toward the Kurds is the direct involvement and support of major world powers; they could influence their foreign policy by friendly and supportive Kurdish lobbies. An influential Kurdish lobby can put forward alternative policies that not only promote the interests of these powers but also the interests of the Kurds. Major realist theorists of international relations such as Mearsheimer and Waltz highlight the role of the Jewish lobby in influencing the policies of the United States in the Middle East (Griffiths and O'Callaghan 2007: 63). Despite the existence of large Kurdish diaspora communities in the western countries and North America, up to very recently they did not have significant influence on the foreign policies of their host countries. An examination and comparison of the socio-economic status of these two lobbies – Jewish and Kurdish – reveals the strong economic power and political influence of the Jewish lobby compared to the Kurdish capacity in similar areas.

The tyranny of geography

The other widely reported reason for the failure of Kurdish aspirations to statehood is the fact that Kurds are the victims of Kurdistan's geography: a mainly mountainous region that is land-locked and surrounded by hostile states. These countries see an emerging Kurdish state in Iraq as a direct threat to their territorial integrity. Lack of access to open seas also limits the capacity for world powers to support the Kurds. Even if there was a willingness among these powers to assist the Kurds, the delivery of such support is largely at the mercy of regional states who remain hostile to outsiders' support for an autonomous Kurdistan.

The hostility of regional powers and their capability for encircling Kurdistan is a significant factor that restrains the Kurdish aspiration for self-rule, not Kurdistan being landlocked in a strictly geographic sense. Countries such as Mongolia, Hungary, and many others do not have access to the sea, yet are functioning independent states. Being a land-locked region with a relatively smaller population, compounded by Kurdish internal disorganization at the beginning of the twentieth century, negatively affected the Kurdish chances for an independent nation state. Surrounded by larger competing ethnic groups, the Kurdish numerical inferiority in the context of a broader Middle East may have reduced their capacity for galvanizing international support. Such a structural weakness was particularly important, as the Kurds were unable to compensate for their numeric inferiority with a superior economy, diplomacy or other relevant factors that are normally considered in the analysis of a nation's power. The lack of unity – something the Kurds are famous for – did not help either.

The Kurdistan region in the context of the post-1991 regional and global changes

Bearing in mind that history can repeat itself, the following questions come to the fore: what are the contextualized similarities and differences between the post-1991 achievements of the Kurdistan region in Iraq and other short-lived

Kurdish accomplishments of the past? Why would the Kurdistan region's current experience with self-rule not fail again? After all, the current quasi-independent status of the Kurdistan region in Iraq follows the same historical pattern. The Kurdistan region came into being as the consequence of a power vacuum and the weakness of the Iraqi central government after the 1991 Gulf war, not as a result of solid political and historical achievements. Nevertheless, the Kurdistan region has been able to solidify its achievements to some extent in spite of the similarities. There are several structural and contextual differences that assist the Kurdistan region in avoiding the familiar rolling back of its achievements and working more firmly toward establishing an independent Kurdish state.

De facto independence

Unlike the previously short-lived Kurdish experiments with autonomy, a prolonged experience of de facto self-rule has strengthened Kurdish national unity. A pro-independence generation has gradually emerged; a generation that has not experienced any direct foreign rule will strongly resist any direct occupation.[11] The Kurdish national consciousness has also evolved and been strengthened by the battle against ISIS – a common cross-border enemy.

The post-2003 developments in Iraq and the current war against ISIS have taken the Kurdistan region's autonomy into a new stage. These developments are largely irreversible without enormous bloodshed; they make the repetition of the historical scenario by the Iraqi state impractical. However, this does not mean that Sunni Arabs and militias of various brands will not challenge the Kurdistan region, particularly in the disputed areas. In fact, the current sporadic clashes between Peshmarga forces and Shia militias in places such as Tuz Khurmato are an early sign of the potential for future conflicts in these areas.

Structural changes in Iraq's political system after 2003

The majority Shia rule in Iraq has created a fundamental shift in the socio-political power structure of post-2003 Iraq. The new Iraqi state is more representative of the real forces in Iraqi society compared with the dictatorship of Sunni minority or foreign-supported kings in previous decades. However, these changes have also divided the Arab-Iraq along sectarian lines and the rising Sunni–Shia animosity is unlikely to subside easily. So far, the overwhelming trend has been a Shia attempt to dominate Iraq as much as possible. This is and will continue to be challenged not only by the Kurds but also by the Sunni Arabs. Therefore, further polarization of Iraq's ethnic and religious communities is inevitable, and it is unlikely that Baghdad can control all of Iraq again. While the Arab-Iraq may be willing to use its classical tactics against the autonomous Kurdistan region, it has less capability to undermine it with the same vigor in the current circumstances.

Globalized context

Following the 1991 Gulf war, the Kurds were displaced on an unprecedented scale. The pressures from international public opinion, touched by the extent of the tragedy, encouraged the Allies to establish a no-fly-zone in parts of the Kurdistan region in Iraq. These developments introduced a new global factor with regional implications: the regional countries could no longer ignore the international community in the way they treated their Kurdish population. It is largely true that regional countries and non-state regional forces – as the recent ISIS massacre of the Yazidi Kurds suggests – are still capable of repeating acts of genocide against the Kurds. However, the post-1990s global sensitivity to the events in Kurdistan-Iraq means that the regional states may not be able to do so without expecting a reaction from the international community.

The events in 1991 forced the major foreign powers to reshuffle their policies in Iraq. This was influenced by the humanitarian crisis. This, as far as the Kurds are concerned, was historically unprecedented. Although humanitarian issues are another foreign-policy tool in the hands of states, in the case of the Kurds in Iraq, humanitarian concerns triggered the reorganizing of realistic policies along their lines of interest rather than against them. The unwritten international commitment to the security of the Kurdistan region was repeated in Kurdistan's fight against Daesh. An inspiring Kurdish resistance against ISIS, and the massacre and enslavement of Yazidi Kurds, have given more vigor to the possibility of an international reaction to Kurdish issues, particularly in Iraq.

In brief, the Kurdistan Regional Government operates in the context of an increasingly globalizing world, both politically and economically. Local events do not go unnoticed by the international community. This makes countries with a Kurdish minority more cautious about repeating their historical anti-Kurdish policies.

Greater Western military presence in the region

Following the 1991 and 2003 Iraq wars, western powers have a large military presence in the Middle East. Even though Americans withdrew their forces from Iraq in 2011, a significant force has been redeployed for assisting the Kurdistan region and the Arab-Iraq in their fight against ISIS. Americans showed their commitment to the security of Kurdistan when they helped the region with arms and air support after the ISIS attack in 2014. The American military presence in Kurdistan and its support for the region's war efforts has, to some extent, shaken the established anti-Kurdish pattern of regional geopolitics. Whether the Western presence in the Kurdistan region has permanently altered the previously hostile geopolitical setting largely depends on the long-term commitment by Western powers to the security of the Kurdistan region. In the current circumstances, at any rate, the presence of western forces in Kurdistan is a deterrent against any overwhelming and direct interference by the neighboring countries in the region.

Strong international presence

Since its establishment, the KRG has followed an effective para-diplomacy and it has rapidly increased its international presence. There has been a historically unprecedented level of diplomatic traffic to Erbil in the last few years, and many countries, including all the permanent members of the United Nation's Security Council, have opened their consulates in the Kurdistan region. The American vice-president visited the Kurdistan region on March 18, 2008. Many high-ranking politicians, including the Turkish Prime Minister and the President of France, have subsequently visited the region. KRG's diplomatic efforts have been particularly successful after the ISIS invasion in August 2014. Such level of international recognition does not have any historical precedence; it can gradually translate into broader regional and global support for the KRG's ambitions for independence.

Kurdistan's oil and EU energy security

The Kurdish failure to solidify their earlier gains for achieving national self-determination has not been due to lack of opportunities, but to their powerlessness to harden and transform short-term gains offered by these opportunities into solid long-term achievements. This has been mainly due to the lack of tangible economic and strategic policy tools that could enable the Kurdish leadership to strengthen the basis of their accomplishments.

KRG's success in developing Kurdistan's oil sector and exporting it to international markets has, for the first time in modern Kurdish history, provided the Kurds with tangible means for strengthening their relationship with their regional and international partners. Oil-consuming nations, in particular EU countries, see in the Kurdistan region an opportunity for diversifying the sources of their oil and natural gas import. This will give another alternative energy supply line to Europe, making Europeans less dependent on other suppliers, particularly Russia. The Turkish Government has also realized that it is much more beneficial to treat Kurdistan, a small but rich region, as a partner instead of a threat. Therefore the oil factor has, to some extent, altered the historical anti-Kurdish geopolitical settings of the region and made a Kurdish bid for self-determination more realistic.

Prospects for independence and the KRG's current socio-economic policies

This chapter has argued that a key failure of the Kurds in the twentieth century was their inability to accommodate the forces that were shaping their destiny. At the beginning of the twenty-first century, this is largely not the case. The current economic and political policies of the Kurdistan Regional Government are predominantly compatible with a global capitalist economy and democratic political system: two forces that are shaping the global economy and politics respectively. Economically, the Kurdistan region is following free market economic policies, the same economic model that has shaped the international political economy in the age of economic globalization. Kurdistan is working towards the regionalization and globalization of its economy and, despite its shortcomings, democracy is gradually consolidating in the region.

The Middle East has also witnessed structural changes in the post-Arab Spring period. A series of simultaneous revolutions in Arab countries have changed the political setting of the Middle East. The post-revolution political similarities of these countries either led to the popular election of Islamist parties (e.g. Mohammed Morsi's government in Egypt) or created chaos and disorder in which the radical Islamic groups flourished (e.g. in Libya). The uprisings in the Arab world were due to the realization of unresolved tension created by the suppression of people by authoritarian regimes in previous decades. This historical tension which lay at the heart of Islamic societies surfaced, and politicized. Extreme forms of religious fundamentalism, combined with criminal tendencies (as evident among ISIS members) has flourished in this period.

The spirit of the Ottoman and Safavid Empires has re-surfaced and Shia-Sunni rivalry, as evident in Iraq, Syria, and Yemen, has revitalized. The Arab countries are increasingly worried about Iran's growing influence in many Arab capitals such as Damascus and Bagdad. There are gradual shifts in the alliance systems in the Middle East. Besides the Turkish and Iranian historical rivalries and their imperial ambitions, a third alliance, mainly composed of Sunni Arab states, is reacting to Iran's influence in the Middle East. Saudi and its Arab allies' response to Iranian involvement in Syria and Yemen are the most obvious evidence.

The Islamic world has never undergone a serious religious reformation similar to that of Christianity in Western Europe, which could redefine the role of religion in society and politics. The lack of genuine reform has led to an inability of these societies to adapt to modernity, something that is manifesting itself in a violent backlash from religious fundamentalists. What is more troubling is that the Middle East is still in the beginning phase of the religious violence, and we are yet to see the full momentum of Shia–Sunni conflict. History tells us that the separation of church from the state, the secularization of politics in the West, was only achieved through enormous bloodshed. Now the Middle East is at war with itself, similar to the religious conflict that led to wars between Protestants and Catholics in sixteenth and seventeenth-century Europe. There is no reason to think that a genuine separation of Mosque from the state will be any less violent.

After ISIS took control of Mosul, Iraq's second-largest city, the Kurdistan region's president tentatively announced the region's bid for independence. If there was not widespread public international support for Kurdistan's aspiration for independence, perhaps what was more curious and interesting was the lack of the usual strong reaction to it. This in itself suggests that both the region and the world are becoming gradually more receptive to an independent Kurdistan.

The slow political evolution that prevented Kurdish nationalists from effectively capitalizing on favorable international and regional conditions in the previous century seems to be truly beneficial to the Kurdistan region in the present circumstances. When waves of radical nationalism took over Europe and the Middle East in the early twentieth century, the Kurds were caught unprepared, and the religious loyalties were still strongly influencing Kurd's political allegiance. The powerful nature of religious identities significantly contributed to the failure of Kurdish nationalist elites to mobilize masses on a nationalist platform that could lead to the establishment of a Kurdish state.

Ironically, now that waves of religious fundamentalism are engulfing the Middle East, Kurdish nationalism is becoming the predominant force for political loyalties in Kurdish-inhabited areas of the Middle East. There are several religious parties in the Kurdistan region with a significant powerbase, but they often promote their political agenda on a nationalist platform. So far, the Shia-Sunni divide has not penetrated the Kurdistan region and all religious sects are living together peacefully. In this respect, the region is providing a glimmer of hope to the international community and is bringing political legitimacy to the rulers of Kurdistan.

When religious fundamentalism and political instability has engulfed the Middle East, the Kurdistan region has proven a stable, reliable, and widely secular partner for the west in general and the United States in particular. The nationalist, yet tolerant and inclusive, Kurdish forces have so far been the only reliable forces in the fight against ISIS. This has brought them international recognition and some degree of support. It has also strengthened both the Kurdish national consciousness and Kurdish defensive capabilities.

Americans are likely to defend their core achievements in the Kurdistan region, even if they disagree with the shape and size of the Kurdistan that the Kurds hope to see. Furthermore, Iraq is divided beyond a returning point. Iraqi Sunnis are gradually realizing that they are now a minority in Iraq. The Sunni Arabs, while a majority in Syria, will not be able to rule the whole country as the Alawites and Kurds will not easily accept that.

The re-emergence of imperial ambition in Turkey and Iran and the Arab world's defensive strategies all suggest that the creation of an independent Kurdistan in one form or another is becoming a possibility, if not a necessary buffer zone with an historical responsibility to mediate between these rivals. The Kurds have also been able to solidify their nationalistic achievements through their oil wealth and its links to European energy security. Turkey is reaping the benefit of the Kurdistan's oil and markets and has little incentive to derail its achievements. In the years ahead, we will see whether Iran will accommodate an independent Kurdistan or will test the Kurdish aspiration for independence through their strong influence in Iraqi Shia militias. Whatever course of action the regional powers decide to take, it is only a matter of time before, as Hegel has famously argued about the nature of nationalism, Kurdish national consciousness will need to actualize through the establishment of an independent Kurdish state.

Conclusion

In this chapter, I have reflected on the causes for the failure of Kurdish nationalists to establish a Kurdish state and tentatively projected my findings on the future, taking into account the recent dynamic changes that have occurred in Iraqi Kurdistan and the Middle East. I argued that due to many factors, including a slow and ineffective Kurdish response to international events and the forces of nationalism that shaped their destiny, the Kurds were unable to establish a state in the last century. Such a state could have gradually re-shaped the Kurdish *ethnie* into the Kurdish nation, unify the language, and address all other aspects of nation-state building. While the Kurds have gradually adopted nationalism, it was not with the speed and efficiency that the historical chain of events required. This led to the failure of Kurdish nationalists to establish a Kurdish state in the early twentieth century.

However, the post-1991 Kurdish achievements in Iraq are marked by a prolonged period of self-rule, increased global sensitivities to developments in the Kurdistan region, structural changes in the Middle East and Iraq, and the presence of western forces in the region. All these factors suggest that Kurdish national accomplishments have been relatively consolidated, in comparison with the previous short-lived Kurdish nationalist achievements in Iraq.

In early twenty-first century Kurdistan, the slow evolution of national consciousness and a nationalist ideology are proving beneficial to the Kurds. In a time when the Middle East is engulfed in reactionary religious fundamentalism, the overwhelming politics in the Kurdistan region is nationalistic, pluralistic and tolerant. In sharp contrast, only fifty kilometers from Erbil, the capital city of the Kurdistan region, ISIS is practising a medieval form of warfare with unparalleled barbarism, including enslaving women and children, beheading, enacting primitive laws and destroying all evidence of past human civilization.

A combination of post Arab Spring geopolitical changes in the Middle East, the KRG's successful diplomatic efforts, the political and economic impact of Kurdistan's oil wealth both regionally and internationally, and the region's fight against ISIS on behalf of the civilized world all suggest that the Kurdistan region in Iraq is closer to full autonomy than any time before in its modern history.

Notes

1 Since the birth of the states of Iraq, Turkey, and Syria they have deliberately tried to distort the historical and geographical realities and avoid using this term. For example, in Iraq it was often referred to as *The North*, or Northern Iraq, rather than Kurdistan. The only exception is a part of Kurdistan in Iran that has historically been named Kurdistan.
2 The term 'Kurd' is spelled differently; different sources assign different meaning to it.
3 A city situated near Hawler (Erbil) in Kurdistan-Iraq.
4 *Kor* means blind in Kurdish.
5 General Sharif Pasha was the president of the Kurdish Delegation to the Peace Conference in Paris on March 22, 1919. In his speech in the Paris Peace Conference, he predicated the problems associated with foreign domination of Kurdistan with a remarkable insight. While declaring the Armenian claim to parts of Kurdistan as 'excessively imperialistic' he argued:

> if those districts where the Kurds are in a majority are to be included in the New Armenia, regardless of their warlike spirit and jealousy of independence, there cannot be the slightest doubt that a chronic state of disorder will reign in Armenia unless the Allies are prepared to occupy the country indefinitely with a strong army, and even then would be subject to all the attacks of guerrilla warfare (Pasha 2001: 130).

6 Fawcett (2001: 11) provides a similar argument.
7 Acting Civil Commissioner, in the Middle Eastern Department of the British Colonial Office 1920–23.
8 For example, in a press release by the KDP politburo on February 2, 1963, Qasim is depicted as a dictator who tries to eradicate the Kurdish nation through military force (Mustafa 2007: 404).
9 In an interview with the Kurdish section of the Voice of America (VOA), Mahmud Othman, then a member of the Iraqi federal parliament, warned against the possibility of the KRG facing a fate similar to what the Kurds faced in 1975 (Othman 2008).
10 Translated from Kurdish.
11 This is evident in the 2005 unofficial referendum on the future of Kurdistan that was conducted alongside the Iraqi general election in which the majority of Kurds voted for independence from Iraq.

References

Anaid, A. 2014. Globalist Nationalism: A Theoretical Approach to the Nature of Nationalism in the Modern Global Political Economy. *European Scientific Journal.* 16(10), 129–145.

Anderson, B. 2006. *Imagined Communities: Reflections on the origin and spread of nationalism.* London: Verso.

Akra'ee, M. S. 2007. 'کورد و دەوڵەتی سەربەخۆ' (in Kurdish: *The Kurds and an Independent State*). Dehuk: Dehuk Khani Publication, 172–173.

Bedr Khan, S. 2004. The Case of Kurdistan against Turkey. *International Journal of Kurdish Studies* 18(2), 42.

Blaum, P. A. 2006. Life in a Rough Neighbourhood: Byzantium, Islam and the Rawwadid Kurds. *International Journal of Kurdish Studies* 20(1–2), 3–4.

Brecher, F. W. 1989. Lawrence of Arabia as History. *Film & History: An Interdisciplinary Journal of Film and Television Studies* 19(4), 92–94.

Cowell, A. 1988. Turkey Offers Temporary Haven to Top Iraqi Kurd. *The New York Times.* 4 September [Online]. Available at: www.nytimes.com/1988/09/04/world/turkey-offers-temporary-haven-to-top-iraqi-kurd.html?scp=7&sq=Kurd&st=cse [Accessed: April 23, 2009].

Dunn, M. C. 1995. The Kurdish 'Question': Is There an Answer? A Historical Overview. *Middle East Policy* 4(1–2), 5 and 73–87.

Edmonds, C. J. 1971. Kurdish Nationalism. *Journal of Contemporary History* 6(1), 87–107.

Eppel, M. 2008. The Demise of the Kurdish Emirates: The Impact of Ottoman Reforms and International Relations on Kurdistan during the First Half of the Nineteenth Century. *Middle Eastern Studies* 44(2), 250.

Erikson, T. H., 1993. *Ethnicity & Nationalism: Anthropological Perspectives,* Chicago: Plato Press, 105.

Eskandar, S. 2000. Britain's Policy in Southern Kurdistan: The Formation and the Termination of the First Kurdish Government, 1918–1919. *British Journal of Middle Eastern Studies.* 27(2), 139–163.

Eskander, S. 2001. Southern Kurdistan under Britain's Mesopotamian Mandate: From Separation to Incorporation, 1920–23. *Middle Eastern Studies* 37(2), 153–180.

Fatah, R. 2006 April 12. The Kurdish Resistance to Southern Kurdistan annexing with Iraq. *Kurdish media* [Online] Available at: http:www.kurdmedia.com/articles.asp?=11980 [Accessed: July 1, 2006].

Fawcett, L. 2001. Down But Not Out? The Kurds in International Politics. *Review of International Studies* 27, 109–118.

Fuller, G. E. 1993. The Fate of the Kurds. *Foreign Affairs* 72(2), 108–122.

Ghasimlow, A. R. 2007. دروك و ناتسدروك (in Kurdish: *Kurdistan and Kurd*). Erbil: Rojhalat Publications, 38–87.

Griffiths, M. and O'Callanghan 2007. Realism. *An Introduction to International Relations.* R. Devtak, A. Burk and J. George. Cambridge: Cambridge University Press, 54–63.

Gunter, M. M. 2004. Why Kurdish Statehood is Unlikely. *Middle East Policy.* 11(1), 106–110.

Gunter, M. M. and M. H. Yavuz 2005. The Continuing Crisis in Iraqi Kurdistan. *Middle East Policy.* 12(1), 122–134.

Hassanpour, A. 1992. *Nationalism and Language in Kurdistan, 1918–1985.* San Francisco: Mellen Research University Press, P.53

Hurriyet. 2009. Iraqi president rules out possibility of independent Kurdish state. *Hurriyet* [Online]. Available at: www.peyamner.com/default.aspx?l=4&id=114969 [Accessed: March 30, 2009].

Kissenger, H. 1979. *White House Years.* New York: Weidenfeld and Nicolson and Michael Joseph, 63.

Martin, T. 2003. Bedouin Tribes and the Imperial Intelligence Services in Syria, Iraq and Transjordan in the 1920s. *Journal of Contemporary History*, 38(4), 539–561.

McDowall, D. 1997. *A Modern History of the Kurds.* London: IB Tauris.

Mustafa, S. K. 2007. دروك و مزيىسعةب (in Kurdish: *Ba'athism and the Kurds*). Sulaymaniyah: Sulaymaniyah Hamdi Publication, 434.

OED. 2008. Embassy to Court of Gt. Mogul T. Roe, 1899. *Oxford English Dictionary* [Online]. Available at: http://dictionary.oed.com.ezproxy1.library.usyd.edu.au/cgi/entry/50128282?single=1&query_type=word&queryword=Kurd&first=1&max_to_show=10 [Accessed: August 1, 2008].

O'Leary, C. A. 2002. The Kurds of Iraq: Recent History, Future Prospects. *Middle East Review of International Affairs* 6(4), 9–13.

Olson, R. 1989. *The Emergence of Kurdish Nationalism and the Sheikh Said Rebellion, 1880–1925*. Texas: Austin University of Texas Press.

Olson, R. 2006. Relations among Turkey, Iraq, Kurdistan-Iraq, the Wider Middle East, and Iran. *Mediterranean Quarterly* 17(4), 13–45.

Othman, M. 2008. دەكاتن حەفتاكانى ئازارى 11 ىەقماننايەقب قل ساب نامسوع دومحەم رۆتكد (in Kurdish: *Mahmud Othman talks about the Declaration of 11th of March*). Voice of America-Kurdish [Online]. Available at: www.voanews.com/kurdish/archive/2008-03/2008-03-12-voa3.cfm [Accessed: March 12, 2008].

Pasha, S. 2001. Memorandum on the Claims of the Kurd People. *International Journal of Kurdish Studies*, 15. 130–137.

Rayburn, J. 2006. The Last Exit from Iraq. *Foreign Affairs*, 85(2), 29–40.

Rubin, M. 2003. Are Kurds A Pariah Minority? *Social Research*, 70(1) 297–370.

Sajadi, A. 2005. شۆڕشەكانى كورد: كورد و كۆمارى عێراق (in Kurdish: *Kurdish Revolts: Kurds and the Republic of Iraq*). Tehran: Atlas Chap, 700.

Smith, A. 2002. When is a Nation? *Geopolitics* 7(2), 5–32.

Stansfield, G., R. V. 2003. The Kurdish Dilemma: The Golden Era Threatened. *Adelphi Papers*, 43 (354), 131–148.

Van Bruinissen, M. 1991. *Agha, Sheikh and Khan – The Social and Political Structure of Kurdistan*. London: Zed Books.

Wadie, J. 1960. The Kurdish Nationalist Movement: Its Origins and Development. *Political Science, International Law and Relations*. New York: Syracuse University, [PhD].

Yavuz, H. and M. M. Gunter 2001. The Kurdish Nation. *Current History*, 100 (642), 33–39.

2 New horizons
Iraqi federalism

Alex Danilovich

The historic injustice done to the Kurds after the collapse of the Ottoman Empire, the ensuing misfortunes and bad luck described in the previous chapter have been perpetuated in various forms in each of the four countries with a substantial Kurdish population. Turkey in its Kamalist efforts to build a strong unitary state denied the Kurds their national identity to the point that officially an ersatz appellation was used to refer to Kurds – 'mountainous Turks', and that despite the fact that the Kurdish language belongs to a distinctly different language family. Kurds constitute some 14 million or 18 per cent of the current Turkish population. Particularly bloody was the relationship between Turkish authorities and the Kurds in the 1920–30s, marked by several Kurdish rebellions.

Until recently, many Kurds in Syria were denied citizenship because they were considered non-native people who had come from Turkey fleeing the Kemalist crash on Kurdish uprisings early in the twentieth century. Thus, 20 per cent of the Kurdish inhabitants of the Al-Jazeera region were non-citizens. A harsh Arabization campaign, similar to that in Iraq, was conducted in Syria. There are about 2.2 to 2.5 million Kurds in Syria making up 10–15 per cent of the Syrian population. In 2014, Syrian Kurds declared three cantons parts of the autonomous Syrian Kurdistan. Under the pressure of the civil war, the government has made significant concessions in order to have the Kurds side with the government against ISIS forces and also against the opposition supported and encouraged by the international community.

The situation in Iran has not been any better. Four provinces within the country are inhabited by Kurds, representing 6–7 million people altogether, or 9–10 per cent of the Iranian population. There have been constant uprisings and infighting between Kurdish dynasties and tribes to keep their self-rule. In modern history, Reza Shah deported Kurdish chiefs and confiscated their lands. In 1945 in the Soviet-occupied zone, a Kurdish state was created in Iran: the Republic of Mahabad. With the withdrawal of the Soviet Army, the central Iranian government defeated the separatists. Nowadays many Kurdish activists, in particular members of the Party for a Free Life in Kurdistan (PJAK) have been executed or are on death row.

The relationship between Iraqi Kurds and Arabs had ranged from violent uprisings in the 1960s to administrative autonomy in the 1970s (promised by the Saddam Government, but never realized), a bitter standoff in the 1980s that culminated in the use of chemical weapons against Kurdish civilians, to a no-fly zone in 1991 and a loose federation since 2005. Iraqi Kurdistan acquired its *de facto* autonomy after the Gulf War in 1991, and was, in a sense, detached from the rest of the country by the establishment of a no-fly zone under UN Resolution 688. After the invasion of Iraq by the Coalition Forces in 2003, Iraq adopted a constitution that introduced a federal system designed to accommodate the Kurds, palliate the deep-rooted ethnic conflict and keep Iraq's territorial integrity.

Federalism: A technological solution to human problems

With the intensification of ethnic conflicts in multi-cultural societies over the last two decades, increased scholarly attention has been given to ways of managing these conflicts. New theories, approaches, and policy recommendations have been profusely advanced. Federalism occupies a place of choice in this booming literature as one that seems to offer a mechanism to deal with divided societies, appease ethnic violence and preserve international borders.

The explosion of federalist studies can be partially explained by the view that federalism has a well-pronounced applied character. Federalism, as a specific institutional arrangement, seems to be quite easy to use for the management of domestic conflicts. It appears that the best way to hold fragmented and crumbling countries together is to share power constitutionally and turn their threatened unitary polities into federations. Even established democracies, such as Great Britain and Spain, consider employing federalism to quell separatist moods. Federal design secures social unity and political stability in deeply divided societies by facilitating both unity and diversity and maintaining 'dual identities' within a single country (Habisso 2010).

The classical characteristics of federalism as described by Riker (1964: 11) remains valid today:

(1) Two levels of government that rule the same land and people.
(2) At least one area of action in which each level is autonomous.
(3) Certain guarantees of the autonomy of each government in its sphere.

Political authority at the regional level is often exercised through a regional legislature, a regional executive, and a regional judicial system. In other words, a federated unit possesses all attributes of a polity as organized society, one step short of full sovereignty.

Federalism is particularly appropriate in transitional societies, as it not only palliates ethnic conflicts, but also enhances the quality of democracy.

According to Brancati, if federalism in ethnically diverse countries functions properly, democracy becomes more stable (Brancati 2004: 13).

Federal accommodation vs unitary assimilative integration

There are two main approaches to dealing with minorities, nationalism and its associated problems: federal accommodation and unitary assimilation (McGarry et al. 2008; Choudhry 2008; Elazar 1984). Obviously, we use this dichotomy only for analytical purposes, as in real life, successful federations simultaneously resort to both. The process of federation building is meant to produce a reasonable degree of common identity, otherwise it makes no sense to create and keep a common state. That is taken to mean that integrationist steps are necessary to certain degree in federations in order to preserve the unity of a country.

As we have seen in the previous chapter, the Kurds have experienced integrative assimilation in all four countries with a Kurdish population. Southern Kurds (Iraq) have recently been offered federal accommodation under the sponsorship of the United States. The Iraqi Kurds, as do many other large ethnic groups in the Third World want more, they want to establish a nation-state following the classic logic well captured by William Safran: *independence – state building – nation building*, 'which was accepted almost as a political law of nature' (Safran 2000: 1). Unfortunately, this seemingly logical and simple sequence of political developments has not proved viable in most places.

The current Iraqi constitution in its federal design fully moderates and tempers ethno-politics. We can give credit to the new federal system for:

(1) ending the civil war, ethnic cleansing and genocide;
(2) truly protecting Kurdish national identity; and
(3) granting considerable political and economic autonomy.

To Elazar, federal accommodation is the most just resolution of ethno-political problems and legitimation of ethnic identities in order to attain 'local and world peace' (Elazar 1984: 3–5). He claims that federalism is likely to become the predominant societal organization in the future while the current nation-state model that implies assimilation becomes obsolete and must yield to federations (Elazar 1982). Only federal solutions can fix seemingly intransigent political problems arising from conflicting national, ethnic, linguistic, and racial claims (Moots 2009: 408).

Symmetrical and asymmetrical federalism

Multinational democracies (ethno-federations) are, most of the time, asymmetrical, which means that in order to hold multinational polities together, constitutions assign different cultural and linguistic competences to different federal units. Mono-ethnic or administrative federations are constitutionally symmetrical because all federal regions have same rights. Liam Anderson finds a serious problem in the Iraqi federal design – insufficient asymmetry in regard to the Kurdistan Region. A formal asymmetrical recognition of the Kurdistan Region in the Transitional Administrative Law was not incorporated into the 2005 Constitution. The rights enjoyed by the Kurdistan Region have now potentially been granted to all parts of Iraq, although this is so far theoretical because there is only one federal region in Iraq's federation (Anderson 2010: 154). In other words, all new would-be federal regions in Iraq will have the same type of autonomy and rights as Kurdistan.

The 'paradox of federalism'

The introduction of a federal system, ethno-federation in particular, has often unintended consequences, as it allows an ethnic group to create in embryo its own state, mobilize resources and thereby prepare for ultimate secession. This phenomenon is known in literature as 'paradox of federalism'. Iraq offers a graphic illustration of how this paradox plays out. The Kurds, who obtained significant autonomy in the new Iraqi federation, now have many of the governmental institutions of a sovereign state – a parliament, a cabinet, specialized departments, including foreign relations, defence and security, all of which would serve them well if the Kurdistan Region decided to break away. Furthermore, federalism has given the Kurdistan region a favorable environment for developing its economy and establishing linkages with governments and businesses worldwide.

Certainly, federalism is employed to avoid a country's break up, but it can also involve a potential risk, as 'federal arrangements can ultimately offer opportunities for ethnic nationalists to mobilize their resources' with a view to breaking away (Stepan 1999: 215). Federalism, warns Donald Horowitz, may be just 'a resting point' on the road to secession (Horowitz 1985: 602). The exact same institutions designed to hold the country together by assuaging secessionism, and removing the possibility of conflict, may actually backfire and work in the very opposite direction. These institutions may give incentives for mobilization in favor of separation, and also provide an infrastructure that can be used for secession. These institutions can transfer into independence, thereby lowering the costs of secession. Federalism, Anderson notes, 'might actually promote secessionism rather than avoid it' (Anderson 2010: 131). Many writers agree that federalism may quell domestic conflicts in the short term, but it will more likely contribute to separatism in the long term (Bunce and Watts 2005; Elazar 1984; Fabry 2008; Horowitz 1985).

Therefore, a key theoretical issue in the study of federalism, as pointed out by Filippov, Ordeshook and Shvetsova (2004) is 'whether it is possible to design federal institutions' that would enable secessionism constraints only (Anderson 2010: 126). How the paradox of federalism plays out in a particular country depends on many variables.

The importance of federal origins and institutional setup

The outcomes of federalism vary in accordance with its origins. At first glance, it may appear that Iraq is a 'holding together' federation, as Iraq has long existed as a unitary state and federalism was introduced to accommodate the Kurds. There is enough reason, however, to argue, in particular from the Kurdish perspective that Kurdistan came into the new Iraq from *de facto* independence under the no-fly zone. Therefore, the Iraqi federation may be also viewed as 'coming together,' as the Kurdistan Region had an independent existence and has consented to joining the new federal state (Anderson 2007: 168). The Iraqi constitution does not mention the right to secession; therefore, a unilateral secession of Kurdistan would be totally unconstitutional. The procedure of constitutional amendments affecting federal relations is intentionally made cumbersome and does not allow a federal unit alone to introduce such an amendment.

The nature of institutional design means that the propensity to secede will not only vary according to differences in the institutional setup, but the implementation will also vary over time as institutions – and their meanings – are transformed (Anderson 2010: 130). In Iraq there are ongoing negotiations over the actual functions federal institutions created post-2003 should carry out; while some of the institutions mandated by the constitution (e.g. the territorial chamber of the Iraqi parliament) have not even been established; some institutions in charge of managing federal relations (e.g. the Iraqi Supreme Court) have been keeping a low profile, eschewing matters related to federal relationships.

Iraqi federalism: Constitutional design and reality[1]

Iraq's federal constitution was adopted in the aftermath of a devastating war and regime change that worsened the country's severe disunity. The process of constitution-making was sponsored by the occupying power and was, at some point, rushed to meet the deadline set by the Coalition Provisional Authority. The Arab Sunnis, the former regime's powerbase, largely boycotted constitution-making and the referendum. Therefore, some claim that many constitutional provisions do not take account of the interests of the entire country.

The constitution and the 'federalism law'

The 2005 constitution proclaims Iraq an Islamic, democratic, federal and parliamentary republic, which represents a radical departure from the tradition of Iraqi statehood and political regimes during the Republic of Iraq (1968–2003): Iraq's political system was secular, unitary and presidential.

The current constitution can be amended via a rather simple procedure, except for the fundamental constitutional principles stated in Section

One: Islamic, democratic, federal and parliamentary – as well as Section Two: the Iraqi Bill of Rights. To protect federalism, the constitution reiterates in an additional provision, Article 126, that it cannot be amended 'if such amendments take away the powers of the regions.'

As mentioned earlier, the new Iraqi federal system has origins as much of holding-together as coming-together. The previous existence of Iraqi Kurdistan as an integral part of Iraq, the introduction of the no-fly zone in 1991, a direct military invasion and subsequent occupation in 2003 blurred the distinction between the two different sources of federalism. The Iraqi federation was conceived by domestic actors as a step to assuage the unforgiving rivalry between Kurds and Arabs, however it was imposed by external forces. The introduction of multilevel governance was meant to diffuse ethnic conflict in the first place and solve 'a high degree of ethno-religious complexity' (Visser 2006: 1).

Article 117 reflects well the coming-together origins of Iraqi federalism:

> First: This constitution, upon coming into forces, shall recognize the region of Kurdistan, along with its **existing authorities**, as a federal region (Emphasis added – A.D.).
>
> Second: This Constitution shall affirm new regions established in accordance with its provisions.

As of today, the Iraqi federal system is more of a federacy than a multi-unit federation, as there is only one federated region – Kurdistan. In other words, the federal Islamic Republic of Iraq consists of two parts: the main Iraq, made up of 15 administrative units called governorates, and the federal Kurdistan Region, made up of three governorates.

The constitution-makers took account of Iraqi Kurdistan's particular relationship with the rest of the country and consented to the creation of one federal region, but at the same time it made possible further federalization. In other words, the constitution has created a federacy, which implies asymmetrical federal relations, yet it allows for an extension of federalism to other regions with the same degree of autonomy, potentially making Iraq a symmetrical federation in which all federal units enjoy the same rights and have a similar relationship with the federal centre. Iraqi federalism was designed as symmetrical, but as of today with only one federal region in place, the federal relationship remains asymmetrical.

The procedure of forming new federal regions is outlined in the constitution and is rather straightforward: one or more governorates have the right to become a federal region. It takes '1/3 of the council members of each governorate intending to form a region' or 1/10 of the eligible voters in each of the governorates intending to form a federal region to make a request. Although the Iraqi constitution sets forth a simple procedure of further devolution of power, it states that the process should be governed by a special federal law to be enacted by the Iraqi legislature within six months after the parliament first convenes following the adoption of the constitution. In accordance with this provision, the Council of Representatives, the national legislature, enacted in 2006 the 'Federalism Law' which sets out in detail the rules and procedures for establishing new federal regions.

As the idea of federalism is contrary to the Iraqi tradition of a highly centralized state, the enactment of the Federalism Law was difficult and surrounded by controversy. First, it took place under occupation; second, its enactment was carried out amidst protests and boycotts. Many political parties had put up a virulent opposition to the very principle of federalism, fearing that the possibility of sectarian federalization would be unhelpful to the nascent process of national reconciliation. Lawmakers from the Iraqi Accord Front, Islamic Virtue Party and Sadrist Movement adamantly opposed the adoption of the law. They believed the Federalism Law would lead to an obstructive partitioning of their country. Some details of the adoption of the law are rather telling. The minimum threshold for the law to pass was 138 out of the 275 deputies who actually took part in the vote. By some accounts, undecided MPs were dragged into the hall where the voting took place while observers and journalists were not given access to the proceedings (Visser 2006). Therefore, in the opinion of many Iraqis, the Federalism Law is not fully legitimate.

Since the introduction of federalism in Iraq through the adoption of the 2005 Constitution and the enactment of the Federalism Law in 2006, the idea of further federalization has been caught up in Iraqi politics. The central government dominated by the Shi'a majority has been blackmailed by various groups who have threatened to proclaim new federal regions. Thus, in June 2011, the Sunni speaker of the Iraqi parliament said that the Sunni community might wish to seek the formation of a Sunni federal region in Salahaddin, Anbar, Nineveh and Diyala – the Sunni-dominated governorates in the center of the country.

Reflecting on further federalization of Iraq, some analysts believe that using the 'one-size-fits-all' formula of the 'Federalism Law' can indeed threaten the survival of the country. Hilterman et al. (2012) are convinced that this formula demonstrates 'intrinsic flaws' in Iraq's federal design. It would have been more reasonable to introduce an asymmetrical federalism that would treat the Kurdistan Region preferentially as opposed to other would-be federal units. Asymmetrical federalism would acknowledge the Kurdistan federal region's particular status and thereby would help to avoid tensions between Erbil and Baghdad. The asymmetrical model could also 'recognize the unique oil-contracting abilities of the KRG while also safeguarding Baghdad's fiscal and monetary powers as well as authority over oil contracting elsewhere' [in other would-be federal regions] (Hilterman et al. 2012).

The federal government

The Iraqi Constitution introduces a parliamentary republic, in which the federal legislative and representative branch is to comprise a Council of Representatives (lower chamber) and a Federal Council (upper, territorial chamber). The Council of Representatives shall consist of 'a number of members, at a ratio of one seat per 100,000 Iraqi persons representing the entire Iraq people' (Article 49), while the Federation Council shall 'include representatives from the regions and the governorates that are not organized in a region' (Article 65). Unlike the Council of Representatives that has been successfully functioning since 2005, the Federation Council exists only on paper.

The federal executive consists of the President – a significantly symbolic figure under parliamentary supremacy, elected by a qualified majority of the Council of Representatives – and the cabinet, formed by the majority block in the parliament. The term in office of both the president and the prime minister ends with the expiration of the Council of Representatives' mandate. Prior to the 2010 legislative elections, the Iraqi Presidency was assumed by a Presidency Council made up of three individuals: the president and two vice-presidents, each representing three main ethno-sectarian communities: Kurdish, Sunni and Shi'a. All members of the Presidency Council had veto power. In other words, any piece of legislation passed by the Council of Representatives had to be unanimously approved by the Presidency Council to be enacted.

Interestingly enough, Jalal Talabani, an Iraqi Kurdish politician served as president of Iraq when the Presidential Council was enacted in 2005. In accordance with Article 138 of the Constitution, the provisional Presidential Council had to be replaced by a presidency assumed by one individual following 'one successive term after this constitution comes into force.' In other words, after the reelection of Jalal Talabani in 2010, the president could sign bills passed by the parliament into law without the consent of his two vice-presidents. This also applies to the current Iraqi President, Fuad Masum, also an ethnic Kurd and a veteran of Kurdish politics.

The constitution accords an outstanding role to the new Iraqi judiciary, which is rather unusual given that Iraq is a parliamentary republic and thereby has what constitutional scholars call 'parliamentary supremacy.'[2] The federal judiciary is proclaimed independent and consists of the Higher Judicial Council, in charge of overseeing the federal court system and of managing its budget, as well as the Federal Supreme Court, the constitutional court of the country, made up of nine justices who are legal scholars and experts in Islamic jurisprudence. In spite of parliamentary supremacy, the constitution endows the Supreme Court with exceptional judicial review powers. The Supreme Court carries out all the usual duties of constitutional courts, oversees the constitutionality of laws and regulations in effect – in other words, judicial review after enactment.[3] It also regulates the relationships between the federal judiciary and the judicial institutions of the regions and governorates, as well as settling disputes that arise between the federal government and the governments of the regions and governorates, municipalities and local administrations. The Court is also expected to resolve matters that arise from the application of the federal laws, regulations, instructions, and procedures issued by the federal authority. Unlike the U.S., the Iraqi Supreme Court is not the highest appellate court. The Iraqi appellate court of the highest instance is the Federal Supreme Court of Cassation.

Given the strong review power of the Supreme Court, and the contradictory obligations under a constitution that proclaims both Islam and democracy the foundation for legislation, the composition of the Court is very important. The type of jurists that will evaluate, interpret, and apply constitutional principles will determine what Iraq is destined to become in the near future. So far, the seats have been divided among the sects, ethnicities and political parties – Shia, Sunni, Kurds and Turkmen – but 'Shia Islamic jurists dominate the institution' (Barzinji 2012).

The Kurdistan Regional Government and politics

The Iraqi Kurdistan Parliament was elected in the first regional legislative elections in 1992, long before the formation of the federal Iraq in 2005. It had enacted Law Number 1 in 1992, by which it established its own powers and size – 111 members. Under Article 8 of the Kurdistan Electoral Law, legislative elections must be held once every four years, the most recent being held in September 2014. Similar to the federal level, the Kurdistan Parliament is elected using proportional representation on a closed-party list. Based on election results, all parties are allotted the number of seats in the Parliament proportional to the number of votes cast for the party.

The KRG's powers are not delegated by Baghdad. Unlike governorates, the largest administrative units in Iraq, the Iraqi Kurdistan Region has its own law-making authority that passes legislative acts. It has a *de facto* presidential form of government, as determined by the actual relationship between the presidency and the legislature; unlike at the federal level, the Kurdistan president is elected directly by the people; the proposed, but never enacted, regional draft constitution suggests a parliamentary system for the Iraqi Kurdistan federal region.

In the absence of a written constitution, political processes in Kurdistan are governed by statutes and bylaws enacted by the regional legislature, as well as by the internal rules of the major political parties, as in a British-style constitution. The KRG Minister of Foreign Relations, Mustafa Bakir, explained in an interview that the Kurdish Parliament had enacted various statutes that regulate Kurdistan's politics and governance: a statute on the Presidency, a statute on the Parliament, and a statute on the Judiciary.

Politics within the Kurdistan Region seem less formally regulated than at national level: the Kurdistan Federal Region does not have an enacted constitution. In a sense, the current political system in Iraqi Kurdistan does not hold on strong governmental institutions, but rather on gentlemen's agreements, treaties between political parties, legislative acts, executive orders and cabinet edicts. In fact, the bulk of the framework within which politics unfolds in the Iraqi Kurdistan federal region was created by the 2006 PUK-KDP

Reunification Accord. This agreement was concluded early in 2006 in an effort to stop the interethnic hostilities between the Kurdistan Democratic Party and the Patriotic Union of Kurdistan that had ravaged the region for over a decade. It was also meant to concert Kurdistan's efforts 'in dealing with the central government' in Baghdad and to act as a united front at the national level (Ahmed 2012: 12). This accord ended open hostilities between the two main political forces, but largely reduced Kurdish politics, leaving out other smaller political groups. Now with the rising popularity of political groups, like Gorran, this dynamic has significantly changed. The constitutional draft explicitly states that Iraqi Kurdistan is a parliamentary system, while the real distribution of power and the way the president is elected directly by the people in a general election point to the fact that the current KRG is a presidential system. What is more, political parties put mid-level members (not top politicians) who do not have the power to make decisions on their electoral lists (Mufti 2015). That assumption is validated by the events caused by controversies surrounding the Kurdish presidency in 2015–16 – a symbolic presidency would not cause such an upheaval. Demonstrations that turned violent early in October 2015 were organized to protest the dire economic situation, but also to demand that the Kurdistan Democratic Party ask Masoud Barzani to step down as the president of the regional government (KRG).

The crisis started when Barzani's presidential mandate expired on August 20, 2015. The KRG Ministry of Justice (sic) extended it for two more years, even though the mandate stated that it could not be prolonged. This provoked an outcry in the second-largest parliamentary party, Gorran. Gorran's excellent performance in the Kurdistan legislative elections in 2014 meant that it had several ministers in the KRG cabinet and its representative was elected Speaker of the House. Massoud Barzani's presidential term had been extended for two more years, from 2013 to 2015 with no right for further extension, a deal agreed by the two most influential political forces at the time – the Barzani KDP and the Talibani PUK. Since then, however, the political landscape has changed. Gorran, (in Kurdish, the Party of Change), came second with 24 seats in the parliament, after the Kurdistan Democratic Party (38), surpassing the Patriotic Union of Kurdistan (18). Obviously, Gorran adamantly opposed the renewal of Barzani's term in office that was not even allowed under the previous arrangement between the KDP and PUK. The situation was compounded by a severe economic crisis caused by the drop in oil prices and strained relations with Baghdad. Gorran's political claims unfolded against the backdrop of economic demands from civil servants (teachers and doctors whose salaries had not been paid for several months), deadly clashes with Islamic State and the influx of refugees from the regions occupied by ISIS.

There were riots in Sulaimaniyah and neighboring villages, the stronghold of the PUK and now Gorran. One office of Barzanis's KDP was set ablaze. Altogether five people were reportedly killed and 200 wounded. The traditionally good relations between Sulaimaniyah and Teheran might have also played a role in the crisis. Nechirwan Barzani, the KRG Prime Minister sacked four Gorran cabinet members. Yusus Muhammed, the speaker of the parliament and Gorran's MP, was not allowed to come to Erbil to carry out his duties. Many considered that a *coup d'etat*, as the Speaker is the highest official in a parliamentary system.

Al Monitor accused the United States as being partially responsible for the escalation of the crisis:

> They are giving weapons to Kurdish parties. This could be one reason for the crisis. The party with heavier weapons could be a threat to others. Don't forget that until today, there hasn't been any state institution in Kurdistan. Everything was done by political parties. One party can instruct the police to prevent a minister from coming to his ministry. This is unprecedented. ... The US and Europe have to press political parties to refrain from threatening others and claiming the upper hand. The US should tell them clearly that it is giving those guns to Kurds to fight IS, not each other.
> (Iraqi Kurdistan's Brewing Crisis www.al-monitor.com/pulse/originals/2015/10/turkey-iraq-kurdistan-economic-political-crisis-kdp-goran.html#)

Power sharing and mechanisms of mediation

Federalism, in the words of Daniel Elazar, is not only about 'separate rules,' but also about 'shared rules' (Elazar 1987: 12, Riker 1964: 11). Shared political authority and cooperation between the federal center and regions are crucial for the unity and survival of a federal state. Two parts of the Iraqi federal constitution specify the respective jurisdictions of each level of government and areas where they share powers – Section Four: Powers of the Federal Government, and Section Five: Powers of the Regions. The exclusive authorities of the federal government are stated in Article 110. These are:

- Formulating foreign policy and diplomatic representation, negotiating, signing and ratifying international treaties and agreements;
- Formulating and executing national security policy, including establishing and managing armed forces;
- Fiscal and customs policy, currency and monetary policy, regulating of commercial policy across regions;
- Regulating issues of citizenship.

The management of oil and gas is also specified in Section Four: Powers of the Federal Government, but not as its exclusive powers. The wording of some provisions is imprecise and ambiguous. Thus, Article 111 reads: 'Oil and gas are owned by all the people of Iraq in all regions and governorates.' Article 112 requires both the central government and producing governorates and regions to establish a joint management of oil and gas, while both levels of government are also expected to 'formulate the necessary strategy that achieves the highest benefit to the Iraqi people ....'

As a result of the ambiguity of these constitutional provisions, Erbil and Baghdad significantly disagree over which level of government can sign contracts with oil companies and how the revenues shall be ultimately used. On August 6, 2007, the Kurdistan National Assembly, the Region's parliament, approved the Kurdistan Oil and Gas Law which was signed into force by President Barzani two days later. At the same time, the federal Hydrocarbon Law has never been passed mostly because of the Kurdistan Region's opposition. Some 50 oil and gas companies have been operating in the Kurdistan Region. KRG-published statistics show that under the terms of the production-sharing contract with the KRG, 'the payback [to foreign oil companies] is more lucrative in Kurdistan than in Iraq....'

(Erbil Governorate website: www.hawlergov.org/en/article.php?id=1361783458)

Article 114 spells out other competencies shared by federal and regional authorities, such as managing customs, running power plants and electric energy distribution, regulation of internal water resources and environment policy, public health and education. The constitution also proclaims that 'all powers not stipulated in the exclusive powers of the federal government belong to the authorities of the regions and governorates...' (Article 115).

The constitution endows formal institutions, like the Federation Council and the Federal Supreme Court, with strong powers that allow mediation of the federal relationship. It also mandates the establishment of several independent commissions, including a commission to guarantee 'the rights of the regions ... to ensure fair participation in managing ... various federal institutions, missions, fellowships, delegations and regional and international conferences. 'The commission shall include representatives of the regions and federal government' (Article 105). The draft constitution of the Kurdistan Region also requires that the KRG president coordinate relations 'between regional and federal authorities' (Rafaat 2012: 198).

There are also informal means that would normally allow fine-tuning and improving the federal relationship, such as an impressive Kurdish representation in the federal government, including a striking presence in the federal cabinet where ethnic Kurds hold important positions. The Iraqi presidency was assumed by Fuad Masum, a veteran of the Patriotic Union of Kurdistan, who succeeded his compatriot and party fellow Jalal Talabani; the former federal Minister of Foreign Affairs is Mr. Hoshyar Zebari. One of the highest-ranked Iraqi army generals, Babaker Shawkat B. Zebari, an ethnic Kurd, used to be the Chief of Staff of the Iraqi Joint Forces.

Protecting other minorities

Article 4 of the Iraqi constitution, the language article, establishes two official languages in the country – Arabic and Kurdish – but it also grants the 'right to Iraqis to educate their children in their mother tongue, such as Turkman, Syriac and Armenian... or in any other language in private educational institutions.' The constitution allows federal regions and governorates to adopt other languages as local official languages if the majority of its population decides to do so in a general referendum.[4]

To promote women's participation in politics and raise their role and status in society, the federal constitution sets out a gender quota in the national legislature at 25 per cent for women (Article 49); the Kurdistan Region's quota is set even higher, at 30 per cent. Currently, there are 34 women MPs in the Kurdistan parliament, which is exactly 30 per cent, or the gender quota requirement, as opposed to 39 in the previous parliament. Eleven seats in the regional parliament have been reserved for Assyrian, Armenian, and Turkman minorities, regardless of the electoral performance of their political parties.

The unfinished constitutional agenda

Several constitutional provisions have not been fully implemented in spite of Article 144 that reads: 'This Constitution shall come in force after the approval of the people thereon in a general referendum... .' The most important unimplemented provision relevant to federalism is that of Article 48, 'The federal legislative power shall consist of the Council of Representatives and the Federation Council,' and Article 65:

> A legislative council shall be established named the 'Federation Council,' to include representatives from the regions and the governorates that are not organized in a region.
> A law, enacted by a two-thirds majority of the members of the Council of Representatives, shall regulate the formation of the Federation Council, its membership conditions, its competencies, and all that is connected with it.

The Federation Council was meant, among other things, to represent regions and enhance their greater voice in the central government. Despite serious domestic and international efforts, in particular by the Iraqi Supreme Court, the United Nations Assistance Mission for Iraq (UNAMI), various conferences and roundtables, the Chamber of Representatives has been unable to shape relevant legislation. As of winter 2016, the federal chamber has not been established, leaving the federal relationship largely unmediated by a specialized entity, as mandated by the constitution. No wonder that the central government in Baghdad chooses to selectively apply certain constitutional requirements as does the KRG in Erbil. This situation can be illustrated with reference to the language provision of the constitution. Article 4 of the federal constitution makes Arabic and the Kurdish the two official languages of Iraq. Yet publication of the Official Gazette is in Arabic only, as are bank notes, passports and stamps. Even in Iraqi Kurdistan many official documents are still in Arabic only.

Out of security concerns, the KRG has introduced a registration procedure for Iraqi citizens visiting the Kurdistan Region, a visa-like residence permit. This practice is standard for foreigners, but is unconstitutional in its application to Iraqi citizens, as Article 24 and Article 44 of the federal constitution guarantee the freedom of movement, travel and residence within the country. This is done for obvious reasons – safeguarding security in the face of ISIS and other threats. Iraqi Kurdistan with a population of 5 million people is now coping with the influx of 1.4 million refugees from the regions invaded by ISIS in Iraq and Syria.

A big blow to Iraqi constitutionalism has been dealt by the non-implementation of Article 140, which mandates the resolution of the thorny issue of disputed territories, Kirkuk in particular.[5] The constitution requires the federal government to conduct a referendum in the disputed territories and implement its results by a specific date: December 31, 2007. However, in the aftermath of the parliamentary crisis followed by Iraq's general elections in 2010, the KRG and Baghdad signed an agreement called the Erbil Agreement. As part of this agreement, Kurdish officials promised to back Prime Minister Nuri Maliki to form a cabinet on the condition that he would implement Article 140. The non-execution of this high-profile constitutional provision keeps protracted tensions lingering and sends a negative message to all Iraqis that the constitution is not sacred and may be simply ignored.

An unexpected 'resolution' of this problem came as ISIS invaded the disputed territories while the Iraqi army fled its offensive in summer 2014. With ISIS targeting Yezidis, Christians and Kurds, the demographic in these areas was changing even more to the detriment of non-Arabs. In 2015, the Kurdish Peshmerga recaptured over 90 per cent of the disputed territories from ISIS. Some Kurds claim now that they are closer than ever to the resolution of the problem and to the implementation of Article 140 of the Iraqi Constitution. '… the Kurdish troops have no intention of leaving the area and we are here to stay' (Rudaw 2015). The Kurds argue that Article 140 has been more or less implemented on the ground and that was done well without civil war with Arabs. The remaining job, they continue, is to convince the federal center to accept this reality, something that can be done through political processes, without violence, they hope.

Several attempts to adopt a regional constitution and thereby institutionalized politics in the Kurdistan region have failed. It is fair to note that a constitutional draft was prepared and published in February 2006. It was approved by the parliament in June 2009 and was meant to be enacted in a regional referendum scheduled at the same time as Kurdistan's provincial legislative elections in July 2009. However, serious obstacles arose with the emergence of strong opposition party Gorran, which questioned the existing political framework in the region: the 2006 PUK-KDP Reunification

Accord. It favored a real parliamentary system, as opposed to the *de facto* presidential form of government, and demanded a full surrender of the two parties' security apparatuses to the Kurdistan regional government.

The issue of disputed territories constitutes another serious hindrance to the adoption of the regional constitution. The Kurds consider the disputed territories theirs, and therefore the Kurdish constitutional draft does not entirely square with the federal constitution in parts that relate to the disputed territories.

However, the absence of a written constitution can be convenient, as Kurdish political players are relieved of constitutional responsibilities when they make certain decisions. This circumstance also allows the KRG not to fear sanctions under Article 13 of the federal constitution:

> Any text in any regional constitutions or any other legal text that contradicts this Constitution shall be considered void.

Even though the Kurdistan Region has no enacted constitution, the existing draft reflects the mindset of the Kurdish elites, including their attitude to federalism. Article 7 of the Iraqi Kurdistan constitutional draft unambiguously binds the Kurdistan Region to the federal democratic Iraq:

> The people of Iraqi Kurdistan shall have the right to determine their own destiny, and they have chosen, out of their own free will, to make Iraqi Kurdistan as a federal region within Iraq....
> Draft Constitution of the Kurdistan Region of Iraq

There is only one precondition set forth in the draft: Iraq should remain a federal, democratic and parliamentary system.

The absence of the Kurdistan Region's own constitution for over a decade of existence within the federal Iraq can be also considered non-implementation of the federal constitution, whose Article 120 reads:

> Each region shall adopt a constitution of its own that defines the structure of powers of the region, its authorities, and the mechanisms for exercising such authorities, provided that it does not contradict this Constitution.

Fostering national identity

National sentiments in Iraq and its unified identity are rather weak, given the vivid memories of recent conflicts between Arabs and Kurds and between Sunni and Shi'a Arabs. These antagonisms have made it all but impossible for a sense of an all-Iraqi identity that all people in the country could eagerly espouse. Therefore, the possibility of a further federalization of Iraq along the ethno-sectarian fault-lines was meant to sooth identity conflicts. However, those who think that Iraq can be further federalized along sectarian lines may be mistaken. Strong regional identities do not coincide with sectarian divisions. Even for the Kurds, their regional identities quite often overshadow ethnic unity and solidarity. Internal regional tensions within Iraqi Kurdistan stand as proof of the existence of strong regional identities that may weaken any sense of Kurdish ethnic unity. The eastern and western parts of Iraqi Kurdistan are still divided and constitute a serious obstacle to otherwise growing Pan-Kurdish feelings. The recent bitter interethnic conflict among political parties is a reflection of a strong regional-tribal identity that can weaken the overall Kurdish ethnic unity.

However, much of the Kurdish national character has been shaped by Islam. The Kurdistan incorporation into Iraq since early in the twentieth century had been presented as Islamic unification, favoring a religious community over ethnic identity. The relationship between Islam and Kurdishness has been, however, rather complex. Aram Rafaat (2012) compiled impressive evidence in support of his argument that Islam in Kurdistan is different from mainstream Islam, including its Sunni branch to which most Kurds belong.

The Kurdish leaders who stake on the Kurdish sense of ethnic belonging consider Islam an obstacle to the fostering of Kurdish identity. In their logic, diminishing religiosity would enhance the sense of Kurdishness. Some already claim that religiosity in Kurds is weak, and 'the Kurdish vision of religion is more similar to that of Europeans than that of Arabs' (Rafaat 2012: 23). This particular relationship of the Kurds and Islam may be explained, according to Rafaat, by history and geography. The Kurdish-specific network of socialization in Islam, called Hajra, was in the past isolated from mainstream Islam due to the mountainous areas where the Kurds traditionally inhabited. For several centuries, Kurds lived in between the Ottoman and Persian empires, enjoying significant autonomy from both. As a result, the Kurdish principalities were more secular than their neighbors. Some call Kurdish Islam an 'un-Islamic form of Islam' (Acker 2004). Today this particular feature of the Kurdish identity manifests itself in the KRG's distant position with regard to sectarian tensions in the rest of Iraq, and in the absence of influential Islamic political parties in the region. KRG officials periodically meet with Kurdish religious leaders to urge clerics and mullahs to 'remain tolerant in face of new social changes' in Kurdistan (*Kurdish Globe*, March 3, 2012). Significantly, the KRG constitutional draft, while restating some features of the Iraqi political system, reads that Iraqi Kurdistan is a federal region of Iraq and is 'a democratic republic with a parliamentary political system,' but does not mention that it is Islamic, as the federal constitution does.

It will be rather difficult for all Iraqis to foster a common unifying identity that all will eagerly associate themselves with. But there is hope – all ethno-sectarian and regional communities in Iraq were able to come together to celebrate the triumph of the national Iraqi football team when it won the Asian championship 2007 by defeating the Saudis.

Conclusion

In this chapter we set about introducing the new Iraqi federal system to the reader. We contend that federalism well serves Iraq and has more potential in the future despite its obvious shortcomings caused by the non-implementation of relevant constitutional provisions, deep-rooted distrust, idyllic hopes for a sovereign Kurdish state and adverse developments in the Middle East.

Federalism is considered a technological solution to deeply rooted human problems. The introduction of a federal system in Iraq, and the creation of the Kurdish federal region more particularly was meant to solve the following problems:

(1) Stop the civil war between the Kurds and Arabs that at some point verged on ethnic cleansing and genocide.
(2) Protect and foster Kurdish identity.
(3) Give the Kurds significant political and economic autonomy.

That was meant to be done through a particular constitutional design and institutional setup. The Iraqi federal constitution provides the Kurds with extraordinary opportunities and only one precondition – the will to learn to live together.

Given many new and unexpected circumstances, some external to Iraq, such as the emergence of ISIS and other adverse regional developments, it is hard to accurately forecast which way the proverbial paradox of federalism will be playing out in Iraq.

We contend that the territorial devolution of power and polycentric governance in Iraq has brought peace between Kurds and Arabs; nascent federalism can be adjusted and fine-tuned through limited constitutional amendments, judicial interpretation, fiscal arrangements and intergovernmental collaboration. The Kurds may eventually learn to live together with their federal partners.

The Kurds decided on their own volition to join in a federal and pluralist Iraq in which they would maintain their considerable autonomy. A tremendous opportunity was presented to them when a new, democratic Iraq emerged from a foreign intervention. The Kurds wholeheartedly espoused the idea of federalism, promoted through their active participation in constitution-making and in the federal government.

Iraqi federalism is in its early days. Many constitutionally prescribed mechanisms and institutions are not fully in place, while some remnants and leftovers from the previous relations that the new constitution tacitly allowed, like the *Peshmarga*, Kurdish armed forces, Kurdistan's representatives abroad may be easily misinterpreted as deliberate attempts by the Kurdistan Region Government to resist or even obstruct the federal relationship. The heavy legacy of distrust and suspicion makes the learning process slow and painful.

As there are no corresponding institutions to watch over and mediate the federal relationship because the territorial/federal chamber of the national parliament intended for this very end has not been established, the only possible umpire of federal relations remains the Federal Supreme Court. It keeps a rather low profile however, and eschews cases associated with the relationship between Kurdistan and the rest of Iraq. One of the reasons why the Supreme Court has adopted this position is the fact that the constitution explicitly imposes contradictory obligations under Article 2.

The dismantlement of the established political system in Iraq and the introduction of bewildering changes have been accompanied by an acute struggle for power. The process is ongoing and engulfs all political forces; it goes along with tensions and violence, as ethnic and sectarian differences are easily caught in politics. The new Iraq is not an established polity; relationships, including the federal relationship, are evolving. Each actor involved attempts to carve out the largest possible niche in Iraqi politics that unfolds under a new set of rules introduced by the new constitution. One of the significant variables in sustaining Iraqi federalism is an impressive representation of ethnic Kurds in key positions in the federal government, from the Iraqi Presidency and the federal Ministries.

The disruption of the state system – the Sunni minority was replaced by the Shii'a majority at the helm of the system; Kurdish nationalism has been legalized and enhanced by federalism; all forces are having a hard time adjusting to the unknown rules and are trying to maximize their influence in the process, sometimes pushing their ambitions too far and creating serious problems for the new system. Iraqi federalism is an ongoing experiment whose outcomes are rather positive, but painstaking efforts and a purposeful fine-tuning are badly needed. A central theoretical question in the study of federalism whether it is possible to design institutions that are efficient in solving conflicts and stable over time, institutions that would eliminate the paradox of federalism is hard to answer in the Iraqi case.

Writing in 2016, we can say that major disputes between Erbil and Baghdad are being resolved by negotiation rather than by force, often after some tough negotiations and even brinkmanship. This has never been easy, as the actors also have to navigate the rocky environment of regional and international pressure and permanent security threats. The external threat emanating from ISIS and other terrorist groups and the current financial crisis caused by the dramatic drop in the price of oil may push Baghdad and Erbil closer together. The federal system remains unstable and shaky, but provides a viable alternative to breaking away into a region in turmoil.

Notes

1 The section that follows is a reworked and updated version of Introducing Iraq's Federal System published in Alex Danilovich 2014. *Iraqi Federalism and the Kurds: Learning to Live Together*. Farnham: Ashgate.
2 Under parliamentary supremacy, the relationship between the legislature and the judiciary can be described as 'principal-agent'. In such a system, judicial review of enacted legislation is impossible, while the Iraqi constitution grants judicial review power to the Supreme Court that can review legislation post-enactment.
3 This type of review means that courts can strike legislative acts enacted by the parliament as unconstitutional, thereby undermining parliamentary supremacy in the system. This type of strong review is characteristic of the U.S. constitutional system.
4 Based on the data provided by Mr. Nazar Hhana, the general director of Syriac Education in Kurdistan, there are 51 schools in which classes are taught in the Syriac language (including a course in Arabic, one in Kurdish and one in English). All the materials are same as those studied in public schools in Kurdish or Arabic. The books are translated and reviewed by special committees from the KRG Ministry of Education. These schools include primary, secondary and high schools of which 19 are in Erbil (mostly in Ainkawa) and 32 are in Duhok. They are all public and tuition-free. There are over a dozen Turkoman primary private schools in Erbil, including four high schools.
5 Kurds claim that as a result of the Arabization campaign in the 1960–1970s, the ethnic balance in many areas and localities in Northern Iraq had been tilted in favor of Arabs. The oil-rich Kirkuk region is said to be particularly affected by the Arabization campaign.

References

Anderson, K. G. 2007. Theorizing Federalism in Iraq. *Regional and Federal Studies*, 17(2):159–171, March.

Anderson, Lawrence. 2005. *Resolving the Paradox of Federalism in Iraq*. Paper presented at the 2005 Annual Meeting of the Mideast Political Science Association. April 2005, Chicago.

Anderson, Liam. 2010. Internationalizing Iraq's Constitutional Dilemma. In: Lowe, R. and Stansfield, G. (eds). *The Kurdish Policy Imperative*. London. Royal Institute for International Affairs.

Aziz, Mahir. 2011. *The Kurds of Iraq*. Tauris Academic Studies.

Brancati, D. 2004. Can federalism stabilize Iraq? *Washington Quarterly*, 27:2, 7–21. Available at: www.federalism.ch/files/documents/04spring_brancati.pdf [accessed June 9, 2012].

Bunce, Valerie and Stephen Watts. 2005. Managing Diversity and Sustaining Democracy: Ethnofederal versus Unitary States in the Postcommunist World. In: *Sustainable Peace: Power and Democracy after Civil Wars*. Edited by Philip G. Roeder and Donald Rothchild. New York: Cornell University Press, Sage House.

Burgess, Michael. 2006. *Comparative Federalism: Theory and Practice*. London: Routledge.

Cameron, David. 2009. The Paradox of Federalism: Some Practical Reflections. In: *Regional and Federal Studies*, 19: 2, 309–319.

Chatfield, Sara and Philip Rocco. 2014. Is Federalism a Political Safety Valve? Congressional Decision Making, 1960–2005. In: *Publius, the Journal of Federalism*. Vol 44, N 1, Winter 2014, 1–23.

Chodosh, Hiram. 2009. From zero-sum conflicts to federalism: Iraqis offer the international community a road forward. *The Daily Star* [Lebanon]. July 9, 2009. Available at: www.dailystar.com.lb/Law/Jul/09/From-zero-sum-conflicts-to-federalism-Iraqis-offer-the-international-community-a-road-forward.ashx#ixzz2AD8ZqOIc

Danilovich, Alex. 2014. Introducing Iraq's Federal System. In: *Iraqi Federalism and the Kurds. Learning to Live Together*. Farnham: Ashgate.

Danilovich, A. 2014. *Iraqi Federalism and the Kurds. Learning to Live Together*. Farnham: Ashgate.

Dent, Martin J. 2004. *Identity Politics: Filling the Gap between Federalism and Independence*. Farnham: Ashgate.

Elazar, Daniel. 1987. *Exploring Federalism*. Tuscaloosa: The University of Alabama Press.

Elazar, Daniel. 1984. Introduction. In: Elazar (ed). *Federalism and Political Integration*. Lanham, MD: University Press of America.

Elazar, Daniel (ed). 1982. *Governing Peoples and Territories*. Philadelphia: Institute for the Study of Human Issues.

Elkins, Zachary and John Sides. 2007. Can Institutions Build Unity in Multiethnic States? In: *American Political Science Review*. Vol. 101, No. 4.

Erk, Jan and Anderson, Lawrence. (eds). 2009. *The Paradox of Federalism: Does Self-Rule Accommodate or Exacerbate Ethnic Divisions?* In: *Regional and Federal Studies*. Vol. 19, No 2, 191–202.

Erk, Jan and Swenden, Wilfried. (eds). 2010. *New Directions in Federalism Studies*. London: Routledge.

Fabry, M. 2008. Secession and State Recognition in International Relations and Law. In: *On the Way to Statehood: Secession and Globalization*. Edited by A. Pavkovic and P. Radan. Farnham: Ashgate, 51–66.

Feeley, Malcolm M., and Edward Rubin. 2008. *Federalism: Political Identity and Tragic Compromise*. Michigan: The University of Michigan Press, 2008.

Funk, A. 2012. *Asymmetrical Federalism: A Stabilizing or Destabilizing Factor in the multinational Federations? A Comparative Study of Asymmetrical Federalism in Canada and Spain*. Available at: www.ie-ei.eu/bibliotheque/memoires2010/Funk.pdf.

Gunter, Michael. 2010. Prospects for the Kurdish Future in Iraq and Turkey. In R. Lowe and G. Stansfield, *The Kurdish Policy Imperative*. London. Royal Institute for International Affairs.

Habisso, Tesfaye. 2010. *Multiethnic (Multinational) Federalism in Plural Societies: Does It Make a Difference?* Available at: www.tigraionline.com/articles/article11002.html

Haddad, Fanar, and Sajjad Rizvi. 2008. 'Fitting Baghdad.' In: R. Visser and G. Stansfield, *An Iraq of Its Regions: Cornerstones of a Federal Democracy?* New York: Colombia University Press, 51–74.

Halberstam, Daniel. 2008. Comparative Federalism and the Role of the Judiciary. In: K. Whittington, D. Keleman and G. Caldeira, *The Oxford Handbook of Law and Politics*. Oxford: Oxford University Press, 142–64.

Hiltermann, Joost, Sean Kane and Raad Alkadiri. 2012. Iraq's Federalism Quandary. In: *The National Interest* 28 February 2012.

Horowitz, Donald. 1985. *Ethnic Groups in Conflict*. Berkeley, CA: University of California Press.

Iraqi Government Profile 2013. Available at: www.indexmundi.com/iraq/government_profile.html

Majeed, Akhtar. Watts, Ronald L. and Brown, Douglas M. 2006. (eds). *Distribution of Powers and Responsibilities in Federal Countries*. Montreal and Kingston: McGill-Queen's University Press.

Mathew, George. 2006. Republic of India. In: Majeed, Akhtar. Watts, Ronald L. and Brown, Douglas M. (eds). *Distribution of Powers and Responsibilities in Federal Countries*. Montreal and Kingston: McGill-Queen's University Press.

McGarry, John, Brendan O'Leary and Tichard Simeon. 2008. Integration or Accommodation? The Enduring Debate in Conflict Regulation. In: Choudhry, Sujit (Ed), *Constitutional Design for Divided Societies: Integration or Accommodation?* New York: Oxford University Press.

McGarry, John, Brendan O'Leary. 2007. Iraqi Constitution of 2005: Liberal Consociation as Political Prescription. *International Journal of Constitutional Law*. Volume 5, Issue 4. pp. 670–698.

McGarry, John and Brendan O'Leary. 2005. Federalism as a Method of Ethnic Conflict Regulation. In: Sid Noel (Ed), *From Power Sharing to Democracy: Post-Conflict Institutions in Ethnically Divided Societies*. Montreal and Kingston: McGill-Queen's University Press.

McGinnis, John and Ilya Somin. 2004. Federalism vs. States' Rights: A Defense of Judicial Review in a Federal System, Northwestern University School of Law. *Public Law and Legal Theory Papers*. Year 2004 Paper 9.

Moots, Glenn A. 2009. The Covenant Tradition of Federalism: The Pioneering Studies of Daniel J. Elazar. In: A. Ward and L. Ward, *The Ashgate Research Companion to Federalism*. Farnham: Ashgate.

Keating, Michael. 2002. *Plurinational Democracy: Stateless Nations in a Post-Sovereignty Era*. Oxford: Oxford University Press.

Kelly, Michael J. 2010. The Kurdish Regional Constitution within the Framework of the Iraqi Federal Constitution: A Struggle for Sovereignty, Oil, Ethnic Identity, and the Prospects for a Reverse Supremacy Clause. In: *Penn State Law Review*, V. 114: 3.

Lawrence, Quil. 2008. *Invisible Nation: How the Kurds' Quest for Statehood Is Shaping Iraq and the Middle East*. New York: Walker & Company.

al-Mufti, Torhan 2015. A Turkoman politician interviewed by *al-Monitor* newspaper in December 2015. Available at: www.al-monitor.com/pulse/originals/2015/12/iraq-kurdistan-turkmen-minister-new-provinces.html.

Rafaat, Aram. 2012. *The Kurds in Post-Invasion Iraq*. LAP Lambert Academic Publishing.

Riker, William H. 1964. *Federalism: Origin, Operation, Significance*. Boston and Toronto: Little, Brown and Company.

Ryan, Erin. 2012. *Federalism and the Tug of War Within*. Oxford: Oxford University Press.

Safran, William. 2000. Introduction. In: William Safran and Ramon Maiz (eds), *Identity and Territorial Autonomy in Plural Societies*. London, Portland, OR: Frank Cass.

Stephan, Alfred. Federalism and Democracy: Beyond the US Model. In *The Global Divergence of Democracies*, by Larry Diamond and Marc F. Plattner, 215–230. Baltimore: The Johns Hopkins University Press,

Visser, Reidar. 2006. Iraqi Federalism Bill Adopted Amid Protest and Joint Shiite-Sunni Boycott (12 October 2006). Available at: www.historiae.org/devolution.asp

Watts, Ronald L. 2008. *Comparing Federal Systems*. 3rd edition. Montreal and Kingston: McGill – Queen's University Press.

Williams, Paul R. and Matthew T. Simpson. 2008. *Rethinking the Political Future: An Alternative to the Ethno-Sectarian Division of Iraq*. Available at: www.wcl.american.edujournalilr24…williams-simpson.pat

3 Rebels without a cause?

A historicist analysis of Iraqi Kurdistan's current political and economic development and prospects for independence

Nigel M. Greaves

A great many excellent books and articles have emerged in recent years providing a welter of empirical detail on the Iraqi Kurdish question (i.e. McDowall 2004, Aziz 2011, Stansfield 2003, 2005, 2007, Natali 2005, 2010, Danilovich 2014, to name but a few). Noticeable for its absence from the literature is, however, an attempt to assemble and rationalise recent economic and political trends according to a larger pattern of historical development. In adopting a historicist approach, this chapter seeks to address this shortfall by investigating where precisely Kurdish society is going.[1]

The Kurds are inevitably embroiled today in the violent turmoil engulfing much of their region. However, this is, for many Kurds, merely the latest episode in a much larger historical pattern of external interference, the effect of which has been to deny them the time and space to determine their own future. But, what future are we talking about exactly? Today, the Kurds can be hardly considered enthusiastic participants in the post-Saddam, Iraqi state project, and a powerful if rather unstructured separatist nationalism is very much in the air. This coincides moreover with many recent visible changes in urban Kurdistan. In its new high rise buildings, modern airports and highways, shopping malls, and indeed in its apparent western-style parliamentary system of government, Kurdistan exhibits today a seductive general impression of modernist transition. But is this the case? This chapter investigates whether, subject to internal dynamics, Kurdish society is undergoing genuine modernisation.

We begin our enquiry with an analysis of the current condition of Kurdish nationalism. Signs of underlying modernist development within Kurdistan might be expected to surface in the current Kurdish nationalist discourse. A major point brought out in Ernest Gellner's work is the functional connection between nationalism and modernity; changes to class relations and power bases, brought on by underlying economic shifts from feudalism to capitalism, disrupt previously 'ascribed statuses', thus necessitating a reinvigorated sense of 'shared culture' (Gellner 1994: vii–viii). Yet, modernity not only necessitates nationalism, it imbues it with specific (critical) content. The rise of modern nationalism in Europe witnessed conflict, for example, with institutionalised religion, which had been instrumental in stabilising the pre-modern social world. The secularist drive which followed was very much caught up in questions of sovereignty and self-determination. However, immediate contradictions, latent or otherwise, between nationalist and religious impulses are difficult to detect in Kurdistan today. Nor is there a noticeable element of self-criticism to be found in the Kurdish nationalist discourse, or indeed in public political culture in general. Modernist nationalism, if that is what it is, might be expected to exhibit distinct critical features directed toward the very pre-modern social and political institutions that continue to dominate Kurdish public life. However, as we shall see, in the wake of would-be independence, Kurdish nationalism is strong in its desire for external recognition of its sovereign ambitions, but it is curiously reticent on the internal implications. For reasons to be explored, Kurdish nationalism is, in this introspective sense, not really radical at all.

Kurdistan's main political parties reflect this inherent conservatism within Kurdish society at large. They are rooted in pre-modern cultural practices and social structures, and show little sign of movement. The main political parties have been cooperating in recent years but they remain firmly tied to a fundamental regional schism which is feudal and patrician (pre-modern) in origin. The more recent emergence of the 'Movement for Change Party' or *Gorran* has complicated the picture, but Kurdish politics remains not only territorial but also highly elitist, and indeed this is part of *Gorran*'s complaint. A tentative cross-party national consensus has endured, but this comprises ultimately an elite governing caste that has become somewhat detached from the largely passive mass of Kurdish society. The democratic process is thus grafted onto pre-modern distributive structures of political, social, and economic power. Hence, the second key question to be confronted is thus: What are the determinants of Kurdistan's seemingly frozen social and political relations? Kurdistan simulates a certain outward modernist veneer, but it lacks, it will be argued, the genuine socio-economic drivers of modernistic change.

Societal immobility originates in the complex relationship between political and economic power in Kurdistan. It is a condition that bears strong resemblance to Karl Marx's description of the 'oriental society' in *Grundrisse* [1939] (1973). Marx's overall idea is that the social relations of the oriental society are so deeply entrenched that they do not respond 'normally' to pressures for change brought on by contact with the outside capitalist world. In fact, the oriental society is stubbornly resistant to change. In that case, how might we account for the fairly rapid material changes that are visibly underway in Kurdistan today?

One hears it mooted occasionally on the Kurdish street that the country is becoming the 'Dubai of the North'. This is it seems by no means entirely fanciful. A case can be made that Kurdistan is developing naturally and seamlessly out of an orientalist background cultural logic towards an oil-based, 'rentier-type' political economy. The social and political structures of Kurdistan already bear some correspondence to the classical Persian

Gulf rentier-state form, as we shall see. The point is that such transition is entirely non-revolutionary since it anticipates little if any impact upon existing power structures. Of course, this in turn would largely explain the absence of introspective critical radicalism in the Kurdish national-independence movement today.

Epistemological authority is derived significantly, but by no means exclusively, from a Marxist analytical paradigm. I rely heavily in places on the analysis of states and societies in transition provided by Antonio Gramsci (1891–1937), and indeed the thinking of Karl Marx (1818–1883), as I have already intimated. Reference is made throughout to 'modern', 'modernity', etc., and the concept is used as an analytical device in which to compare current and possible future social conditions in Kurdistan. There are a number of closely related thematic attributes to the 'modern' which have been subject to different emphases by different thinkers. For example, for Marx the modern is closely associated with a transition from a feudal to a capitalist 'mode of production', and the creation of an entirely new revolutionary class of historical actors. In contrast to the previous social certainties of feudalism, there is such a sustained and totalising cultural overhaul that as Marx tells us in *The Communist Manifesto* [1848]: 'all that is solid melts into air' (1977: 224). For Max Weber (1864–1920), on the other hand, the bases of social and political power changes profoundly from that of tradition and 'accident of birth' to one based on law and reason. The historical transition is one from low social mobility and largely static social relations to high mobility, typical of the meritocratic society. Modern society becomes 'rationalised', rule-governed, impersonal, and dynamic.

These and other conceptual approaches to the 'modernist revolution', when juxtaposed to contemporary Kurdistan, tend to support the conclusion that society is not undergoing modernisation in any typical, historical sense. It is rather, that such change as there is today represents both an outgrowth and a continuity of localised social, political, and economic practices and assumptions.

Kurdish nationalism and difference

As Kurds are all too aware, independence for Kurdistan has fallen victim in the past to larger external geo-strategic concerns and interests in the region beyond their control.[2] However, impossible as it is to disregard this important point, the failure of the Kurds to develop nation-statehood hitherto cannot be wholly attributed to external determinants. In what amounts perhaps to an uncomfortable fact, Kurdish national development has been equally impeded by internal factors.

The traditional power structuring of Kurdish society has hitherto thwarted the prospect of creating a national monopolising force capable of transcending the 'quarrels and jealousies inherent in tribalism' (McDowall 2004: 222). Indeed, tribal allegiance and the feared loss of localised autonomy are sentiments resistant to the transfer of identification and loyalty to the national community, and necessarily to the institutions of a nation-state. This fundamental shortfall in internal unity is however disguised appreciably today by a common distrust of all things 'Iraqi', and this is the place to begin.

The identification of the 'other' is certainly a stage any modern national movement has to pass through. Otto Bauer argued that during the nineteenth century the immediate source for the integration of modern nation-state institutions and their peoples in Europe was the widespread perception of external domination. He writes: 'the subordination to the alien power becomes clearly visible and consequently unbearable' (Bauer, cited in Nimni 1991: 174). The 'external' imposition therefore fosters dialectically 'internal' rejection. In other words, in Bauer's view, nationalism becomes dependent initially on a symbiotic relationship in which a negative affirmation arises: 'we are we *because* we are not they'. Kurdish nationalist sentiment today has certainly attained this rejectionist level of development, and indeed is not limited to it.

The identification and rejection of the *other* naturally sets in motion collective introspection in which the 'nation' commences to search for, and give expression to itself. John Breuilly (1993) sees self-awareness as a pivotal precondition of national development, whereby:

(a) There exists a nation with an explicit and peculiar character.
(b) The interests and values of this nation take priority over all other interests and values (Breuilly 1993: 2).

Condition (a) is fairly secured. The Kurds have distinctive ('peculiar') customs and rituals, distinctive traditional dress the *Kurtak u Sharwal*, and so forth. These peculiarities are necessary anthropological features of what Armstrong famously defined as 'mythomoteur', or the ethno-symbolic logic of national identity underpinning local social and political authority (1982: 8–9).

The social and political task of nationalism is of course to extend the range of identification from the tribe to the level of the nation. In *Philosophy of Right* [1835], Hegel recognised this necessity as a fundamentally modern problem. The sheer human scale of the modern nation state necessitates nationalism. Nationalism allows individuals to extend their emotional and intellectual scope beyond the family and immediate community to conceive of 'belonging' to a much larger community of people they do not know, and for all practical purposes, are incapable of knowing (Hegel 2001: 51).

Anthony Smith stresses moreover the importance to the nationalist logic of terrain, or 'ethnoscape', which bestows on the land a strong spiritual attachment fuelled by the collective act of remembering 'battles, heroes, and sages' (Smith 2000: 67). Ethnoscapism is thus a compound of people and place, and it has great emotional charge in Kurdistan today. Indeed, the Kurds are fond of repeating a lament: 'the Kurds have no friends but the mountains'. The mountains in question, to the north and east of the Kurdistan region, offered protection for the Kurds, for example, during the genocidal campaign against civilians of the Saddam Hussein era of the late 1980s. This period perhaps more than any other in Kurdish history cultivated a sense of isolation, and common suffering. It was at this time also, and not without reason, the Kurdish security force, the *Peshmerga*, gained its almost mythological reputation.

Kurdish nationalism and Islam

Kurdish nationalism in the context of Breuilly's (1993: 2) second precondition (b), above, is more contradictory due to Islam. The interests and values of the nation are strong sentiments in Kurdistan, so too though is the counter-particularism of religion. Islam is cosmopolitan in that believers are expected to ultimately forego other loyalties and confer final allegiance to an authority beyond that of nation-state, or indeed any human construct. Nothing could be more human in construction than the nation, of course.

The birth of modernity in Europe, which drew much of its radicalism from the scientific turn of the Enlightenment, involved an intellectual struggle with established patterns of thought – principally religious – for control of society and state. Hence, central to the formation of the modern nation-state in Europe was a secularist drive. This represented the dismantling of the ideological and institutional grip of religious cosmopolitanism on society, and the transfer of popular allegiance to a state. Religion was, of course, the focal point of feudal ideology and performed the function of endorsing the feudal distribution of socio-economic and political power. As Tocqueville observed of the French Revolution of 1789, so closely enmeshed were religion and the socio-economic power of the *ancien régime* in France, that when the latter collapsed, the mass lost much of its previous religiosity (Welch 2009: 375).

Notwithstanding the considerable religious diversity of Kurdistan today, the majority of Kurds are Sunni Muslims of the *Shafi'i* school, and Islam remains the focal point of public morality (see Kreyenbroek 1996). Whilst expressed as a civil code, the ethical basis of law is ultimately *Sharia*. As a symbolic example, the Kurdish Regional Government (KRG) institutions do not work to a predetermined business calendar because the dates of religious holidays must be declared first by authorities in Saudi Arabia, according to Koranic tradition – i.e. the first sighting of the crescent Moon, and so on. By contrast, in Turkey, the dates of religious holidays are declared by state institutions well in advance; this is arguably indicative of a more unambiguous recognition of the nation-state as an immediate, if not exactly exclusive, public authority and law-giver.

It is nonetheless highly significant that there is a distinct lack of taste among the Kurdish people for the conflation of religion and politics practiced by neighbouring states, such as Saudi Arabia and Iran. Three self-declared Islamic parties fought the Kurdish elections of 2013 (Kurdistan Islamic Union, Kurdistan Islamic Group, and Islamic Movement of Kurdistan) and secured only 17.6% electoral support between them, resulting, under Kurdistan's proportional representation system, in a combined total of 17 seats out of 111 (see www.investingroup.org/publications/kurdistan/overview/diplomacy-politics). All three Islamic parties shun militant Islam. More uncompromising and reactionary indigenous Islamic groups sympathetic to *Al-Qaeda*, such as the former *Ansar al-Islam* formed in 2001, have never enjoyed popularity, nor made any inroads into mainstream Kurdish political life.[3]

Indeed, it is not easy to take issue with Aziz's claim that 'Kurds are not particularly religious people in the sense of abiding by dogma' (Aziz 2011: 10). Woman in Kurdistan, for example, are not commanded by law to cover their heads in public places or state buildings, and a great many women exercise this freedom. Any disapproval involved in abandoning head covering is confined largely to the conservative remote rural villages, the immediate vicinity of mosques, and the bazaar quarter of Erbil. In any case, headscarf-less women might encounter staring, although scarcely more than that.[4] There are also no formal impediments to women's educational and employment opportunities. Islamic strictures prevail – i.e. the public display of affection between the sexes is typically taboo, as is the visible consumption of alcohol, or blatant daytime eating and drinking during the month of Ramadan – but, at the risk of a generalisation, Kurds are remarkably phlegmatic, placid and mild-mannered people, and are not normally given to belligerence, certainly not of a religious kind.

There is in any case no evidence of a conflict of national and religious loyalties in Kurdistan today. The two sources of identity are not discernibly antagonistic and, in a deeper historiological context of modern development, this is significant. As Burke (2005: 37) has noted, historians and sociologists have long searched in vain for an adequate means to measure religiosity, but there are nonetheless sufficient historical grounds to assume that religiosity becomes more strident when its authority is threatened by the rise of modern institutions. As suggested above, Kurds have certain temperamental features which might resonate well with modern secularism; however, this is somewhat misleading. The implication is more accurately that there is no impetus to push religion back because no disruption to current Kurdish power distribution is imminent. Hence, the terms of social, political and economic domination in Kurdistan today is undergoing no appreciable organic pressure which might otherwise necessitate a reformulation of the relations between religion and state. The lack of critical bite in Kurdish nationalism today is, however, not merely confined to attitudes toward religion.

Modernity and ideology

Modernity represents a distinct break with the static nature of traditional pre-modern societies. In the pre-modern world, the social, economic and political rhythms were/are repeated generation upon generation. By contrast, in the modern capitalist era, humans enter into a continually changing relationship with nature and with themselves. As Callinicos puts it:

[t]radition-bound social relations, cultural practices, and religious beliefs find themselves swept away in the ensuing maelstrom of change (1989: 29).

New ideological forms emerge immediately as a means to apprehend the changing world, and they all begin life as social criticism. Calinescu is even led to the conclusion – a not entirely accurate one, but one not without foundation either – that the modern era is the 'age of ideology' (Calinescu 1987: 206). Liberalism in particular has performed the function of a modern 'religion' in some respects by offering the predominant conception of one's place in the world, and as an informant of social conduct.

During the modernist transition in Europe, the passive, subjective 'membership' status offered by religion weakened in favour of a conception of active 'citizenship' and inclusion, which bestowed on individuals tangible new rights and entitlements. Such changes were initiated in the eighteenth, nineteenth and twentieth centuries in countries in which an emergent bourgeoisie sought to exert specific ideological direction on the national discourse. Demands arose for a package of political liberties to match the conception of choice and self-determination already inferred in the dynamics of a developing free-market economy. This is the ideo-political context of modernity of course which was given philosophical expression in the liberal political economy of such figures as John Locke (1632–1704), Adam Smith (1723–1790), and Charles-Louis Montesquieu (1689–1755).

A society undergoing genuine modernist development might be expected to display therefore a confrontation between ideas which attempt to defend the outmoded, decaying pre-modern way of life and those of the radical forces of change. Kurdish nationalism and the direction given to it would become central to this struggle. Nationalism of itself is not really ideological at all in this specific context. Nationalism conforms to the logic of social enclosure and, in its alter-ego, to the logic of exclusion. Its purpose is to mark off a people and territory, but it can do little more than that. Modernist nationalism, however, would at the outset embody libertarian impulses articulating the emergence a new class of would-be mobile social actors. This is what Gellner is essentially driving at when he writes:

> nationalism is not the only character on the ideological scene. Men are or are not nationalists, but they also have their attitudes to … traditional institutions, to the imperative of economic development, to the issue of the availability of universal truth or, on the contrary, the validity of relative local truths (1994: viii).

Nationalism in the modern context simply provides idiomatic alignment to a host of new opinions and attitudes that seek expression, and thus axiomatically political emancipation.

It would be negligent however not to mention that other national revolutionary scenarios are possible, including the authoritarian. A casual glance at twentieth-century history reveals that modernist pressure can be subverted into fascist-type solutions. These typically project an aggressive nation-statism, but with much less emphasis, if any at all, on civil rights and protections. Indeed, the recent history of the Middle East is replete with examples of authoritarian regimes predicated politically on exaggerations of national identity, while utterly devoid simultaneously of 'personal freedoms and political liberties' (Cleveland 2004: 538). Memories of the Saddam Hussein period and Ba'athist nationalism still haunt the Kurdish psyche, but this offers no guarantees of future immunity from past 'administrative errors' and injustices.

However, it is important to appreciate that in seeking guarantees it is not merely a question of promoting certain political liberties in abstraction. Rights are borne by individuals and groups in the act of leading, or desiring to lead, a certain way of life. This exposes, of course, a developmental problem in Kurdistan. Whom or what in Kurdish society is leading, or is pressing to lead, a way of life which in turn requires fundamental constitutional and attitudinal changes? There appears to be nothing significant in this regard on the horizon; and without concrete social actors to carry them, it is surely doubtful if meaningful political rights and liberties can develop in Kurdistan much beyond their current level.

Kurdish political parties and political culture

The role of political parties is crucial to the foregoing discussion. Gramsci viewed the political party as the 'nomenclature for a class' (1971: 152). Parties represent particular class interest which attempt to become states. In this regard, the political party represents a social formation to which it attempts to give political expression in the form of a programme for government. By 'expression' is meant the articulation of values and interests that conform to the life-conditions of the people who necessarily brought the party into being and support it. In this respect, political parties represent ideological positions aligned to distinguishable class interests. The commitment by the party to become the state involves what Gramsci termed a 'war of position' (Gramsci 1971: 231–2) in which an attempt is made to project the specific class interests onto the notion of the general national interest. This involves 'hegemony', or the attempt to disseminate a worldview or *weltanschauung* of a particular class throughout society. Gramsci coins the phrase 'national popular' to describe a condition in which a political party achieves the broad uptake of its values and ideas throughout society to become the basis of a national course of action (Gramsci 1971: 113).

Notably, Kurdish political parties do not provide overt hegemonic leadership in the Gramscian sense of directing and educating society towards certain national goals. However, we should bear in mind that such a task becomes necessary when there is an historical transition and transfer of power underfoot which requires society to be pre-conditioned to accept. In terms of meeting the future needs, interests and aspirations of Kurdistan's independence movement, no hegemonic programme – which would normally be carried by a radical political party – is historically necessary. This is because the Kurdish mass is already raised to a level of hegemonic acceptance of the terms of post-independence social, political and economic power distribution. In other words, no hegemonic conditioning is necessary because again no significant transfer of social, political and economic power is imminent.

Kurdish politics has been dominated by two main parties, the Patriotic Union of Kurdistan (PUK) led by Jalal Talabani and the Kurdistan Democratic Party (KDP) led by Masoud Barzani, which is currently the largest party in Parliament. *Gorran* formed in 2009 emerged from the 2013 elections in second place, pushing the PUK into third. *Gorran* complicates the picture, but is in many ways merely a more critical and radical offshoot of the PUK. The KDP and PUK leaderships are structured around ruling families rooted in certain geographical areas. This has crystallised over the years to produce dynastic-type authority (Mullitt 2012: 323). The parties depend for support more on regional and largely tribal affiliations. The PUK is traditionally associated with the city of Sulaymaniyah and its environs in the south of the KRG region, whilst the long-standing KDP base is in the capital city of Erbil and the territory to its immediate north and east bordering Turkey and Iran. *Gorran* has made some effort to break the partisan mould but has effectively wrought more political damage to the PUK than the KDP, and indeed its power-base is largely 'southern'.[5] The PUK is traditionally identified, albeit vaguely, with leftists and liberal progressives, whose appeal has, of course, been challenged in this regard recently by *Gorran*; on the other hand, the KDP is regarded equally ambiguously as rather more agrarian and conservative (Stansfield 2007: 68).

However, an ideological stand-off necessary to format the political agenda and animate a competitive democratic culture is barely detectable today in Kurdish party political life. The current Prime Minister is quoted as having remarked:

> [t]he programmes of both parties are virtually identical, and the goals are the same. The problem is one of who has power, and this may be solved by either elections or violence ... Believe me, there is no apparent external difference between the KDP and PUK, it is a personal matter (Nechervan Barzani, cited in Stansfield 2003: 114).

The phrase 'a personal matter' is revealing. Ostensibly, in modernist terms, it is not entirely clear why there have until recently been two rival parties in Kurdistan. There is no ideological distinction. The divide is not characterised by class division, or radical forces of modernity versus conservative traditionalists. The nearest to a reason Stansfield is able to find is that there is a rough correspondence to a 'division of dominant dialects' (Stansfield 2005: 199). Hence, we can be reasonably confident that Kurdistan's main political parties are tied to expressions of territoriality. The loyalties underpinning the PUK and the KDP – which have in the past been shown to be fierce – are forged in pre-modern socio-economic practices tied to the aristocratic and elitist logic of landed power (i.e. feudalism).

To take Gramsci's truism that political parties are states-in-waiting (Gramsci 1971: 152), in Kurdistan the two main political parties do not truly compete in the same political space. Each party conducts itself not so much as a national state-in-waiting as much as a sectarian state-already-formed. Each party has its own security services, courts, and militias. The parties have even established their own separate trading relations (Stansfield 2005: 211). It is true that the current war with ISIS has stimulated a greater collective effort between the two parties, but it remains the case that Kurdish political life is deeply schismatic. Max Weber's famous definition of the state in *The Profession and Vocation of Politics* [1919] is instructive in this regard. It is a:

> human community which (successfully) lays claim to the monopoly of legitimate physical violence within a certain territory.
> (Weber 1994: 310–11)

There is however little evidence of a contest for the monopoly of the state in Kurdistan today. This is in itself indicative of the fact that outside of the sub-region in which they predominate, the parties have very little else on which to base or broaden their appeal to the level of would-be national popularity. In effect, an ethno-political subdivision has formed between Erbil and Sulaymaniyah (Stansfield 2005: 199) and, rather than rectifying it, any newly independent Kurdish state would be simply imposed upon it.

We might recall at this juncture Lipset and Rokkan's (1967) acclaimed thesis that political parties represent and articulate what they call social 'cleavages' within the national community. What prevents the otherwise fracturing of the national community along a cleavage fault-line, such as the protracted regionalism we see in Kurdistan today, is the cross-cutting effect of other allegiances. For example, the territorial cleavage can be offset by a socio-economic class fault-line which cuts across it (rather than running parallel to it). This cross-cutting effect is, Lipset and Rokkan argue, for example, what holds an otherwise divided modern Belgian state together (1967: 48–9). Indeed, the modern states of the west became, if anything, more cohesive following their modernist revolutions because although this created new fault-lines (i.e. aristocrat versus bourgeoisie versus proletariat) these cross-cut the former social fractures of religion and ethnicity (Lipset and Rokkan 1967: 14). One could argue, therefore, that a key reason why the north–south divide in Kurdistan is the key political focal point is because there is an absence of modern offsetting and cross-cutting through social cleavages.

Gorran and tradition

The 'Movement for Change' Party or *Gorran*, which emerged in 2009, represents in some ways an attempt to break free of such party regionalism, although that might not be a self-conscious aspect of its agenda. *Gorran* represents a growing suspicion, not merely confined to one region, that government in Kurdistan is self-serving and self-interested. It is noteworthy that a campaign by *Gorran* to widen public awareness was not well received by the KRG's security services. *Gorran*-sponsored public demonstrations in Sulaymaniyah and Erbil in 2011 exacted a swift and heavy-handed response. This event served to remind western observers that basic liberal-type freedoms of speech and opinion are, as yet, nowhere near established in Kurdistan. Malcolm Smart, Amnesty International's Director for the Middle East and North Africa was moved to state:

> [w]hat happened ... was the latest stage in an ongoing clampdown on freedom of expression and protests ... which has been marked by excessive use of force against those who dare to protest in support of demands for political and economic change and an end to corruption among those holding power.
> (See www.amnesty.org/en/articles/news/2011/04/independent-investigation-urged-police-violence-iraqi-kurdistan)

There is certainly much scope for *Gorran*'s case. In *Economy and Society* [1922], albeit a heavily Euro-centric analysis, Max Weber contrasts the practices of the traditional society with what he calls the 'rational–legal' principles of organisations characteristic of the modern era (1978: 218). Typically, Weber goes into labyrinthine detail but what emerges is clear enough. All positions of authority in modern societies (i.e. those positions which command the legitimate use of power over others) are governed by clear and precise rules which are both logical and transparent. Such rules affect not only the process in which the authority is taken, but also what is done with authority once gained. Typical of the traditional society, political authority in Kurdistan remains largely hereditary in character with transfers of power 'bound to the precedents handed down from the past' (Weber 1978: 244).

Indeed, Kurdistan is a 'traditional society', by Weberian definition. Typically, nepotism is common throughout Kurdish political and public life, with particular resonance in its governing elite (Gunter 2007: 35, Mullitt 2012: 323). For example, the current President Masoud Barzani is the current Prime Minister Nechervan Barzani's uncle. Both men command tremendous and very genuine public respect, but the basis of their authority differs from the rational-legal system wherein what is important is the 'office', how it is attained, and the power it bestows. The latter contrasts for Weber with authority that is based on traditional practices, which in Kurdistan is typically heavily clannish and ancestral. In rational-legal societies, the office holder, be it president or schoolmaster, derives authority from the legitimacy of the process of his/her selection. Office-holders are selected on the basis of technical competence according to meritocratic principles. Rational-legal systems are hierarchical, and based on a chain of command, but the structure is open to competition (Weber 1978: 217–19). By contrast, family and personal connections remain crucial to political or indeed any type of advancement in Kurdistan. Modernist meritocratic appointment to positions of importance remain largely antithetical to the Kurdish tradition, where it is commonly far more advantageous, to coin a phrase, 'to know *someone* rather than to know *something*'.

It is true that *Gorran* represents an attempt to break with such tradition, but it is probably unwise in modernist terms to expect too much of it. Whilst radical, *Gorran* is essentially a resistance or protest movement. It is committed to negative campaigning, and whilst its constituency is largely Kurdish youth and an educated, liberalised intelligentsia, which might indeed crosscut the old tribal fault-line, it cannot be said to offer anything resembling a coherent ideological position of its own. As with the dilemma of all the other political parties in Kurdistan, there is no clear-cut radical, modernising social agency struggling for change to which *Gorran* can become attached.

Governmental elitism

Gorran's challenge to the two-party governing axis that has dominated Kurdistan's political life hitherto is ongoing, but Kurdistan's democratic system remains otherwise fundamentally elitist. The cross-party coalition-type governments of recent years has been inclusive at the apex of government, but this has led in turn to the distancing of government from governed. Gramsci dubbed this phenomenon *trasformismo* ('transformism') (1971: 58). Italy's conflicting social divisions necessitated the formation of a national coalition between the elites of its party-political establishment. Hence, parties which began life thoroughly distinguishable ceased to have any substantive differences thereafter as their respective leaderships gravitated toward one another and became transformed by the trappings of office. Powers of patronage were invoked – the issuing of jobs, titles, material reward, prestige, and so on – and were intended to bind the heterogeneous agents comprising government to the general interests of the 'nation'. Gramsci's point is, of course, that the 'national interest' ends up receiving definition from a very thin, elite stratum of society.

Typically, the transformed coalition members derive their power and value to the coalition by virtue of the human capital they command in their constituencies, or power bases. The party elites exercise effectively a disciplinary function over the lower rank and file within the specific party, corporate and/ or regional structures. What results is a continuation of a horizontal bond across the top of the national elites, which facilitates stability of government, but this often comes at the price of the 'decapitation' of the leadership of the political party from its mass base, with the resultant distancing moreover of the governing class from the general populace (Gramsci 1971: 59).

The entrenchment of elitist political culture in Kurdistan differs from the Italian experience of the early twentieth century in one crucial respect. The Italians were desperate to arrange the stability necessary to effect a modernist transition in economic and social life. There is no evidence in Kurdistan that modernity is as yet struggling to be born, and so *trasformismo* is logically serving a modified stabilising function. It ensures that the democratic process remains under the aegis and control of the dominant social and political elite, which is otherwise divided by a territorial rift. *Trasformismo* in Kurdistan thus functions to legitimise pre-modern social conditions by essentially pseudo-modernist, democratic means.

Closely related to *trasformismo* is Gramsci's concept 'passive revolution' (Gramsci 1971: 59). This can be gauged relevant to Kurdistan's independence movement due to the fact that it is being led, orchestrated and conducted by a transformed elite in which the mass of Kurdish society remains passive (i.e. 'the fact that a State replaces the local social groups in leading a struggle of renewal' (Gramsci 1971: 105–6)). Whilst it is not correct, I think, to regard the Kurdish mass as indifferent to the imminent national revolution, far from it, it is, however, currently non-participatory. The political leaders in Kurdistan can be assured that the public in general will throw its weight behind the independence movement, and it does so morally already, but that is surely the limit of its current and future participation. The independence movement will be orchestrated as it is now by the elite national coalition, from the top down, into post-independence. In this scenario, sovereignty will pass to the Kurds, but when the dust has settled, the transition will appear largely seamless since no significant interruption to the terms of political domination will be likely to occur. The change will be constitutional, not 'historical' in the sense that there will be no significant transfer of power to different social and political agents.

Economy and orientalism

The conservative nature of politics in Kurdistan is, however, reflective of deeper-lying socio-economic realities. For Marx, a pre-capitalist society such as Kurdistan would be considered to be 'feudal'. It is a society that derives its wealth, power and prestige from land and its ownership. There is moreover a crucial distinction between a feudal and a capitalist mode of production. The nature of exploitation in the feudal mode is not determined economically, as an inherent feature of production. The feudal relations of production are produced wholly politically (Vali 1993: 57, Hindess and Hirst 1975: 194).[6] That is to say, possession of the mode of production is not intrinsic to the social relations of production. Ownership of the mode of production is a political construct born of a mixture of despotic force and traditional modes of thought grounded in the obscurities of antiquity. The landlord enjoys economic conditions that are derived from his status 'in the hierarchy of political power' (Vali 1993: 58). Thus, the possession of social, political and economic power reaches a more natural equilibrium than in the capitalist mode of production. In the capitalist mode of production, as Gramsci has illustrated, economic and political power cannot be assumed to spontaneously correspond. Hence, ideological validation of the socio-economic relations becomes an active and ongoing political project, where the advantages of economic power are exploited to affect the way society regards, in moral terms, the source of those advantages. In the case of feudalism, by contrast, the social relation derives politically from the start, and ideology attuned to the distribution of social and political power is already embodied in the assumption of the basis of that economic power.

Kurdish feudalism shares this characteristic with its European historical counterpart, but there is a distinctive point of departure. In *Grundrisse*, Marx talks about 'oriental despotism' which is characterized by the dominant role of a large and bloated state acting as 'landlord' in economic life and sponsor of all public projects, and a corresponding underdevelopment of a private urban sector (Marx 1973: 404). The oriental society is based on 'propertylessness', which is, in fact, a sort of inverse of communal ownership of the land-resources by the 'clan', whose authority is condensed ultimately into a person or group of persons to whom feudal tribute accrues (Marx 1973: 404). The economy becomes self-sustaining, containing all the necessary conditions for reproduction within itself, resulting in a freezing of social relations (Marx 1973: 404–5).

Pre-capitalist European conditions were different. Cities were, for example, established around skilled artisans, free trade and the principles of private ownership and exchange, which eventually created the space for the growth of an industrial bourgeoisie. Cities became, in other words, giant productive units based on private individual initiative. By contrast, the oriental city, argues Marx, is an artificial creation of the state, one not linked organically to the economy as much as the mode of administration – the state bureaucracy – and becomes an outlet for the exchange of 'surplus product' for goods and services by the governing elite, and as a terminal for external trade (Marx 1973: 405).

Erbil today rather typifies the 'oriental' city in this regard. Shopping malls and retail outlets abound, but it lacks an industrial heart. Private property is present but it is largely distributed on the basis of state patronage. Property as land, for example, is often granted as part of a retirement package for public-sector employees. The Kurdistan Board of Investment (BI) has in the last decade stimulated growth in economic sectors such as industry, agriculture and tourism, but control of none of this is given over in any case to the initiative of private agents (see www.investingroup.org/publications/kurdistan/overview/economy).

Private initiative, where it exists, is promulgated through inward investment in Kurdistan by companies whose motive is to make a profit, which

Rebels without a cause? 71

is subsequently exported back to the country of origin. This has little or no lasting impact on the domestic socio-economic structure.

Foreign companies set up camp and commonly bring their own labour-expertise. This often leaves Kurdish university graduates with qualifications and transferable skills but highly restricted career opportunities. There have been numerous demonstrations by Kurdish graduates outside Parliament in Erbil in recent years seeking to bring this problem to the attention of government. It could be argued that this in itself is indicative of the orientalist case in that it is assumed, in the absence of private sector job opportunities, to fall within the government's scope to take the necessary action to create jobs.

Dubai-ification

The oft-vaunted 'Dubai-ification' of Kurdistan mentioned above refers to a seemingly harmonious transition already underway, and it is one that can be attributed to the presence of oil. Many of the key conditions for the development of a so-called 'rentier state', as described in the seminal work of Beblawi (1990), are either already in place or are in the process of development in Kurdistan. The rentier state embodies a contradiction in that it projects powerful progressive imagery and dynamism whilst retaining a deeply immobile and conservative underlying social and political structure. Modern roads and highways, parks and gardens, and typically lavish and ostentatious construction work creates a visual impression which actually belies the ossified and stationary social relations which maintain a fierce controlling influence behind the material façade. Rentier-ism is the means by which many of the oil-rich pre-modern and deeply conservative societies of the Middle East, particularly those of the Persian Gulf, have managed the modernist pressures associated with contact with western capitalism.

The ultimate source of 'tribute' of the rentier state is of course oil – rent is paid by foreign oil companies to the state in the form of licence payments and royalties, and this becomes by far the most dominant source of wealth generation. Kurdistan has large oil and gas reserves within its current geographical boundary, and it is projected that by 2019 it has the potential to export two million barrels of oil per day, seemingly more than enough to sustain a population of 5.3 million people (see www.investingroup.org/publications/kurdistan/overview/economy). Thus, it is distinctly feasible that the Kurds may in the future forego their current 17% share of Iraq's national oil revenue, as would be required following independence, and export oil from their own sovereign territory to more than make up for the shortfall. Either way, dependency on oil is already showing signs of a developmental trend towards a 'Gulf-state' model of society.

As has been suggested, Kurdistan has already a number of characteristic symmetrical features with the classical rentier state. The self-sustaining economy depends on rent from external sources which is payable on the basis of some internally pre-established process whereby a particular clan has assumed the status of a state administration (Beblawi 1990: 87). Few ultimately receive and control the rent. Thus, the narrow basis of ownership is reflected in the narrow basis of political domination that was inherited from oriental feudalism. Almost the entire wealth of a 'rentier state' can be in the control of one ruling family or clan, and there is no immediate perception of a potential conflict of interest, as would be found in modern rational-legal societies. External rent of course curtails the need for the development of a domestic productive sector because the state is not dependent on income from an internal economy at all (Luciani 1990: 71–72).

Rentier states are indeed usually the major employer of the community, to the extent that they rival former socialist states (Beblawi 1990: 91). Government bureaucracy becomes an important means to redirect oil revenue. Moreover, with government jobs comes prestige and usually decent salaries and conditions, good pension payments, and so on, that can be used as instruments of state patronage and reward. Civil service jobs are certainly highly coveted as stress-free 'jobs for life', quite beyond the reach of the disciplines of market forces. As Beblawi observes:

> [c]ivil servant productivity is, understandably, not very high and they usually see the principal duty as being available in their offices during working hours.
>
> (1990: 91)

One of the key features of the rentier state, and one which provides the means for the ruling elite to maintain its ascendency over society is the absence of taxation (Beblawi 1990: 90). Typically, Kurds today do not pay taxes on income or purchases. The rentier state itself actually asks little of its people. On the reverse side of this coin, of course, the voting public has no direct material stake in government. Joseph Schumpeter made the point long ago that the best way to comprehend the relationship between people and state is to observe the struggle over 'public finances' ([1918] 1990: 101). In capitalist economies, governments are not generally wealth creators themselves. The question of the distribution of the state's resources therefore takes on a practical and indeed ethical immediacy; since the state is effectively spending money that is not its own. By contrast, the rentier state *does* create its own wealth independently of the wealth creativity of the rest of society. Government spending, particularly on welfare and social policy, is then perceived popularly as modernistic perhaps but one actually thoroughly commensurate with feudal paternalistic benevolence:

> [a] long tradition of buying loyalty and allegiance is now confirmed by an *etat providence*, distributing favours and benefits.
>
> (Beblawi 1990: 89)

Rebels without a cause? 73

Wealth does not originate internally from the industry and effort of the mass of people in rentier states. Wealth distribution is thus not tied to the social responsibilities involved in its creation. Luck and the principle of good fortune predominate distribution. Essentially, the hereditary or accident of birth principle operates to determine who gets what, and this is the way Kurdistan with its dynastic tradition has long operated. If there is a powerful religious sentiment functioning to legitimise power and wealth distribution in Kurdistan it is surely that of 'Inshallah' (God willing). It indicates a perception of a lack of agency in that what one gets from life in general is predetermined and not subject necessarily to any voluntary activity on the part of the individual. This idea sits very easily of course with the hereditary principle of distribution. However, one serious consequence of the fatalistic approach to social justice is that it fosters a general apathy towards individual effort. In rentier states there is no clear-cut linkage between effort, attainment, and reward; a *quid pro quo* which provides the motivation factor of modern meritocratic societies.

Moreover, as a consequence, modernist terms of political obligation do not develop and become based on clear principles of social justice and conceptions of citizenship. Rentier societies are, like Weber's traditional type, deeply patriarchal and paternalistic. The key to political obligation is merely to obviate the likelihood of popular opposition, and with vast material resources the state is able to mobilise a popular perception of generosity and largesse. Kuwait is typical in this regard. Not only is there no need to tax its citizens, the state provides a range of services and benefits: free social security, healthcare, education, good infrastructure, and citizens enjoy generally a very high standard of living (Beblawi 1990: 90).

Welfare provision is currently becoming commodified in Kurdistan, most noticeably in the health sphere, with generally a distinctly inferior state sector providing residual cover. However, this policy might change, particularly if it becomes politically expedient to do so. From the perspective of government, there is undoubtedly a seductive quality to the idea that with most of the people's material needs catered for, so-called political rights and entitlements, if they are considered at all, can be readily dismissed as unnecessary philosophical abstractions of western origin.

Conclusion

This chapter has sought to establish whether the powerful independence movement gathering momentum in Kurdistan is situated in larger background historiological changes. Kurdistan is undergoing visible change, undoubtedly, but what is its historical significance? We searched for clues to modernist development in the Kurdish nationalist discourse, where it was argued we ought to find both secularist causes and a broader ideological struggle for control of the state. The investigation in this regard proved rather barren. Nationalism is strong but it is not revolutionary. The national discourse is not associated with a specific group of social actors proposing change to the current distribution of social, economic and political power in Kurdistan.

The social grounding and function of Kurdistan's political parties and culture was subsequently analysed. The parties remain tied to pre-modern social interests producing a highly conservative political culture. There is no sign of attachment to social forces seeking concrete change here either. In fact, democracy has produced a balancing act between two deeply polarised regional constituencies that are feudal in origin and character. The main parties are largely inseparable ideologically, which poses the question as to their role and function. It was argued that the party hierarchies have combined, albeit on occasion uneasily, as a single 'transformed' governing elite operating a policing function over their respective constituencies. This has brought about political stability but at the cost of distancing of the governing class from the Kurdish mass. Kurdistan is one of the few functioning democracies in the region, but this process is distorted by the social backdrop in which it operates. Democracy tends to confer retrospective modernistic-type legitimacy on thoroughly pre-modern social and political relations. *Gorran* has arisen as an attempt to combat Kurdistan's conservatism and stagnant political life. However, there is every possibility that this Party will become transformed itself in time. This is because *Gorran* like any other party is unable to attach itself to truly radical social forces in Kurdish society whose future development depends upon effecting substantial institutional and cultural changes. The parties might talk 'modern' but who and where exactly are the 'modernisers'?

A modernist transformation of society would find its ultimate cause in economic life, and yet here again we find no evidence of its development. It was argued that Kurdistan conforms in certain respects to Marx's model of the oriental society. The key element here is the conflation of economic and political power. Economic power is contrived politically through the legitimisation of land ownership. The ownership of land confers monopolistic economic control in turn because the absence of private property eliminates the space for the growth of a modern bourgeoisie. These economic conditions coupled to the massive influx of oil it is argued is propelling Kurdistan towards a rentier state model of development. Rentier states interface with modern capitalist economies whilst preserving their deeply pre-modern social structures. Here the economy is based predominantly on external revenue generated by foreign oil companies and little if any economic revenue is sourced internally. The internal economy is turned over to retail and services in a series of sub-feudal type landlord – serf relations.

Contrary to what we might expect in societies undergoing genuine modernist historical transition, ordinary Kurds seem destined to remain the subjects of paternalistic government, that is, rather than developing into an objective participating citizenry and drivers of social and economic change in themselves. Political independence will thus take the form of a 'passive revolution'. Genuine popular participation and input is what is lacking. Kurdish political life is, and will likely remain for the foreseeable future, essentially paternalistic in character.

Overall, the move toward an independent Kurdistan and fully-fledged rentier state is unlikely to bring about any fundamental restructuring of Kurdish society and politics. The explanation is ultimately economic, but the political effect will be a continuation of conservatism and resistance to change in society. Future independence will likely result therefore in 'business as usual' with few appreciable differences to the existing Kurdish way of life. The only distinctive internal uncertainty in all this appears to rest on the durability of Kurdistan's 'transformed' cross-party governing elite. Ironically, genuine modernisation might be the enduring solution to this problem, but to engage in what would be required to bring this about would alas necessitate a separate study.

Notes

1 Hereafter the terms 'Kurdistan', 'Kurds', etc., refer to Iraqi Kurdistan and Iraqi Kurds. The chapter does not address Kurdish pan-nationalism involving the Kurds of Turkey, Iran and Syria.
2 This aspect of the discussion is beyond the scope of this chapter, see: Aziz (2011). A good account of the complexity of the relationship between the Kurds and the new federalised state of Iraq can be found in Danilovich (2014).
3 This group dissolved and merged in 2014 with the Islamic State of Iraq and Syria (ISIS), which is known to Kurds by the Arabic acronym 'Da'ish'.
4 Note: the practice of so-called 'honour killing', despite government initiatives to eradicate it, remains fairly common in Kurdistan. Strictly speaking, it is unclear if honour killing is doctrinal or cultural in origin.
5 Note that a potential political row is brewing due to President Barzani's controversial two-year extension to his term of office, although this is claimed to have been a deal struck between the KDP and 'strategic partner' (*sic*) the PUK (see Karem and Chomani 2015).
6 See also Avinieri (1968).

References

Amnesty International. 2011. *Independent investigation urged into police violence in Iraqi Kurdistan*. Available at: www.amnesty.org/en/articles/news/2011/04/independent-investigation-urged-police-violence-iraqi-kurdistan/ [accessed: 8 June 2015].
Armstrong, J.A. 1982. *Nations before Nationalism*. Chapel Hill: University of North Carolina.
Avineri, S. 1968. Introduction, in *Karl Marx on Colonialism and Modernization*, edited by S. Avineri. New York: Doubleday, 1–28.
Aziz, M.A. 2011. *The Kurds of Iraq: Ethnonationalism and National Identity in Iraqi Kurdistan*. London: IB. Tauris.
Beblawi, H. Al. 1990. The Rentier State in the Arab World, in *The Arab State*, edited by G. Luciani. London: Routledge, 85–98.
Breuilly, J. 1993. *Nationalism and the State*. Third Edition. Manchester: Manchester University Press.

Burke, P. 2005. *History and Social Theory*. Second Edition. Cambridge: Polity Press.
Calinescu, M. 1987. *Five Faces of Modernity: Modernism, Avant-garde, Decadence, Kitsch, Postmodernism*. Durham, NC: Duke University.
Callinicos, A. 1989. *Against Postmodernism: A Marxist Critique*. Cambridge: Polity.
Cleveland, W.L. 2004. *A History of the Modern Middle East*. Boulder, CO: Westview.
Danilovich, A. 2014. *Iraqi Federalism and the Kurds. Learning to Live Together*. Farnham: Ashgate.
Gellner, E. 1994. *Encounters with Nationalism*. Oxford: Blackwell.
Goldcrest Executive. 2013. *Overview: Kurdistan Region – Diplomacy-politics*. Available at: http://www.investingroup.org/publications/kurdistan/overview/diplomacy-politics/ [accessed: 21 June 2015]
Goldcrest Executive. 2013. *Overview: Kurdistan Region – Economy*. Available at: http://www.investingroup.org/publications/kurdistan/overview/economy/ [accessed: 21 June 2015].
Gramsci, A. 1971. *Selections from the Prison Notebooks*, edited by Q. Hoare and G. Nowell-Smith. London: Lawrence and Wishart.
Gunter, M. 2007. *The Kurds Ascending: The Evolving Solution to the Kurdish Problem in Iraq and Turkey*. Basingstoke: Palgrave.
Hegel, G.W.F. 2001. *Philosophy of Right*, translated by SW. Dyde. Kitchener, Ontario: Batoche.
Hindess, B. and Hirst, P.Q. 1975. *Pre-Capitalist Modes of Production*. London: Routledge & Kegan Paul.
Karem, H. and Chomani, K. 2015. *Massoud Barzani's Controversial Presidency*, The Kurdistan Tribune, April 24. Available at: www.kurdistantribune.com/2015/massoud-barzanis-controversial-presidency/ [accessed: 22 June 2005].
Kreyenbroek, P.G. 1996. Religion and Religions in Kurdistan, in *Kurdish Culture and Identity*, edited by P.G. Kreyenbroek and C. Allison. Atlantic Highlands, NJ: Zed Books, 85–110.
Lipset, S.M. and Rokkan, S. 1967. *Party Systems and Voter Alignment: Cross National Perspectives*. New York: Free press.
Luciani, G. 1990. Allocation vs. Production States: A Theoretical Framework, in *The Arab State*, edited by G. Luciani. London: Routledge, 65–84.
Marx, K. 1973. *Grundrisse*. Translated by M. Nicolaus. London: Penguin.
Marx, K. 1977. *Karl Marx Selected Writings*. Translated and edited by D. McLellan. Oxford: Oxford University Press.
McDowall, D. 2004. *A Modern History of the Kurds*. London: IB Tauris.
Mullitt, G. 2012. *Fuel on the Fire – Oil and Politics in Occupied Iraq*. London: Vintage.
Natali, D. 2005. *The Kurds and the State: Evolving National Identity in Iraq, Turkey, and Iran*. New York: Syracuse University.
Natali, D. 2010. *The Kurdish Quasi-state: Development and Democracy in Post-Gulf War Iraq*. New York: Syracuse University.
Nimni, E. 1991. *Marxism and Nationalism – Theoretical Origins of a Political Crisis*. London: Pluto.
Schumpeter, J. [1918] 1991. *The Crisis of the Tax State, the Economics and Sociology of Capitalism*, edited by R. Swebberg. Princeton, NJ: Princeton University.
Smith, A.D. 2000. *The Nation in History: Historiographical Debates about Ethnicity and Nationalism*. Hanover, NH: University Press of New England.
Stansfield, G.R.V. 2003. *Iraqi Kurdistan: Emergent Democracy*. New York: Routledge Curzon.

Stansfield, G.R.V. 2005. Governing Kurdistan: The Strengths of Division, in *The Future of Kurdistan in Iraq*, edited by B. O'Leary, J. McGarry and K. Saleh. Philadelphia: University of Pennsylvania, 195–218.
Stansfield, G.R.V. 2007. *Iraq, People, History, Politics*. Cambridge: Polity Press.
Vali, A. 1993. *Pre-Capitalist Iran: A Theoretical History*. New York: New York University.
Weber, M. [1922] 1978. *Economy and Society*, edited by G. Roth and C. Wittich. Berkeley, CA: University of California.
Weber, M. [1919] 1994. *The Profession and Vocation of Politics*, edited by P. Lassman and R. Spiers. Cambridge: Cambridge University Press.
Welch, C. 2009. Tocqueville, in *Political Thinkers from Socrates to the Present*, edited by D. Boucher and P. Kelly. Second Edition. Oxford: Oxford University Press, 362–380.

4 Erecting buildings, erecting a state
Public perception of Kurdish statehood

Umut Kuruuzum

'Everything has changed a lot,' is a phrase I often heard while conducting my fieldwork among ordinary citizens in Erbil, the capital city of the Iraqi Kurdistan Federal Region. When I asked what exactly had changed, I was always told essentially the same thing: 'Look at those high-rise modern buildings, none of them were here a decade ago!' Indeed, the change is visible to the eye if one compares the skyline of the city today, crowded with construction cranes and partially completed high-rises, to the pastoral view of the city in pictures only a decade ago. Towering office buildings, spacious shopping malls, residential developments, and proliferating hotels seem to have changed the city's landscape beyond recognition.

In recent years, scholars have increasingly drawn attention to the role of material artefacts in political life.[1] Materials are no longer the passive and stable foundation on which politics takes place; on the contrary, they play a lively and often unpredictable role in political disputes (Barry 2013:1–2). In this chapter, following these scholars, I have attempted to analyse the material change with the proliferation of modern high-rise buildings in the city and its impact on the popular understanding of politics. Throughout my ethnographic fieldwork carried out between November 2014 and July 2015 in Erbil, I focused on the physical characteristics of new modern high-rise buildings and a series of narratives that surrounded them. As a result, I came to the conclusion that these buildings, together with images on billboards, magazines, the Internet, and TV have come to animate political debate and provoke passionate discussions among ordinary citizens in the city regarding the Kurdish state.

Most of the recent work on Kurds and the state has focused on the analysis of religious and ethnic conflict, nationalism, and state-building efforts (see Danilovich 2014; Shareef 2014; Gunter and Ahmad 2013; Kirmanj 2013; Bengio 2012; Lowe and Stansfield 2010; Romano 2006; Natali 2005). In this chapter, I have attempted to contribute to the literature by paying particular attention to the cultural construction of the state, that is how local people perceive the state, how their understanding is shaped by their particular locations and encounters with state practices, and how the state manifests itself in their lives (Sharma and Gupta 2006:11). An anthropological perspective allows us to see the modalities by which the state comes to be imagined and symbolically represented at a local level, offering a critique of the conceptualization of the state as a universal, monolithic and unitary entity.

In this chapter, I have employed the issue of corruption surrounding the recently erected modern buildings to demonstrate how the Kurdish state comes to be imagined in a cultural context. I argue that while modern highrise buildings are often interpreted as images of modernity and progress to a much-desired Kurdish state, they also generate rumors of corruption and conspiracy, and create doubts about the Kurdish statehood among ordinary citizens. They produce suspicions that the state is inseparable from the interests of the ruling families, which works against the idea of a state as an entity, agent, function or relation over and above the society, operating according to its own logic, dictates, and priorities (Nugent 1994:199).

The chapter is divided into two main sections. In the first section, I will look at the local construction sector and explain a new form of urban fragmentation that accompanied selectively territorialized investment in the city. In the second section, I will look at the specific meanings attributed to the various aspects of modern high-rise buildings and illustrate the insight they offer into ordinary people's perceptions about Kurdish statehood. While the first section is about the material change in the city, the second section is about how it is perceived and constituted as one mechanism through which the Kurdish state is discursively erected in public culture and challenged accordingly by its citizens. These two sections are followed by a conclusion with attempts to draw out larger theoretical inferences.

Modern buildings in Erbil

Being in a transition period from a marginalized region within the old Iraq to a new autonomous region within a federal Iraq, the first Kurdish government has seen its goal as promoting entrepreneurship at every level, supposedly to speed up the development of an economically self-sustainable polity in the north of Iraq. Economic expansion through international companies and their investments has been considered an essential condition for stability, welfare, and security in the region. The introduction of market norms alongside a discourse of political stability rendered neoliberal economic transformations not only feasible and legitimate but also normatively desirable and necessary for building an affluent Kurdish society.

The Kurdistan Region Investment Law was passed in July 2006 and the Board of Investment was created in the same year to attract more foreign investments and assist investors in the region.[2] The establishment of the Ministry of Natural Resources (2006), the formation of the Kurdistan International Bank for Investment and Development (2006), and the introduction of the Kurdistan Hydrocarbon Law (2007), which opened up Kurdish oilfields to international companies through production-sharing agreements, have not only created incentives for foreign entrepreneurs to step in, but also offered an attractive economic system through which international capital can flow in and out. In addition, the relative stability and security of the Kurdistan region has also played a substantial role in the economic expansion and creating confidence on the part of investors.

The construction sector and the hydrocarbon industry have been two key investment areas which have benefited most from the business-friendly policies and a comparatively stable and secure environment in the Kurdistan Region over the last decade. According to figures that I have taken from the Kurdistan Board of Investment, around $42.5 billion was invested in Iraqi Kurdistan between August 2006 and September 2015, 33 per cent of which (approximately $15 billion) has gone into the housing sector. The large-scale return of the Kurdish diaspora, the influx of Iraqi nationals living in areas suffering from higher security risks, the arrival of expatriate workers in the region, increased urbanization, and a shift in local preference towards single-family homes have created a high demand for housing. However, it seems safe to say that the majority of the housing projects were designed as luxury villas or expensive apartment complexes for high-income groups rather than addressing the escalating demand by middle- or low-income groups. The sudden influx of petrodollars has resulted in a significant inflation of real estate prices, which has not only transformed property and land into a form of investment and one of the quickest ways to attain wealth, but has also led to the privatisation of public land.

During this process, the west side of Erbil seems to have emerged as the city's new central business district. It contains dozens of villas and several high-rise apartment buildings, attracting most of the current residential and commercial real estate projects in the region (See Figure 4.1 next page). Erbil's west side is located away from the city's old and cultural centre, the Citadel of Erbil, where local businesses and people tend to cluster. In the new district, international companies are currently leasing residential villas clustered within the Italian Village, the English Village, Dream City and the American Village and standalone office buildings on Gulan Street and 100m Road within close proximity to Erbil International Airport. In addition to being close to work, the expat community favours the West Side because the new district is within easy reach of many facilities and services such as world cuisine, shopping malls, gyms, yoga centres, cafeterias, and pubs. The city's new franchise knockoffs, such as the creatively named MaDonal, Dominoes Pizza, PJ's Pizza, Burger Queen, Krunchy Fried Chicken, and Costa Rica Coffee, have mushroomed around the walls of the gated communities. The TGI Friday near Naz City, an American restaurant chain focusing on casual dining, is a recent addition to the American-style food culture burgeoning in the west side of Erbil. In the American restaurant, burgers, ribs, steaks, and fajitas are served by English-speaking East Asian staff in a new style of décor with red-striped canopies, brass railings, and Tiffany lamps. Well-matched with its motto, 'Thank God it's Friday,' the restaurant is especially popular for lunch after jum'ah prayers on Friday, a legal holiday in Iraqi Kurdistan.

Erecting buildings, erecting a state 81

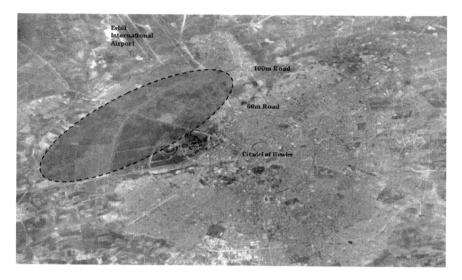

Figure 4.1 The west side of Erbil, Erbil's Emerging business and modern residential district
Source: Figure by the author.

Average rental rates within gated compounds in the west side of Erbil are typically between $2,000 and $6,000 per month depending on the location. Villas and apartments within gated compounds are transacted on the secondary market starting from $600,000 per unit, prices similar to London, Munich, Houston, and Dubai despite the lower quality of construction materials used. However, since the beginning of 2014, the real estate market in the region has experienced stagnation and a relative decline due to the economic downturn. Prices have fallen in the past several months and the current economic and political situation indicates that this downward trajectory may continue for some time.

Within the construction sector, the great majority of the companies operating in the region originate from Turkey, with most of the construction labourers coming from Turkey's economically depressed Kurdish areas. Erbil International Airport, the new Department of Justice, the Governor's Office buildings, Divan Hotel (one of two five-star hotels in Erbil), Naz City, and the Park View Project, which consists of 12 multi-storey luxury apartment buildings situated above a shopping facility, are outstanding examples of residential complexes in the city erected by real estate development companies from Turkey. Most of the construction materials utilised in the region, including cement bricks, concrete blocks, gypsum, ceramic, and cobble, as well as prefabricated construction elements such as windows, plumbing supplies, and electrical appliances, are also imported from Turkey. Real-estate development companies from the United Arab Emirates have also been involved in various large-scale projects in Erbil. One of the major examples is the $3 billion downtown Erbil project, which covers an area of roughly 541,000 square metres with 15,000 homes, hotels, and a shopping mall andis undertaken by Emaar, the developer of Downtown Dubai, home of the world's tallest building the Burj Khalifa (see Figure 4.2 below).

The majority of the current construction caters to the consumption preferences of those at the higher end of the income spectrum. This has resulted in the rapid spread of 'high security' and 'ultra luxurious' designs of proprietary urban communities which have been variously termed 'gated communities' (Low 2003; Davis 1992), 'enclosed neighbourhoods' (Landman 2000), 'private cities' (Glasze, Webster and Frantz 2011), or 'city of walls' (Garreau 1991). These developments have emerged as a new trend in the city with varying characteristics that reflect a new set of socio-cultural features such as status, privacy, security, and the feeling of belonging to a special place.

The city has been developing with intense heterogeneity through its urban housing sector, transforming the previously integrated urban space into enclaves with exclusive collective spaces which are secure, modern, and globally integrated such as Dream City, the American Village, the Italian Village, the English Village, the German Village, Empire World, Park View Residences, Naz City and Royal City (see Figure 4.3 next page). Essential to this emerging enclave urbanism is the introduction of social, legal and physical boundaries where affluent groups, what the local community call the 'nouveau riche', actively separate themselves from the rest of the urban population, often reflecting a fear of crime or simply a desire to be, and to appear

Figure 4.2 Downtown Erbil project by Emaar Properties in the west side of Erbil
Source: www.stergroup.com/projects/downtown-erbil.htm

Figure 4.3 New Park View residence compound
Source: Photograph by author.

to be, exclusive. Most of these enclaves are physically separated from surrounding areas by walls; there are security cameras as well as 24-hour armed personnel. The enclaves offer top-quality facilities such as a grand entrance boulevard, perimeter landscape and fencing, a central park with distinctive cafés, restaurants, and supermarkets and English-style gardens, recreational vehicle parking, efficient sewage and water networks with underground sewage treatment, along with housekeeping and garbage collection.

Houses and infrastructure in the rest of the city, especially in the east and south sides and quarters such as *Mamzawa, Kuran, Kurdistan, Kasnazan Shawase, Pirzen,* and *Bnaslawa*, suffer from chronic underfunding. Many households have unsatisfactory centralised sewer systems or facilities for the collection of solid household waste. The technical condition of existing water, sanitation systems, and municipal services are inadequate. There is a lack of stable electricity and water supply; many households have access to electricity for only a few hours a day and water every other day. Many of the roads are currently in poor condition due to the government's lack of investment in transportation infrastructure. In addition to the acute infrastructural problems and dilapidated housing conditions, the east and south sides of the city have also seen a large-scale proliferation of slums and illegal housing developments, hence worsening the existing inequality in the city.

Enclave urbanism seems to be a global trend in the real estate, housing, industrial, and retail markets. Erbil looks like just another city going through the processes of urbanisation, disintegration, and fragmentation. Nonetheless, enclave urbanism often serves different purposes and expresses distinct cultural meanings in each context, so they have to be studied in relation to the associations with which they emerge in specific cities (Wissink 2013:4). For instance, urban enclaves reproduce racial segregation and exacerbate social divisions in the U.S. (Low 2003); create exclusive compounds for emerging elites in Bulgaria and China (Low 2003); reflect the post-metropolitan lifestyle in Cairo (Almatarneh 2013; Denis 2006); provide a secure lifestyle in the face of extreme poverty in Southeast Asia (Low 2008); house Canadian age-segregated communities in retirement villages (Townshed 2004); and separate foreigners in Saudi Arabia with different religious backgrounds from the dominant Islamic culture (Glasze and Khayyal 2002). Enclave urbanism may be interpreted as a global trend, but to grasp its precise form, meaning, function, and effect in different environments, it is essential to examine the context in which gating takes place and let local people tell their stories about the city they live in.

Narratives of modern buildings

In a culture with a rich tradition of oral storytelling, several themes surfaced during my conversations with local people regarding the proliferation of high-rise buildings in the city, most of them revolving around the numerous corruption charges against the Kurdish government, particularly those against the ruling families in the region. Following Gupta (1995:376), I take corruption as a mechanism through which 'the state' itself is discursively constructed instead of considering corruption as a dysfunctional feature of state organizations. The proliferating narratives of corruption revolving around themes, such as 'Who is making money out of these constructions?' 'Where does all the essential money come from to finance these projects?' 'Who lives in these modern luxurious buildings?' and 'How can they afford it?' not only structure people's imagination of what the state is and how it is demarcated, but also enable people to develop strategies of resistance to this imagined state (Sharma and Gupta 2006:17).

Erbil's central bazaar, the city's traditional market, is one of the largest covered markets in the Kurdish Region, filled with stalls selling Kurdish cheese, honey, fresh fruit or clothes, electronics, and money exchangers who set up small tables along the main roads. In the dusky maze of narrow alleys, there are various coffee houses where people traditionally go to relax after shopping. Since shops in the bazaar are often very small, these coffee houses also serve as a meeting point for most shopkeepers. In a typical conversation I had in the bazaar, one of my informants asked me to look at the catalogue of a housing project in which he was planning to invest with his older brothers. The house in the catalogue had its own private garage and a subtropical garden with a barbeque area. I asked if he was serious, as the price was high. He smiled faintly down at me, with a flicker of irony in his eyes and a touch of bitterness, and said, 'I will buy it when the bubble bursts.' The discussion about the real-estate bubble in Erbil articulated into a long discussion about whether the government should regulate the housing prices and offer incentives to developers to build affordable housing in the city. At one point, he interrupted the flow of our discussion. He lowered his voice and started to explain staring straight at the catalogue in my hand:

> There is no state here separate from the interest of the ruling families. The government cannot regulate the housing prices because the ruling families themselves are making millions of dollars out of these buildings. The entire bureaucracy furthers the interests of them and their close allies. They are behind all the lucrative business in the region. Nobody can do a big business here without offering them bribes. However, they keep denying involvement in any commercial enterprises. Well, it is true if you consider the official documents, but not if you consider behind-the-scenes negotiations. How would we trust the thought that the Kurdish state could act in our interest?

What my respondent believes is that the ruling families and their close allies became rich from the creation of monopolies, subsidies, and privileged access to the real estate market in the region. For him, they control huge swathes of public land and the network of infrastructures in the city, which puts them in a privileged position vis-à-vis foreign investors and entrepreneurs. Any foreign investors and entrepreneurs who wish to enter the market have to cooperate with the ruling families and their close allies to run a lucrative business in the region, in return for a share of the investment. He considers that these processes produce diverse, behind-the-scenes negotiations whose outcome is entirely different from the official bureaucratic processes; this creates a shadow state being drawn directly into the revenue streams of the official state (Bear 2011). As a result, he sees the range of public institutions and processes as mechanisms that further the interest of the ruling families in the region, not a neutral bureaucracy separated from society and the economy aimed at the general or public interest.

In the case outlined here, there emerges a public understanding of the state, a sense of the local level functioning of the state, where everyday interactions with state bureaucracies mixes with familiar routes of street talk, gossip, humours, conspiracy theories, projections, and the media. Local people handle their documents and approach the law of their regional government and its administration, practices, procedures, and implementations with a doubt quite apart from the implicit assumption that the state is a neutral arbiter of public interest. They suspect the range of institutions and processes that would conventionally be understood as the state in reality lacks coherence, unity, and neutrality (Nugent 1994:199). There are formal rules and procedures, but local people believe that these are not applicable at all times, which makes the economic and political system particularly ambiguous and opaque in the popular imagination of ordinary people. Some even argue that the government diverts public funds into construction projects to create cheap, fast ways of raising income and extracting revenue towards the political centre, the politburo of the political parties. Notice, for example, this short passage from one of my interviews with a government official:

> There is no transparency for how public funds are spent. Where does our money go? The number of fancy malls, enormous shopping centres, and elevated skyscrapers are noticeably on the rise in the city. I believe that these investments are funded by hundreds of thousands of public funds. If not, why not conduct an investigation to let the public know how and by whom all these business projects are funded? Can these public funds be better used on more vital priorities? Don't we need equal access to employment, education opportunities, a superior health care system, and solutions to water and electricity shortages? Citizens should decide how public money is spent rather than the ruling families themselves for their own interests.

Taxi driving is one of the more popular jobs in Erbil. There is no requirement for a taxi-driving license and there is also no licensing committee to set a limit on the number of taxis in the city. Hence, automobiles have become a form of investment which generates an additional income source for local people living in and around the city. Below is another passage from one of my informants who is a taxi-driver on a trip to a village, which I visited as part of a convoy of picnickers. I interviewed the taxi driver in the context of the unpaid salaries of civil servants, including peshmerga on the frontlines in the war against the ISIS. Indeed, he was also a peshmerga nominated by, and receiving his salary from, the government. At that time, the government was three months behind on payments, once again blaming the financial crisis due to the fall in oil prices, the costly war against ISIS, and the dispute with Baghdad over its budget share as well as an influx of refugees and displaced Iraqis to the region. He explains here why he feels uneasy about the proliferation of modern buildings in the city and takes them as a sign of a corrupt political system:

> Who is making cash out of these buildings? Let me say, the Turks. They fund the construction of these buildings and then make millions of dollars behind the Kurds' back. In the North, Kurds have had a long history of discrimination, persecution and even massacres perpetrated against them by the Turkish government. Turkey also opposes independence, opposes a Kurdish state. Why is, then, our government cooperating with the Turks? The ruling families are making millions of dollars out of these buildings together with the Turks, but cannot pay the salaries of peshmerga on the frontlines in the war against the ISIS. I am dreaming of an independent Kurdish state caring for its own citizens and separated from the interest of the ruling families in the region.

He was only one among many other respondents who criticized the ruling families in the region for co-operating with Turkish construction companies in order to raise income and extract revenue for their own interests. According to several respondents, co-operation with Turkish construction companies is not aimed at rebuilding the country, but instead at making short-term profits and filling the ruling families' own pockets. The government's good relationships with Turkish politicians and its co-operation with Turkish construction companies fuel the conspiracy theories and corruption allegations voiced by my informants. Notice, for example, another passage from one of my interviews with an instructor in one of the universities:

> The ruling families of the region are giving public lands to Turkish construction companies in order to develop residential and commercial real estate projects. Once the project is finished, the construction companies give a number of shares back to the ruling families. This is another way of privatizing public lands and transmitting common wealth into private hands. The Turks are making millions of dollars in cooperation with the ruling elites against the wealth of the commons. How can one trust a state which is cooperating with foreign companies against its own citizens? Is this a path to freedom or slavery?

Al-Iskan Street is the centre of Erbil's famous nightlife for men who stay in cafeterias, especially in the ones offering wireless Internet access, until the early hours of the morning during the long, hot summer days. Apart from the local Kurds, the lively street is busy with young Syrian Kurds who had to flee their country and have ended up working in food trucks selling snacks, immigrant workers from the Southeast Asia selling watches, sunglasses, and prepaid *Korek* telecom top-up cards, and Arab tourists from the southern provinces of Iraq. In a typical conversation in Al-Iskan Street, one of my informants who referred to himself as a 'pious Muslim' expresses below his uneasiness with the new lifestyle in modern housing compounds and accuses the Kurdish state of 'blending Islam with Christian habits'.

> This is not the way we used to live. The Kurdish Islamic life is spoiled. The Kurdish Islamic tradition is corrupted. Look at the advertisements all around the city. What kind of life do these buildings offer us? The people in the advertisements wear clothes like Western people do. They live alone apart from their families. They socialize in shopping malls. We see neither mosques nor Islamic practices in these advertisements. Why does the Kurdish state let our Muslim culture decay? They are making millions of dollars out of these buildings through promoting Western lifestyles, but spoiling at the same time our Islamic Kurdish culture.

What he meant by the advertisements all around the city are the billboards standing in front of construction sites depicting what life will be like when the

Figure 4.4 Billboards depicting the future life of a residential complex
Source: Photograph by author.

construction is finished. Computer-aided designs of would-be buildings are superimposed onto photographs of existing environments to represent what that locale will look like in the future. These billboards surround almost all the construction sites in the city. In the simulations of these future dreamlands, women are typified by light hair, light skin, blue eyes, tall stature, and a narrow nose, wearing business-casual wear and working at offices besides their male colleagues; going to the gym wearing workout pants and sports bras; and shopping in malls wearing tight skirts and sheer blouses (see Figure 4.4 above). The men wear dark sunglasses and talk on their mobile phones while relaxing by the swimming pool. Nuclear families consisting of a pair of adults and their children are represented in these advertisements rather than extended families all living in the same household (see Figure 4.5 next page).

It is highly uncertain when or if these dreamlands will be realised. The buildings may continue to represent an imagined future of abundance, but it seems that today there are only a limited number of rich people who can enjoy the comfortable, modern, and luxurious lifestyle seen on billboards all around the city. After being marketed for sale or for rent for months, concrete shells of unfinished constructions have abandoned due to the economic downturn in the region since February 2014. As of today, unfinished buildings are occupied by hundreds of displaced Iraqis (see Figure 4.6 on page 90). More refugees try to move out of camps into these abandoned buildings in search for a better life and job opportunities. The uncomfortable space between the advertiser's dream and reality serves as a critique of the state. Notice, for example,

Figure 4.5 Billboards depicting the future life of a residential complex
Source: Photograph by author.

another passage from one of my interviews with a Kurdish journalist in the region:

> Political parties have their own companies here. They are doing business through their companies. However, they are ruling the country at the same time. There is a conflict of interest here. They are involved in multiple interests, financial interests which corrupt the motivation of public interests. They are erecting these buildings in order to make millions of dollars. However, few people could afford these residential complexes. Most of them also remain empty due to the financial crisis in the region. Refugees are sleeping in these half-constructed, abandoned buildings. People need affordable housing. There is a discrepancy between what citizens need and what the state does.

In 2015, the KRG became the largest employer in the region, providing monthly salaries to an estimated 2 million people (i.e. nearly 40% of the population working in the public sector). It is argued that half of public employees are 'ghost employees' who collect a salary without working. Most of my respondents believe that the recruitment of public employees is not based on merit or competence, but on patronage. The ruling political parties in the region aim to build networks of supporters by founding particularistic relationships with citizens through the exchange of public material benefits, particularly government jobs. Patronage employees engage in political activities that support ruling political parties (patrons) because their fates are tied to

Figure 4.6 Refugees living at a hotel construction site near the Dream City
Source: Photograph by author.

the political fate of their patrons. In the absence of an effective formal government bureaucracy, patronage networks are the most readily available, and most advantageous, means of getting access to employment in the public sector (Leezenberg 2006:23). Most people believe that they cannot afford a life in modern high-rise residential complexes without some connection to the ruling elites. This is illustrated by the middle-aged street seller who works in a food truck on Al-Iskan Street.

> If you are somehow connected to the ruling families, you can be rich overnight. You live in a luxurious villa and drive an expensive car. If you are not connected, most likely you live in a poor neighbourhood without electricity, water, or salary. How can one otherwise afford a house in the Dream City? Who is living in these luxurious buildings? Those who have good connections with the ruling elites! Most of them are foreign people. They are all given good jobs in the government. What happened when DAESH came? They all left. They ran away without looking behind their backs. Now they come back to make money again. In order to run again after they make money? Who did make war against DAESH? Those who suffered for years, and are still suffering, stayed and made war against DAESH without having their salaries. Who can deserve the good life in these buildings?

He often punctuated his statements by turning to the others and rhetorically asking, 'Have I said anything wrong?' At the end, he stood up and pointed to the west side of Erbil where high-rises are popping up and said, 'They enjoy.' By foreigners, he did not refer particularly to expatriates coming from Western countries who are temporarily residing in Erbil. He also accused the Kurdish diaspora coming into the region for governmental posts, economic partnerships, or conducting business. In his view, they had fled Iraqi Kurdistan during the war and came back to the region during the economic boom. In this context, he accuses the political elites of cooperation with the Kurdish diaspora recruited in the public sector as consultants and business partners, and justifies the social inequality between the Kurdish diaspora and the local Kurds as a sign of corruption in the Kurdish state.

In Iraqi Kurdistan, traditional houses are built in two-storey modules representing the public and private realms. A single doorway that leads into to the courtyard provides the entrance; windows are generally placed high enough so that passers by cannot see inside. At the entrance to the house, there is usually a place of sitting called *majlis* where guests sit either with cushions placed directly on the floor or upon a raised shelf. Most families take pride in making their guests comfortable because hospitality is taken seriously in Kurdish culture. On the walls, there often hang calligraphy of verses of the Qur'an or pictures with the names of Allah and Mohammed beside pictures of Mustafa Barzani. There is little evidence of an absolute separation of public and private spaces and the segregation of men and women within traditional houses, yet these separations are physical architectural designs that ultimately guide behaviours (Campo 2009: 312). These separations have been eliminated in the architectural design of modern apartments, posing a serious threat to local identity and culture according to some of my informants. Modern dwellings with western-inspired decors typically consist of three rooms, one kitchen, and one or two bathrooms, which are connected through an entrée and a corridor without a separation.

From a conversation with a Turkish architect, I learned that in recent developments, his company cancelled full-sized balconies and put in French balconies instead (actually a false balcony with doors that open to a railing and a view of the surrounding scenery below). He maintained that the most recent trend is to build studio flats in a contemporary design with one bedroom for expatriate workers who live temporarily in Erbil. The modern architectural designs are locally referred as 'copying of the Western lifestyle', which assumes that the core of the household is the nuclear family of husband, wife and children. Some of my informants argue that these buildings create misunderstanding and a lack of attachment between parents or elder people and the younger generation; they accuse the ruling elite of supporting the societal decay.

For example, one of my informants in his late 60s was concerned about his son's plans to move into MRF apartments, one of several residential complexes in Erbil located on 100m Street near Empire World. He does not want to live in an apartment, but if he refuses, he is afraid of living alone. He had grown up in a house with his grandparents and had never lived anywhere but his father's home. His house is located in a nice neighbourhood where he has lots of friends, although some of them have already passed away. He is unsure about what to do as houses are abandoned in favour of apartments, while the traditional extended family seems to give way to a nuclear family in these modern apartments:

> Nowadays young people like to live in luxurious apartments, but they are quite small, only constructed and designed for small families. In the past as the family gets bigger, we used to enlarge our house horizontally by building new rooms or vertically by adding another flat. What will my son do? Is he going to add another room for us? If not, how can he able to afford a flat for me next to them? These buildings are changing our cultural habits, dividing our large families, and making us live our life just like Western people. The Kurdish politicians are no longer giving importance to the Kurdish culture, Islam, and old habits. They are instead caring about how much money they make with their Western counterparts.

It is fair to say that none of my informants witnessed any incident of bribery, reported the misuse of funds in the government budget, or provided any record of officials who abuse their power. Regardless of their validity and reliability, the narratives of corruption are vehicles for ordinary citizens to challenge their changed situations vis-à-vis the newly created lifestyle and social inequality. Notice that not everyone imagines the state in quite the same way. Sometimes the discussion dealt with the exploitation of Kurdish society by international companies in co-operation with the ruling elites of the region; at other times with the state's role in promoting a 'Christian culture' and imposing Western values and lifestyles on Islamic Kurdish society; at still other times with who is likely to be appointed to a certain position and live an affluent life. Yet, they all perceive the Kurdish state to be acting against their interests and imagine it as an entity inseparable from the interest of the ruling families of the region; therefore, deploy the discourse of corruption to resist the manner in which the state organisations function. In such a historical and cultural context, recently erected high-rise buildings give a concrete shape and form to the Kurdish statehood and enable certain constructions of the state in the imagination and everyday practices of ordinary people.

Conclusion

In this chapter, I focused on the materiality of recently constructed modern buildings and a series of narratives that surrounded them. In the first section, I looked at the local construction sector and explained a new form of urban fragmentation that accompanied selectively territorialised investment in the city. I argued that the city has been developing with intense heterogeneity through its urban housing sector, transforming the previously integrated urban space into enclaves with exclusionary collective spaces. In the second section, I examined the proliferating narratives of corruption regarding recently erected modern high-rise buildings in the city and came to the conclusion that these buildings have become what Geertz (1973) calls 'a public symbol' through which members of society communicate their beliefs to one another, and a key arena in which the state comes to be imagined in public culture. I argued that while modern high-rise buildings are often interpreted as images of progress to a much-desired Kurdish state, embodying the many facades of 'modernity' and 'westerness', they also generate ideas of corruption and conspiracy, and doubts about the Kurdish statehood among ordinary citizens in Erbil. Due to their visibility, buildings display the process of change and represent an imagined future of abundance, yet, at the same time they cause suspicions that the state is inseparable from the 'behind-the-scenes' interest of the ruling families.

By focusing on the discursive construction of the Kurdish state, I wish to draw attention to larger theoretical issues raised in the chapter. First, an anthropological approach to the study of the state allows us to see it as a cultural construction in contrast to the Weberian argument which tends to see culture as produced by the state (Sharma and Gupta 2006; Fuller and Harriss 2000). Therefore, ethnography of the state suggests that an adequate understanding of any actually existing state requires careful consideration of the ideological and material aspects of state construction (Nugent 1994). This helps us arrive at an historically specific and ideologically constructed understanding of the state being in contrast to the à priori assumptions about the constitution or taxonomy of the state (Gardner 2012). Despite the fact that the range of symbolic representations, material manifestations, and bureaucratic processes that would conventionally be understood as the state does, in reality, present in Iraqi Kurdistan, local people do not believe that the state is a neutral entity which is separated from the interest of ruling families. This is quite apart from the implicit assumption that the state is a neutral arbiter of public interest. Second, the cultural construction of state not only shapes people's imagination of what the state is and how it is demarcated, but also enables people to develop strategies of resistance to this imagined state (Sharma and Gupta 2006:17). Local people perceive the Kurdish state to be acting against their interests and deploy the discourse of corruption to attack the manner in which government organizations function. The insufficient financial transparency in Iraqi Kurdistan both heightens the accusations and blocks efforts to find any evidence of malfeasance, which contributed to the popularity of the proliferating narratives and counter narratives of corruption among ordinary citizens. In this context, the proliferating narratives of corruption draw our attention to less-organized, more pervasive, and more 'everyday forms of resistance' (Scott 1985) facing off the ruling families. Finally, the state comes into being not only through ideological constructions but also material artefacts. In the case outlined here, modern buildings and their physical properties give a concrete shape and form to the newly established state, which otherwise can be an abstraction. In other words, they give the state a relatively fixed locus, and a degree of objectivity, that it did not have before and allow us to see one modality by which the state comes to be imagined. They have become public symbols because of their visibility, vehicles for meanings through which the members of a society construct their ideas about the state, communicating their worldview accordingly (Geertz 1973). In this respect, buildings, as material artefacts, fabricate a particular texture of relationship between persons and states in an historically and geographically specific context. Buildings function as a 'state effect', a practice that makes the state appear to exist as a transcendental entity, which appeals to a notion of Leviathan chartered to bring an imagined future of abundance (Mitchell 2006). However, they also move beyond Foucault's notion of 'governmentality' and 'work against the grain of the sterilisation and desensitisation of materiality' (Navaro-Yashin 2012:33) because they are charged with a particular sense of feeling that the state is inseparable from the interests of ruling families in Iraqi Kurdistan.

Notes

1 See Barry 2013 for oil and gas pipelines in Azerbaijan, Georgia, and Turkey; Weszkalnys 2013 for the materiality of oil in São Tomé and Príncipe; Navaro-Yashin 2012 for abject materials and uncanny dwellings in Northern Cyprus; Kelly 2006 for identity documents in the Israeli-Palestinian conflict; Verdery 2006 for lively politics around dead bodies in the post-socialist period in the former Soviet bloc; Pelkmans 2006 for state in Ajaria; Harvey 2005 for the materiality of state-effects through an ethnography of a road in the Peruvian Andes; Mitchell 2012 for how oil shapes the body politic both in the Middle East and those places that have the greatest demand for energy.
2 According to the Investment Law No.4 of 2006, the foreign investor and capital shall be treated as the national investor and capital. The foreign investor shall have the right to own the entire capital of any project that he establishes in the region under this law (Article 3). The project shall be exempted of all non-customs taxes and duties for a period of 10 years as of the date on which the project begins offering its services or as of the day of actual production (Article 5). The Board of Investment may, for the requirement of the public interest in the region, grant additional incentives and facilities to investment projects that are licensed under the provisions of this law in accordance with the rules set by the board for this purpose (Article 6). The foreign investor shall be allowed to transfer the profits of and the interest on his capital abroad in accordance with the provisions of this law (Article 7).

References

Almatarneh, R.T. 2013. Choices and changes in the housing market and community preferences: Reasons for the emergence of gated communities in Egypt: A case study of the Greater Cairo Region, Egypt. *Ain Shams Engineering Journal*, 4 (3), 563–583.

Barry, A. 2013. *Material Politics: Disputes Along the Pipeline*. Oxford: Wiley-Blackwell.
Bear, L. 2011. Making a river of gold: Speculative state planning, informality and neoliberal governance on the Hooghly. *Focaal*, 61, 46–60.
Blakely EJ and Snyder MG. 1997. *Fortress America: Gated Communities in the United States*. Washington, DC/Cambridge, MA: Brookings Institution Press and Lincoln Institute of Land Policy.
Campo, J.E. 2009. *Encyclopaedia of Islam*. New York: Infobase Publishing.
Danilovich, A. 2014. *Iraqi Federalism and the Kurds: Learning to Live Together*. Ashgate. Aldershot, Brookfield: UK/Burlington, VT: USA.
Denis, E. 2006. Cairo as neoliberal capital? From walled city to gated communities, in *Cairo Cosmopolitan*, edited by D. Singerman and P. Amar. Cairo: AUC Press, 47–71.
Davis, M. 1992. *City of Quartz: Excavating the future of Los Angeles*. New York: Vintage Books.
Fuller, C. J. and J. Harriss 2000. For an anthropology of the state, in *The Everyday State and Society in Modern India*, edited by C. J. Fuller and V. Benei. London: Hurst and Company, 1–25.
Gardner, A. 2012. Rumour and myth in the labour camps of Qatar. *Anthropology Today*, 28(6), 25–28.
Garreau, J. 1991. *Edge City: Life on the New Frontier*. New York: Doubleday.
Geertz, C. 1973. *The Interpretations of Cultures: Selected Essays*. New York: Basic Books.
Glasze, G, C. Webster, and K. Frantz. 2011. *Private Cities: Global and Local Perspectives*. London: Routledge.
Glasze, G. and A. Alkhayyal 2002. Gated housing estates in the Arab world: Case studies in Lebanon and Riyadh, Saudi Arabia. *Environment and Planning B Planning and Design*, 29(3), 321–336.
Gunter, M. and A. Mohammed. 2013. *The Kurdish Spring: Geopolitical Changes and the Kurds*. California: Mazda Publishers.
Gupta, A. 1995. Blurred boundaries: the discourse of corruption, the culture of politics, and the imagined state. *American Ethnologist*, 22 (2), 375–402.
Hansen, T. B. and F. Stepputat. 2001. Introduction, in *States of Imagination: Ethnographic Explorations of the Postcolonial State*, edited by T. B. Hansen and F. Stepputat. Durham and London: Duke University Press, 1–38.
Harvey, P. 2005. The materiality of state-effects: An ethnography of a road in the Peruvian Andes, in *State Formation: Anthropological Perspectives*, edited by C. Krohn-Hansen and K. G. Nustad. London and Ann Arbor: Pluto Press, 123–141.
Kelly, T. 2006. Documented lives: Fear and the uncertainties of law during the second Palestinian intifada. *Journal of the Royal Anthropological Institute*, 12, 89–107.
Kirmanj, S. 2013. *Identity and Nation in Iraq*. Boulder: Lynne Rienner Publishers.
Kurdistan Investment Law. 2006. Available at: www.kurdistaninvestment.org/docs/Investment%20Law.pdf (last accessed: 10 August 2015).
Leezenberg. 2006. Urbanization, privatization, and patronage: The political economy of Iraqi Kurdistan, in *The Kurds: Nationalism and Politics*, edited by Faleh A. Jabar and H Dawod. London: Saqi Books, 151–179.
Lowe, R. and G. Stansfield. 2010. *Kurdish Policy Imperative*. London: Royal Institute of International Affairs.
Low, S. 2003. *Behind the Gates: Life, Security, and the Pursuit of Happiness in Fortress America*. New York: Routledge.

Low, S. 2008. Behind the gates: Social splitting and the 'other', in *The Way Class Works: Readings on School, Family, and the Economy*, edited by L. Weis. London and New York: Routledge, 44–60.

Mitchell, T. 2006 [1991]. Society, economy and the state effect, in *The Anthropology of the State*, edited by A. Sharma and A. Gupta. Oxford: Blackwell Publishing, 169–186.

Mitchell, T. 2011. *Carbon Democracy: Political Power in the Age of Oil*. London: Verso.

Navaro-Yashin, Y. 2012. *The Make-Believe Space: Affective Geography in a Postwar Polity*. Durham and London: Duke University Press.

Natali, D. 2012. *The Kurds and the State: Evolving National Identity in Iraq, Turkey and Iran*. Syracuse: Syracuse University Press

Nugent, D. 1994. Building the state, making the nation: The bases and limits of state centralization in modern Peru. *American Anthropologist*, 96, 333–369.

Pelkmans, M. 2006. *Defending the Border: Religion, Identity, and Modernity in the Republic of Georgia*. Ithaca: Cornell University Press.

Romano, D. 2006. *The Kurdish Nationalist Movement: Opportunity, Mobilization and Identity*. Cambridge: Cambridge University Press.

Scott, J. 1985. *Weapons of the Weak: Everyday Forms of Peasant Resistance*. New Haven: Yale University Press.

Shareef, M. 2014. *The United States, Iraq and the Kurds: Shock, Awe and Aftermath*. London: Routledge.

Sharma A. and A. Gupta. 2006. Introduction, in *The Anthropology of the State*, edited by A. Sharma and A. Gupta. Oxford: Blackwell Publishing, 1–41.

Townshed I. Gated common interest communities in Canada: The retirement village, in: The privatization of urban space: gated communities – A new trend in global urban development? Annual symposium of the Universities of New Orleans and Innsburk, 26–28 February, New Orleans, LA, 2004.

Verdery, K. 2006. *The Political Life of Dead Bodies: Reburial and Post-socialist Change*. New York: Colombia University Press.

Weszkalnys, G. 2010. Re-conceiving the resource curse and the role of anthropology, in signification of oil in Africa: What (more) can anthropologists contribute to the study of oil? edited by A. Behrends and N. Schareika, *Suomen Antropologi: Journal of the Finnish Anthropological Society*, 35, 87–90.

Weszkalnys, G. 2013. Oil's magic: Contestation and materiality, in *Cultures of Energy: Power, Practices, Technologies*, edited by Sarah Strauss, Stephanie Rupp, and Thomas Love. Walnut Creek, CA: Left Coast Press, 267–283.

Wissink, B. 2013. Enclave urbanism in Mumbai: An actor-network-theory analysis of urban (dis)connection. *Geoforum*, 47, 1–11.

Yildiz, K. 2012. *The Future of Kurdistan: Iraqi Dilemma*. London: Pluto Press.

Part II
Iraqi Kurdistan in Middle Eastern politics

5 Oil, the Kurds, and the drive for independence

An ace in the hole or joker in the pack?

Francis Owtram

Introduction: Oil, independence and the divisive lines of Sykes-Picot

In 2011 the Kurdistan Region of Iraq (KRI) was described by Tony Haywood, former Chief Executive of BP, as 'arguably...the last big onshore "easy" oil province available for exploration by private companies anywhere in the world, the last easy frontier' (Wearden 2011). Indeed, it is not just oil that is found in abundance in Kurdistan. Vast pockets of gas are now known to lie under the foothills of the Zagros mountains. This chapter examines the role that hydrocarbon resources have played in the Kurds' struggle for an independent state in the era of the contemporary Middle East state system. This system dates from the collapse of the Ottoman Empire at the end of the First World War, the formative correspondence and subsequent treaties (notably Hussein-McMahon, Sykes-Picot, Balfour Declaration, Sèvres, Lausanne) and the resulting League of Nations French and British mandates for Syria and Lebanon, Palestine, Jordan, and Iraq. From the ashes of the Ottoman Empire a Kurdish state was almost kindled as anticipated by the Treaty of Severe (1920). However, subsequent Turkish military victories under Atatürk and other developments poured cold water on this prospect. There was no mention of a Kurdish state in the Treaty of Lausanne (1923) which officially ended the conflict between Turkey and the British and French empires and accorded recognition to Turkey within its current boundaries. Instead of a Kurdish state, the former Ottoman *vilayet* of Basra, Baghdad and Mosul were cobbled together in a new League of Nations-endorsed mandate in which Shi'a Arabs, Sunni Arabs, Kurds as well as a mosaic of other ethnic groups and religions were ruled by a British-imposed monarchy, in the Kingdom of Iraq. Under the Treaty of Lausanne, Kurds were distributed in the successor states to the Ottoman Empire as a geographically concentrated minority (that is, they formed a majority in the areas they inhabited) in Iraq, Turkey, and Syria (see Natali 2005). In 2016, the one-hundredth anniversary of the Sykes-Picot correspondence, these are still the same internationally recognised boundaries of these states as they were formed after the First World War.

The chapter seeks to answer a seemingly paradoxical question: in the metaphorical poker game of the politics of state independence, do the hydrocarbon resources of the KRI provide a card that would insure the indisputable win or a card whose consequences are unpredictable in outcome: an ace in the hole or a joker in the pack? It might be asked how could such resources not be an asset in attaining independence? In pondering this question the chapter engages with the literature relating to the impact of oil resources on development – namely the *rentier* character of the economy and politics – coined euphemistically as 'the curse of black gold'.

It is important at this point to note that the economic, political and strategic importance of the hydrocarbons for the KRI cannot be seen in complete isolation from the international relations of the global political economy. Rather, they must be seen in their context first, as part of the vast hydrocarbon resources of the rest of Iraq, and second, in the wider context of the resources of Kuwait, Saudi Arabia and the other Gulf states. In many ways Tony Haywood's comment echoes an earlier assessment of the oil reserves of Saudi Arabia which were described by the State Department in 1945 as 'the greatest material prize in history' (Yergin 1990). It is these resources as a whole – of good quality and technically easy to develop – which have put Iraq and the Gulf at the heart of the strategic plans of the Great Powers since they were first discovered.

In terms of perspective this chapter is embedded in a global political economy approach that sets the story of the Kurds and oil within an analysis of the process of state formation in the modern Middle East. Namely, the role that the Middle East's vast oil resources have played in attracting external power involvement, and shaped those powers' interaction with the peoples and polities of the region, both during the impact of formal imperialism and thereafter into the regional power politics of the contemporary Middle East (see, for instance, the accounts by Bromley 1990, 1994; Halliday 2005; Hinnebusch 2003; Luciani 2009). Concomitantly, whilst the chapter's primary focus is on the KRI, oil and Iraq, the 'Kurdish Question' in the Middle East and its relationship to oil cannot be treated in isolation by focusing exclusively on the Kurds in one of the contemporary states: there are wider regional and international ramifications which are addressed as necessary.

Analytical aims, theoretical framework and structure of the chapter

To be specific, the historical narrative of this chapter which contextualises the contemporary period is framed using the middle-range theorisation offered by Halliday's (2008) 'post-colonial sequestration', Harvey and Stansfield's (2011: 13) theorising on unrecognised states and natural resources, and the insights of Luciani (2009) on the impact of oil on the politics and international relations of the Middle East. The historical narrative outlined deploys their theoretical insights by succinct reference to the intersection between oil, politics and international relations since 1918, focusing primarily on the period since 2011. In so doing, it gives an assessment of these issues on the one-hundredth anniversary of the Sykes-Picot correspondence, which still stands as the origin of the contemporary Middle East state boundaries. In developing this analysis, the chapter stands on the shoulders of the exposition by Hinnebusch (2003) in which he deployed a combination of several conceptual approaches to capture the unique complexity of the international politics of the Middle East.

The outlining of this theoretically framed historical narrative in turn enables the chapter to address the second task: to answer the question as to whether the oil resources found in the KRI have constituted a help or a hindrance since the First World War for the achievement of an independent state by the Kurds of Iraq. In so doing, it reflects on the notion of 'the curse of black gold' by analysing the role that oil has played in the historic and contemporary political and developmental trajectory of the Kurdistan Region of Iraq. In short, can we say that the possession of hydrocarbons is an 'ace in the hole' or 'a joker in the pack' for the Iraqi Kurds? The metaphor here refers to a card game in which a card, once revealed, has the certain effect of winning the game. This card is 'the ace in the hole'. In contrast, the 'joker in the pack' could lead to different, unexpected and unpredictable outcomes.

In this metaphorical usage, oil – its associated revenues and measures to control it – is a card which has been both played by the Kurds and also one which has been played against them. It can be added here that it seems fair to conclude that the players in the game of Middle East politics, nearly always perceive that they are playing in a zero-sum game. It is a tragic fact that the violence that has attended external intervention and internal reaction, has made, and will make, the development of co-operative modes of thinking and win–win solutions, far more difficult. The requisite pre-condition for co-operative wins – personal and political trust – has been severely depleted by repeated cycles of external, intra-state and inter-communal violence almost to the point of exhaustion.

The structure of the chapter is as follows. First, I briefly highlight the oil resources of the KRI, to depict its abundant reserves. I then present the theoretical constructs developed by Harvey and Stansfield (2011), Halliday (2008) and Luciani (2009) in order to tease out the key questions which this chapter seeks to address. There then follows a brief review of the historical context in which these questions sit, which highlights key episodes from the end of the First World War to the end of the Cold War, in which oil has been a card played for or against the Iraqi Kurds. This includes those instances of the oil card when the 'Kurdish issue' – invariably linked to territory, oil and state allegiance – has been played by the neighbouring states in the competition and conflict between themselves. We then proceed to an extension of the narrative in the period when the Kurds of Iraq first developed autonomy. This is followed by the main focus of the chapter: an assessment of the role of oil in contemporary times. First, in the period since the attacks on the Twin Towers and the Pentagon (from 9/11 to US withdrawal from Iraq) and, second, in the period since 2011 – a year which is shorthand for the Arab Spring and the ending of the US Stationing of Forces Agreement. There follows a section drawing together the theoretical arguments before a final conclusion on the topic under consideration.

The argument advanced throughout the chapter is that, on balance, the presence of oil has been a hindrance to Kurdish aspirations for Kurdish statehood for the following reasons: oil has drawn in external parties with vested interests and fuelled internal divisions of the Kurds; it has also encouraged corruption in Iraq and the wider Middle East, hindering the development of human capital – the rentier character of development. In other words, far from being an ace in the hole, the oil resources of the KRI have played out as a joker in the pack.

Underlying this argument is the understanding that this region, in common with much of the global south, has suffered greatly from the imposition of artificial borders by the colonial powers. Britain and France, as elsewhere in their empires, deployed a divide-and-rule policy within the colonial administrative entities they created to facilitate political supremacy and exploitation of natural resources (see Cammack, Pool and Tordoff 1994); these carried on for a time as post-colonial states beyond *de jure* independence. In the case of the Middle East this is encapsulated in the Sykes-Picot legacy: the agreement reached in 1915/1916, by the Foreign Ministers of Britain and France, Mark Sykes and François Georges-Picot, to divide the Ottoman Arab lands between them. International society (due to the example and implications in a world of artificial states) has a default antipathy to the creation of new states even though the existing borders only have superficial and instrumental meaning for the populace, for whom sub-state identities of tribe or sect hold far greater resonance. Indubitably, this international recognition lends a great deal of endurance to the dysfunctional regional state system even if there is a massive mismatch between nation, state and identity (Hinnebusch 2003).

The Kurdistan region of Iraq: The last 'easy frontier' of onshore oil

We turn now to briefly consider the nature and extent of the hydrocarbon reserves of the Kurdistan Region, a region whose exact borders within Iraq are not fully defined. For initial clarification, there are the three provinces which form the undisputed territory of the Kurdistan Region of Iraq: Dohuk, Erbil and Sulaimaniya. Additionally, there are territories that are claimed by the Kurdistan Regional Government (KRG) to constitute part of the KRI: the disputed territories (see Zandalis 2012). The KRI's oil and gas reserves are relatively modest (although new discoveries are being made frequently) compared to the rest of Iraq (Mills 2013). The reserves of Iraq excluding the KRI are estimated at 143 billion barrels of oil (bbl), the fifth largest in the world and probably increasing to 200 billion barrels, as well as 127 trillion cubic feet (Tcf) of gas (twelfth largest in the world).

In contrast, the Iraqi Kurds anticipate finding 30–60 billion bbl. Excluding the Kirkuk field, which remains in disputed territory, they currently have 12 billion bbl of oil and 22 Tcf of gas. Large fields include the Shaikan field, Bardarash and Khor Mor and Chemchemal with 10 Tcf of gas. The most developed fields are the Norwegian (DNO) Tawke field, Taq Taq held by Turkish company Genel (with Tony Hayward as CEO), and Khor Mor which supplies gas for local needs. These resources have been developed since 2005 by a range of international oil companies (IOC) including Esso. The KRG's Ministry of Natural Resources has offered attractive Production Sharing Contracts to IOCs from a wide range of countries that have had a high success rate in discovering commercially viable wells. Although holding only a tenth of the reserves of the rest of Iraq the KRI has a population of approximately 5 million, so its reserves certainly provide the potential foundation for a national economy in an independent state or the basis for a prosperous autonomous region. A key point to note is that if the resources of the Kirkuk governorate are added, then this massively increases the oil resources of the KRI.

Unrecognized states: 'Post-colonial sequestration' and the resource factor

In his brief, but brilliantly perceptive, article Halliday (2008) outlined his notion of 'post-colonial sequestration'. It refers to the phenomenon where due to bad luck or timing, countries or peoples fail to gain independence at times of major change in the international system such as the end of wars, colonial withdrawal or revolution. Once this moment of change has passed, then these countries or people find that they are in effect sequestered (legally possessed) into a state system, until the next moment of systemic change unveils a new opportunity. He also notes that the list of independent states of the world does not conform to any possible rational criteria for statehood whether it be size of population, economic viability, internal legitimacy, and so on. In other words, there is nothing 'natural' about statehood, it can be an accident or seemingly unfair. Thus the Government of Somalia has a place at the United Nations, yet it has little internal legitimacy and most of its putative territory is controlled by a variety or warlords (see Owtram 2011). At the other end of the spectrum, there are peaceful micro-states in the Pacific with a population of a few thousand which again have a place in the United Nations (UN) General Assembly (see Owtram 2011). In contrast, the Kurds with a combined population of 30 million, a distinct cultural identity and potentially a viable economy, have no seat at the UN and have suffered extreme repression and genocide from the states in which they found themselves since the post- First World War settlement (see also Stansfield 2013).

In outlining their global political economy approach to the theorisation of unrecognised states – of which the Kurdistan Regional Government forms a notable example – Harvey and Stansfield note that sovereignty over natural resources is a vital factor in the politics of independence and a key source of contestation. Thus, drawing on Harvey and Stansfield (2011) and Halliday (2008), this analysis is informed by a combination of an awareness of the resource factor and the awareness that there is nothing 'natural' or inevitable about state formation and boundaries. Having failed to achieve a state in the aftermath of the First World War, the Kurds since then have subsequently felt the wrath of genocidal regimes and movements determined to forcibly integrate them and obliterate their identity. The Arab Spring and its resulting conflicts represents a decisive moment of international change in the Middle East, whose implications were intensified in Iraq, as it intersected with the withdrawal of US military forces from Iraq in December 2011.

To clarify, the phrase 'curse of black gold' or 'oil curse' refers to the paradox whereby, a natural resource that on the face of it might be assumed to give great benefits to the people in whose land it is found, actually only brings anguish: war, corruption, mismanagement, apathy, misery and destitution. This phrase (it is used in the title of a film about the despoliation of the Niger Delta by oil companies) finds equivalence in the academic literature in that body of work focusing on the *rentier* state or rentier economy. Luciani (2009) has summarised the role of oil in the Middle East in a number of aspects including state formation and division of the Arab world into 'haves' and 'have nots' with the attendant consequences for inter-Arab relations. There is also the impact of oil on domestic politics and economy – the rentier state thesis. In summary form, this argues that the possession of a natural resource sold by the state on the world market to achieve a revenue source (or rent) will mean that the state is not dependent on extracting a surplus from society by taxation. The state does not therefore need to negotiate a social contract with society in which representative institutions are offered in exchange for taxation.

Oil, the Kurds and the creation of the modern Middle East state system

To recap, with the collapse of the Ottoman Empire after the First World War and the occupation of the former Ottoman territories by Britain and France, the Kurds seemed poised to obtain a homeland as reflected in the Treaty of Sèvres. However, with Turkey resurgent a few years later under the leadership of Kemal Atatürk and a string of military victories and accompanying land gains strengthening his hand, the subsequent Treaty of Lausanne, omitted any reference to a Kurdish homeland. Instead it created states – Turkey, Syria and Iraq – where the Kurds were a large peripheral minority set within the overall area of the state but a majority in the lands which they inhabited. Thus, a massively destabilising force was built into the state structures created at that time.

Furthermore, oil attracts the attention of external powers and provides the motivation to involve themselves in the politics of a region in order to pursue and protect their own interests of reliable access to oil. Anderson and Stansfield contend that in the absence of the discovery of oil in Kirkuk the British might have supported the creation of a Kurdish state (2009: 23):

> To emphasize the importance of oil in the story of Kirkuk, it is worth briefly reconsidering Kirkuk's modern political history by imagining a scenario without oil. If the underlying geology of the province had contained water aquifers instead of oil fields, it is unlikely that the enforced population movements caused by the policy of Arabization would have taken place, while the democratic issues that are now so problematic to resolve would have been of a different, lesser magnitude. This counterfactual "Kirkuk without oil" scenario warrants developing a little more deeply. It is possible, for example, that in the aftermath of World War I and the occupation of Kirkuk following the signing of the Mudros Armistice in 1918 that the British would have supported the creation of a Kurdish state – even extending northward of the current Iraqi border to Lake Van, deep into Anatolia. However, as it became more apparent that unknown but probably vast amounts of oil lay underneath Kirkuk, the British position toward the Mosul vilayet changed, which is one of the reasons it was incorporated into the Kingdom of Iraq.

If this contention is correct, it represents the first instance of the 'curse of black gold' for the Kurds.

The artificial state thus created, inevitably pitted the Kurds in the north against the government in Baghdad. It set up a recurring pattern, or what could perhaps be better classified as a recurring nightmare for the Kurds. When the government in Baghdad is weak, concessions are offered to the Kurds; when the government in Baghdad is strong, it withdraws those concessions and seeks to resolve the underlying tension by force. This dynamic, was set in motion and fostered by the structure of the state system created by external powers after the First World War. All states are artificial to some extent but the salient point to be made here is that whereas state formation in Europe took place over hundreds of years, and was forged through wars and dynastic marriage, in the Middle East most of the current states are the result of external imposition following the collapse of the Ottoman Empire. In 1916. the British Navy had converted from coal to oil, immediately elevating the Middle East into new strategic perspective. Oil had been discovered in Persia in 1909 by the Anglo-Persian Oil Company and it was thought that the lands of Turkish Arabia also held promise. Following the invasion of Basra, the occupation of Baghdad, and demise of the Ottoman Empire, the British took on the League of Nations Mandate for Iraq. British imperial officials on the ground such as Gertrude Bell and Arnold T. Wilson sought to fashion a state and create new administrative machinery to facilitate their rule through façade institutions (Cammack, Pool, and Tordoff 1994) and allow the development of the natural resources, particularly the now strategically vital resource of oil. This strategy was shown not to be misplaced with the discovery of the massive Kirkuk oil dome in 1927 – the British created the Iraqi monarchy and co-opted the Sunni landowning elite, pulled the strings of the Iraq Petroleum Company, and independent Iraq was launched in 1932. The British had cobbled together a state, in which the Sunnis maintained their dominance, as a vehicle to exploit a vast quantity of the resource that was to become the life blood of the global economy for the next century.

In their occupation of 'the land of the two rivers' the British encountered major resistance including rebellions by the Kurds in the north of Iraq: a major uprising after the First World War, and later again during the Second World War, when forces led by Mustafa Barzani gained control of large parts of Erbil. RAF bombers dropped their heavy load on the population below in contempt for this outbreak of resistance causing the rebels to flee over the border into Iran. In 1946 the sunshine of the flag of Kurdistan briefly flew over the Mahabad Republic until it was crushed ruthlessly by the Shah and Barzani departed the Middle East for exile in the Soviet Union.

The brutal overthrow of the Iraqi monarchy in the revolution of 1958 marked the end of the British-organised Baghdad Pact designed to contain the Soviet Union and ushered in a new phase of nation and identity building (see Kirmanj 2013). The development of Iraq as a regional power under the Baath party controlled by Saddam Hussein (with his inner circle from Tikrit) using nationalised oil resources proceeded apace in the 1970s. The 1970 Iraqi-Kurdish Autonomy Agreement on paper offered meaningful autonomy but on the ground an Arabisation programme of Kurdish areas was implemented and the Kurds and their *Peshmerga* under Masoud Barzani took up armed rebellion once more. In this they received support from the Shah of Iran who played the Kurdish card against Saddam Hussein – providing safe areas in Iran for them to launch attacks against the Iraqi army. In order to cut off this Iranian support for the Kurds of Iraq, Saddam made concessions to the Shah on the border line between Iraq and Iran on the Shatt al Arab waterway codified in the 1975 Algiers agreements. Saddam then proceeded to easily crush his Kurdish rebellion. During this time and for various reasons, Jalal Talabani split off from the Kurdistan Democratic Party to form the Patriotic Union of Kurdistan (PUK). Thus, an intense and sometimes blood rivalry was inaugurated within the Kurds of Iraq, with rival *Peshmerga* forces and networks of patronage (see Natali 2005).

The Shah's *rentier* state was overthrown in the 1979 revolution and the Islamic Republic of Iran founded under Ayatollah Khomeini; during this time of turmoil, Saddam could not resist the opportunity to attack his Iranian neighbour to try to press home his advantage and obtain boundaries more favourable for Iraq (see Hinnebusch 2003). The Soviet intervention into Afghanistan prompted President Carter to enunciate his doctrine: the oil resources of the Gulf constituted a vital US national interest and any threat to them would be met by any means, including military force if necessary. After Iraq's invasion of Iran, a bloody war of First World War proportions ensued in which Saddam was seen as an Arab bulwark against the export of

Iranian and Shi'a revolution and was supported by the Arab Gulf states and intermittently by the US, UK and France. Again, the Kurdish card was played by the Iranians against Saddam who vowed to find a solution to his troublesome Kurds. The murderous 1987 Anfal campaign saw Kurdish villages depopulated and genocidal chemical attacks launched against Halabja. The Iran-Iraq war left Saddam's regime bankrupt and expecting to be forgiven debts by the Kuwaiti al-Sabah, bankrollers of his war, he found instead to his bitter disappointment, that repayment was expected. Misreading American intentions, Republican Guard forces rolled into Kuwait City in a clear threat to dominate the oil resources of Kuwait and potentially Saudi Arabia (Tripp 2002). The US and the UK, along with other nations and the Arab Gulf states, implemented the Rapid Deployment Force capabilities they had been developing since the early 1980s, to evict Saddam from Kuwait under unambiguous UN authorisation.

There was, however, no authorisation for regime change and an awareness in George H. Bush's administration (for example, expressed by Dick Cheney) that removing Saddam Hussein from power could open up a can of worms of inter-communal conflicts. Instead, George H. Bush encouraged the brutally suppressed Shia in the south and the Kurds in the north to rise up. When they did so, Saddam Hussein initiated new repressive measures including the draining of the southern marshes and dispatching of helicopter gunships to gun down the opposition; once again the Kurds fled to the highest points of the peaks of the Zagros in affirmation of their enduring refrain, 'no friends but the mountains'.

The Kurds and western intervention, 1991–2001: From no-fly zones to regime change

Images in Western media of Kurdish families huddled in the winter snows of the high Zagros range seeking shelter from the helicopter gunships of Saddam Hussein led to an international uproar (the CNN effect). These reports compelled the leaders of the Western liberal democracies to put before the UN proposals for the creation of 'no-fly zones' in the northern and southern parts of Iraq. Baghdad withdrew all governmental services from the Kurdistan Region and erected a blockade. This erosion of the sovereignty of the Iraqi state emboldened the Kurds to take their opportunity, and out of necessity led to the creation of two Kurdistan Regional Governments formed by the KDP in Erbil and the PUK in Sulaimainiyah. This mirrored the dominance of the two families and associated political parties: the Barzanis and KDP in Erbil and Dohuk, the Talibani and PUK in Sulaimaniyah and Kirkuk. The intense rivalry between these two families, associated political parties, and accompanying patronage networks led to the Kurdish civil war in the mid-1990s; the intensity of this conflict partly concerned the control of millions of dollars of US aid derived from Iraqi oil sales under the UN 'oil-for-food' plan. In another version of the 'Kurdish card' the KDP invited the

Saddam regime forces to enter Erbil to evict the militias of the PUK. Iraqi army tanks rolled in and the rose gardens of the parks flowed red with rivers of blood once more.

Convened under US auspices, the signing of the 1998 Washington Agreement committed Kurdish political parties to resolve their differences, act in a unified manner against the threat of Saddam, and work together for his overthrow. Following the election of George W. Bush in 2000, a neo-conservative agenda was firmly on the table (articulated most clearly in the Project for a New American Century), which sought to go beyond Clinton's 'dual containment' of Iraq and Iran, to bring about regime change.

From 9/11 to US withdrawal from Iraq

September 11 led to a swift response against the Taliban in Afghanistan and their 'guest' Osama bin Laden, and was also the perfect opportunity to implement regime change in Iraq, a long desired neo-con objective. The necessary intelligence assessments were procured and invasion initiated without much thought for planning after Saddam's regime was toppled. For the Kurds, the US-led invasion was undoubtedly a liberation as it sent their oppressor Saddam Hussein to the gallows and provided an opportunity to develop as an autonomous region and conduct its own paradiplomacy (on KRG foreign relations, see Khalil and Owtram 2014; Danilovich 2014); however, it shattered Iraq as a country, and the efforts to reconstruct it in a new federal form are a work in progress whose prospects are as yet entirely uncertain. A key question is that posed by the 'paradox of federalism': Are the various measures of federal systems designed to alleviate tensions in deeply divided societies through allowing autonomy, likely to increase the probability of secession? (see Danilovich and Owtram 2014; Danilovich 2014).

Just as the British had 80 years earlier, the Americans now faced the task of building an administration that would cope with the centrifugal forces and fissiparous tendencies of Iraq's deeply divided society (see Choudhry 2008) and allow the exploration of the vast oil resources of Iraq. However, no coherent pre-planning had been put in place for post-invasion reconstruction, as the neo-con worldview was that if Saddam was removed, then a democratic Iraq would effortlessly take root and become a beacon for the rest of the Middle East. In this the Bush administration, as well as Tony Blair in the United Kingdom, ignored any counsel on the dangers of a post-Saddam Iraq from Middle East experts in government and academia.

Imperialism 101: Lessons from the nineteenth century

Exactly the same pattern has occurred in Libya and Afghanistan. The US with British support has invaded or decapitated the state but without any coherent plan in place for post-invasion reconstruction. Once the common enemy is gone, then the various rival factions start fighting each other and attacking the erstwhile liberators, now despised as occupiers, who become pressurised into a hasty withdrawal. As former Labour Minister Kim Howell noted, tasked with the British development programme in Afghanistan, no British imperialist of the nineteenth century would entertain the idea that a country could be invaded and then withdrawn from in the space of five to ten years. Of course, the norms of international society have changed now: after initial euphoria in Iraq, chaos and anarchy began to take hold, and resentment at being occupied by a foreign military force with no discernible plan in place for the continued functioning of government in Iraq. Following the toppling of Saddam's statue in March 2003 it took two months for Paul Bremer to be tasked with the creation of the Coalition Provisional Authority which came into being on 21 April 2003. Bremer had no Middle East or conflict zone experience and his previous posting was as Ambassador to the Netherlands. He issued two decrees (drawn up in Washington he contends) that turned out to be disastrous. The first was the de-Baathification measure that barred all members of the Baath party, at whatever level, from government. At a stroke, the people that could administer Iraq were removed. The second measure was the sacking of the entire Iraqi army which immediately placed a large group of armed men, many from the Sunni community, on the street with no way of earning a living; ultimately this was to contribute to the Sunni insurgency and the rise of the Islamic State (IS).

Further measures to give Iraqis a say in their governance saw the creation of the Iraq Governing Council, the Iraq Interim Government and the Iraq Transitional Government (see Zedalis 2012) culminating in the referendum in October 2005 that approved the draft constitution which thus replaced the Transitional Administrative Law. The Iraqi Constitution contained a number of articles which addressed the highly contentious issue of the management of oil, many of which were contradictory and deliberately vague or ambiguous (for further detail see Owtram 2014 and Zedalis 2012) in order to allow the fractious negotiating parties to sign it. This included the Articles 140 and 143 on Kirkuk which allowed for a referendum on its place in the new federal Iraq as well as including a mechanism to handle the process of Arabization that had taken place there. We now turn to the period since the Arab Spring which, it is argued, can be designated a major change in the regional and international system – a chance to change the 'postcolonial sequestration' issuing from Sykes-Picot and the Treaty of Lausanne?

Iraq, the Kurds and oil resources since the Arab Spring

A feature of the Middle East states prior to the revolutions, conflicts and wars of the Arab Spring in 2011 was the high proportion of unemployed young men who were struggling to make a living and establish a family. The strictures of the neo-liberal prescriptions for the ills of the region defined the medicine: the removal of government services – but this only made them further vulnerable to poverty and motivated to find some means of social welfare. Time and again, we see across the Middle East that the populace look to a group that can provide them with basic services: electricity, water, foodstuffs. The inability to procure these basics of life despite great industry potentially can lead to various extreme forms of behaviour.

The Arab Spring: A self-immolation and the incineration of the dynastic republics

When a young vegetable seller Mohammed Bouazizi set himself on fire in a desperate protest at his inability to make a living, few people suspected that the flames fanned by social media would ignite a bonfire under the regimes of every state in the Middle East and North Africa. Prior to the Arab Spring the 'dynastic republics' (see Sadiki 2009) of Tunisia, Egypt, Libya and Syria all seemed to have achieved a sort of authoritarian stability in which repressive measures contained the people's sense of disenchantment and alienation, and even transmogrified it into placid acceptance of the status quo. The well-entrenched rulers in these putative republics seemed to be successfully grooming a son to take over the mantle of power by offering them as candidates at the ballot box in elections. It had become a touchstone of Western diplomacy that it would imprudent of Western governments to jeopardise this by allowing concerns about human rights to unnecessarily qualify their substantive support. Starting in 2011, the protests and revolutions of the Arab Spring caused a massive seismic shift in the regional social and political system which had existed since the collapse of the Ottoman Empire. Underlying much of this protest was a demographic trend of a youthful population and lack of employment opportunities in a neo-liberal economy (see Coates Ulrichsen and Held 2011); this was coupled with an awareness of the apparent nepotism and corruption of the state's leadership. The Kurdistan Region of Iraq was not immune to these pressures.

The Kurdistan Region's rentier economy and dynastic republicanism

Unsurprisingly, in the Kurdistan Region of Iraq the issue of oil revenues and ruling parties is also present. Partly as a legacy of Saddam's policies, the population of the KRI was not encouraged to be active and entrepreneurial; the expectation of the social contract was that it was the responsibility of the governing parties to provide administrative positions in return for support. Over 80% of the population was employed by the KRG, the payment of whose salaries, is entirely dependent on oil revenues (see Natali 2010). With the disputes between Baghdad and Erbil over oil payments coupled with the slump in the price of oil, the strain on the finances of the KRG has intensified and made the *rentier* model less sustainable. KRG attempts to develop direct exports capacity via Turkey were virulently opposed by Baghdad and a tanker of Kurdish oil lay moored off the American coast subject to legal action by the federal government. The receipt of these oil revenues into the KRG bank accounts has remained opaque and the accrual of wealth by the Barzani and Talabani families is unclear.

While in Tunisia, Egypt and Libya, the dynasties of Ben Ali, Mubarak and Ghaddafi have been swept away by protest, in the KRI we can still observe what appears to be dynastic republicanism operating. Masrour Barzani, the son of the current President of the KRI (Masoud Barzani), is Chancellor of the Kurdistan Region Security Council. Masoud Barzani's nephew, Necherwan Barzani, is the deputy head of the KDP, was Prime Minister of the Kurdistan Regional Government in 2006 and again now since 2012. Qubad Talabani, the son of the leader of the Patriotic Union of Kurdistan and until 2013, the President of Iraq, Jalal Talabani, is Deputy Prime Minister in the KRG. His brother, Pavel is head of the security service in the Sulaimaniah region. To appreciate how dynastic republicanism operates in Iraqi Kurdistan, requires an understanding of what has been termed the 'hidden force' of Middle Eastern society: *wasta*. This refers to being well-connected and to be able to use those connections to access resources such as jobs or business contracts. Masoud Barzani and family relatives control a large number of enterprises, for example, Korek Telecom. Many of the most profitable companies, like those overseeing construction projects, are owned by a Barzani or Talibani; this patronage system alienates and excludes much of the population. In 2015 and 2016 there have been continued protests against corruption and economic mismanagement as the KRG's proposals to cut salaries threaten the *rentier* social contract. This is illustrated most vividly in Kirkuk's salary predicament where employees of the federal government were getting paid whereas employees of the Kurdistan Regional Government were not paid and had the prospect of cuts to their salaries (Natali 2016). All this has intensified the crisis over the Kurdistan Regional Presidency, the tenancy of which by Masoud Barzani, officially came to an end in August 2015 (Stansfield 2015). Opposition to the KRG leadership and their distribution of oil revenues also came from another source which targeted the leadership of Iraq and Syria from a sectarian basis but also tapped into widespread disaffection with the status quo: the Islamic State of Iraq and Syria.

The origins and establishment of the Islamic state of Iraq and Syria: Farewell to Sykes-Picot?

One beneficiary of this upturning of the old order was the Islamic State of Iraq and Syria, which subsequently declared itself to be simply, Islamic State (IS), as it received declarations of allegiance from Libya to Afghanistan (see BBC 2015). Two fatal mistakes made by the Bush presidency and Paul Bremer shortly after the US-led 2003 invasion laid the basis for the eventual rise of IS. First, the ruling that no member of the Baath party could be involved in the government even at junior levels led to chaos and anarchy: the Americans had removed the one group which could have provided some kind of administrative stability and continuity. Second, the entire Sunni dominated army was disbanded, throwing 1 million men onto the streets with their guns but no way of supporting themselves. These two decisions combined with the Sunni disenchantment with the post-2003 order, spawned the Sunni insurgency which subsequently morphed into IS.

The US placed the early insurgents in Camp Bucca, including one Abu Bakr al- Baghdadi. At the time he seemed inconsequential and they allowed him to lead seminars with his fellow prisoners at which he disseminated his radical interpretation of Islam. A decade later Abu Bakr al-Baghdadi re-emerged, this time as the Caliph of the Islamic State of Iraq and Syria. The creation of this organisation used a deep rooted Baathist networks, techniques of surveillance and the use of extreme brutality (see Natali 2015). As they stormed back into Iraq from Syria in August 2014 to occupy Mosul, Iraq's second city, Islamic State celebrated their removal of the Sykes-Picot borders by dismantling the frontier checkpoints and allowing the Sunni tribesmen on each side of the former border to visit their cousins.

All the actors have their own agendas, and their own, sometimes opaque reasons as to whom they support. As is often the case there is a great deal of complexity and constantly shifting alliances depending on the military situation on the ground. Russia is supporting its ally, Bashar Assad, from whom they derive access to a naval base on the Mediterranean coast. A US document obtained under the Freedom of Information Act notes that the US anticipated the emergence of a Salafist principality in eastern Syria and that there could be some benefits in terms of exerting pressure on the Assad regime. There would also be benefits for the US and Israel from the central lands becoming a patchwork of mini ethno-religious statelets (Salt 2013).

Fuelling Jihad: The Erdogan family and the sale of ISIS oil

Reports suggest that Erdogan's son, Bilal, owns a fleet of petrol tankers which sell ISIS oil from the Syrian oil fields they control to third parties at 50% of its market value. Russian intervention to support its ally Bashar Assad involved blowing up the tankers being used to transport the ISIS oil to Turkey. Turkey warned Russia to desist. When Russia refused to comply, Erdogan gave the order to have the Russian jet shot down, enraging Vladimir Putin. The split between Turkey and Russia has gone beyond political and is now personal. President Putin caustically commented that 'President Erdogan wouldn't resign if he had stolen oil smeared all over his face' at the press conference to show satellite imagery purporting to be ISIS tanker convoys loading up in Turkish ports. Charges that Russia is targeting anti-Assad rebels also prompted Turkey to summon Russian ambassador for crisis talks.

Shooting down the Russian jet may be a dangerous form of payback for Vladimir Putin's two-month bombardment of ISIS, Turkey's ally. Although a NATO member country, a raft of evidence suggests that Turkey is in fact using ISIS and has helped the terror organization by providing safe passage and financing via black market oil sales. The United States has requested Turkey seals its border, but aware of its status as a NATO member and its critical role in the region, the Erdogan government continues its *de facto* support of ISIS with impunity. To illustrate, $800 million worth of ISIS oil has been sold in Turkey, and ISIS oil truck convoys are routinely allowed to cross back and forth between the Islamic State stronghold of Raqqa and Turkey. When the YPG threatened to extend their control of the border lands and seal the border, Turkey suddenly climbed aboard the idea of bombing missions in Syria. It immediately repelled the Kurdish forces and prevented a stretch of the border between Turkey and Syria from being closed off, thus allowing the supply routes to continue between Turkey and the Islamic State capital of Raqqa and then onto Mosul.

According to reports there is compelling evidence that the Turkish President's son, Bilal Erdogan, is intimately involved in the ISIS oil sales. As Nafeez Ahmed documents (Ahmad 2015), a large cache of intelligence recovered from a raid on an ISIS safe house confirmed direct dealings between Turkish officials and high-ranking ISIS members. Attacks by Russian bombers on ISIS oil tanker convoys and ISIS operated oil fields cut in half the income ISIS earned from oil. Consequently, Erdogan personally gave the order to shoot down the Russian jet which crossed into Turkish territory for 17 seconds. Before this the US had not dropped one bomb on an ISIS oil tanker; it even airdropped warning leaflets to inform the drivers about an impending bombing. In a single day the Russians destroyed 1000 ISIS oil tankers and subsequently cut in half ISIS's income from oil.

The emperor has no clothes: The Iraqi army and the fall of Mosul to the Islamic State

The lamentable result of the American attempt to create a national army for Iraq becomes clear when considering the following statistics from the US Inspector of Iraq Reconstruction: the soldiers of the Iraqi army, on learning of the approach of ISIS forces, literally took off their uniform and fled; this was after the spending of US $26 billion on training and equipment. The two Iraqi divisions outnumbered the 800 ISIS fighters by a ratio of 30:1 but the Iraqi army simply left the high tech kit provided for them by the US to the ISIS fighters who then paraded through the streets with this equipment including over 2,000 Humvee Armoured vehicles, over 50 US M198 Howitzer artillery guns with GPS and intelligent capability, Black hawk helicopters and missile launchers. ISIS gained a war chest of millions of dollars from the sacking of the National Bank of Iraq in Mosul to add to their vast income from the sale of smuggled oil from fields they controlled in Iraq and Syria.

It was manifestly apparent that those fighting in the army did not have the commitment or will to fight in its uniform as soon as the going gets tough. Fundamentally they do not believe in or have any commitment to the Iraqi state except in the most instrumental of ways. In contrast are the fighters of the different Shia militias who would fight to the death under the Mahdi's flag; it was the Shia militias funded by Iran who stopped Islamic State's march on Baghdad – they believed in the identity they were fighting for.

The fighters of the Islamic State are also highly motivated for a number of reasons, and not only their religious beliefs. The provision of livelihood also explains in part some of the attraction of IS. For example, the greatest percentage of foreign fighters in IS come from Tunisia; the $1,500 a month which the foreign fighter receives enables him to send back money to his family. In the absence of other avenues to earn a living, this prospect is not without its attractions. Furthermore, through its attack on the tourism industry, the main income of Tunisia, IS actively and strategically seeks to erode the ability of 'non-terrorist industries' to offer employment. The prospect of religiously endorsed booty of Yazidi girls as sex slaves is also an attraction as well as the prospect of martyrdom and the bonus of 92 virgins in paradise according to their beliefs. Tellingly, the all-women units of the Peoples Protection Units (YPJ) in Syria strike fear into the IS fighters as to be killed by a woman in battle deprives them of entry to paradise in their beliefs.

Similarly, the Kurdish *Peshmerga* believe in fighting for Kurdistan to defend their land and families and those who shelter within it including Christians and other ethnicities and religious groups in federal Iraq (see Danilovich 2014 on the issues of federal status pertaining to *Peshmerga* forces). But even the *Peshmerga* are not invincible (Natali 2015c) – it was only frantic telephoning by Kurdish officials and the presence of the US consulate in Erbil that led President Obama to authorise the US Air Force to 'degrade' the columns of ISIS forces advancing rapidly on Erbil narrowly preventing the city falling to the marauding thugs of the Islamic State intent on mass executions and cultural destruction. The onslaught of ISIS had been stopped at the gates of Baghdad and Erbil and attention turned to turning the tide. Precision US military strikes in coordination with Baghdad and Erbil have pushed back the radical Islamic group and attention has turned to how institutions can be designed and deals done to reconcile Shiites, Sunnis and Kurds (see Choudhry 2008). Natali notes that 'stabilizing Iraq in the face of IS will ultimately require a deal not only between Baghdad and Erbil, but also among Iraqi Arab, Kurdish and other minority group leaders over boundaries and the revenues and resources linked to them' (Natali 2015). The problem here is that US occupation and the onslaught of IS have done immense and possibly irreparable damage to the relationship between the different communities. Whilst it is unlikely that the fragmented groups of Iraqi society will develop a cohesive identity in the near future, Natali (2016) outlines the many reasons why Iraqi nationalism should not be underestimated due to the opportunities afforded instrumentally by the Iraqi state structures. Countering caution over the 'end of Iraq thesis' or even an assumption that the country will be divided into three areas Natali contends that President Barzani's call for a move beyond the boundaries of the Sykes-Picot era and announcement of a referendum on independence should not necessarily be taken as indicating an impending declaration of independence. The durability of state borders and the dependent nature (see Natali 2010) of the KRG means that the phase of post-colonial sequestration of the Kurds will not necessarily come to an end.

Post-colonial sequestration and the resource factor

This chapter has used Halliday's concept of post-colonial sequestration combined with Harvey and Stansfield's analysis of the resource factor to frame an account of the state formation process affecting the Kurds in the era of modern Middle East politics: the state system originating in the Sykes-Picot correspondence signed in 1916. It has been shown how oil is a hugely important factor in this state formation process which has had, and will continue to have, immense implications on the Kurdish drive for independence. As President Barzani calls to move beyond the Sykes-Picot era and initiates a referendum to marshall preferences on KRG independence, it would be well to note Halliday's injunction. Namely that:

> If the concept of post-colonial sequestration holds, then it carries a vital lesson: only if there is a major political shift in the hegemonic state that has committed the sequestration, and which has secured some international indulgence for it, is there a realistic prospect of post-colonial annexation being reversed (Halliday 2008).

That is, until changes within Turkey lead to an acceptance of Kurdish identity and statehood, the prospects for any declaration of independence is meaningless. Halliday further enjoins that, if democratic (including federal) rights and freedoms can be accorded to the Kurds in Iraq, as well as Syria and Turkey, then all options can be freely placed on the table. This begs the question as to what are the prospects for the consolidation of these democratic and federal rights for the Kurds and all the peoples of Iraq under its nascent federal system.

Whither Iraq: A house of cards?

Looking forward, the 'end of Iraq' thesis in its simplest terms posits that Iraq is an artificial country, created by the British in the 1920s as a vehicle for the development of the oil resources. A foreign king was imposed as a consolation prize for missing out on the crown elsewhere. Ever since then its identity and nation building projects have failed. It is an extremely fragile polity liable to collapse beyond repair under the strain of civil war.

Advancing a complex and nuanced analysis, Natali (2010, 2015a, 2015b, 2015c, 2016) posits the strength of Iraqi nationalism and also urges a cautionary note against the assumption that the KRI is poised for independence. In contrast, she argues persuasively that stalemate rather than statehood may be the defining characteristic for the KRI in the current situation due to the constraints of geo-politics and the benefits accruing to all parties involved, including revenues from the sale of oil (see also Owtram 2014; Danilovich and Owtram 2014; Danilovich 2014).

The US invasion of 2003 by decapitating the regime of Saddam Hussein without much thought for reconstruction, led to anarchy and a Hobbesian state of war of all against all, in which pre-existing sectarian identities have become very salient. The international community's reluctance to see Iraq broken up lends a certain inertia to the state structures that include the Iraqi state and even give it certain advantages over rival bodies in the competition to be seen as the legitimate authority of the territory. Most likely the US will continue to throw good money after bad as it painstakingly tries to construct, reconstruct and maintain this house of cards, in the absence of better alternative policy options.

Conclusion

This chapter has surveyed how the Kurds have been involved in a prolonged and drawn-out poker game since the First World War in which the prize of state independence has remained elusive as they have come to terms with the terrible hand dealt to them by more powerful players in an earlier rendition of this game. Those who took part in the Sykes-Picot Agreement of 1916 are long gone from this world but their legacy continues to confound the search for peace, prosperity and stability. The Kurds see this as the time to banish the ghosts of Sykes-Picot.

This has been a game of high stakes in which Kurdish leaders have had to deal with powerful protagonists across the table all of whom have been ready and willing to deploy strategies to encourage Kurdish division. To name them: brutal and wily regional players such as the genocidal regime of Saddam Hussein and Syria, a Turkish state with a compulsive tendency to deny Kurdish identity; a powerful Iran under first the follies of the Shah and then the austerities of theocratic rule, the ambivalence of the Saudis and the Gulf states; the capriciousness of great powers such as Great Britain, France, Russia and the United State; and currently the existential threat posed by the death cult of the Islamic State.

The view advanced in this chapter has been, on balance, that – although oil seemingly provides economic resources for the development of an independent state, and therefore might represent 'an ace in the hole' – such apparent benefits have not accrued to the Kurds in general, and specifically to the Kurds of Iraq. Due to the constraints of geo-strategy, the vagaries of international politics, the intensification of pre-existing divisions and rivalries, and the ensuing erosion of human capital, oil for the Kurds brings 'the curse of black gold'. Rather than representing the lucky ace in the hole, it can more accurately be described as the joker in the pack. For the Kurds to banish the ghosts of Sykes-Picot will take the ability to play well the bad hand they were dealt. In the coming years, it remains to be seen how this will play out in the ancient and ever-enduring game of high-stakes poker, which constitutes – and at the same time creates – the politics and international relations of the Middle East.

References

Ahmed, Nafeez. 2015. Nato Is Harboring the Islamic State. *Insurge Intelligence.* [Online, 19 November 2015]. Available at: https://medium.com/insurge-intelligence/europe-is-harbouring-the-islamic-state-s-backers-d24db3a24a40#.kkvlwxgwn [accessed: 14 February 2016].

Anderson, Liam and Gareth Stansfield. 2009. *Crisis in Kirkuk: the Ethnopolitics of Conflict and Compromise.* Philadelphia, PA: University of Philadelphia Press.

BBC. 2015. Islamic State [Online, 2 December 2015]. Available at: www.bbc.co.uk/news/world-middle-east-29052144 [accessed 14 January 2016]

Bromley, Simon. 1990. *American Hegemony and World Oil.* PA: The Pennsylvannia State University Press.

Bromley, Simon. 1993. *Rethinking Middle East Politics.* Cambridge: Polity Press.

Cammack, P., Pool, D. and Tordoff, W. *Third World Politics: A Comparative Introduction,* 2nd edition. Manchester: Manchester University Press.

Charountaki, Marianna, *The United States and the Kurds: International Relations in the Middle East since 1945.* London: Routledge.

Choudhry, Sujit. 2008. *Constitutional Design for Divided Societies.* Oxford: Oxford University Press.

Coates-Ulrichsen, Kristian and Held, David. Arab Spring: 1989 Revisited. [Online, 27 September 2011]. Available at: www.opendemocracy.net/kristian-coates-ulrichsen-david-held/arab-1989-revisited [accessed 16 September 2015].

Cunningham, Robert and Yasin Sarayrah. 1993. *Wasta: The Hidden Force in Middle Eastern Society.* New York: Praegar.

Danilovich, Alex. 2014. *Iraqi Federalism and the Kurds: Learning to Live Together.* Farnham: Ashgate.

Danilovich, Alex and Francis Owtram. 2014. Federalism as a Tool to Manage Conflicts and Associated Risks. In Alex Danilovich, *Iraqi Federalism and the Kurds: Learning to Live Together.* Farnham: Ashgate.

Fawcett, Louise. 2009. *International Relations of the Middle East* (ed). Oxford: Oxford University Press.

Halliday, Fred. 2005. *The Middle East in International Relations: Power, Politics and Ideology.* Cambridge: Cambridge University Press.

Halliday, Fred. 2008. Tibet, Palestine and the Politics of Failure. [Online, 13 May 2008]. Available at: www.opendemocracy.net/article/tibet-palestine-and-the-politics-of-failure [accessed: 16 September 2015].

Hinnebusch, Raymond and Ehteshami, Anoushirivan. 2002. *The Foreign Politics of Middle East States.* Boulder: Lynne Rienner.

Hinnebusch, Raymond. 2003. *International Politics of the Middle East.* Manchester: Manchester University Press.

Kirmanj, Sherko. 2013. *Identity and Nation in Iraq.* Boulder: Lynne Rienner Publishers.

Luciano, Guancomo. 2009. Oil in the International Political Economy of the Middle East. In Louise Fawcett, *International Relations of the Middle East.* Oxford: Oxford University Press.

Mohammed, Herish Khalil and Francis Owtram. Paradiplomacy of Regional Governments in International Relations: The Foreign Relations of the Kurdistan Regional Government (2003–2010). *Iran and the Caucasus* 18 (2014) 65–84.

Mills, Robin M. 2013. Northern Iraq's Oil Chessboard: Energy, Politics and Power. *Insight Turkey* 15.1 (2013): 51–62

Natali, Denise. 2005. *The Kurds and the State: Evolving National Identity in Iraq, Turkey and Iran.* Syracuse: Syracuse University Press.

Natali, Denise, 2010. *The Kurdish Quasi-State: Development and Dependency in Post-Gulf War Iraq.* Syracuse, NY: Syracuse University Press.

Natali, Denise. 2015a. The Islamic State's Baathist Roots. *Al Monitor* [Online, 24 April 2015]. Available at: www.al-monitor.com/pulse/originals/2015/04/baathists-behind-the-islamic-state.html [accessed: 13 August 2015].

Natali, Denise. 2015b. Statemate, Not Statehood, for Iraqi Kurdistan. *Lawfare* [Online, 1 November 2015]. Available at: www.lawfareblog.com/stalemate-not-statehood-iraqi-kurdistan [accessed: 26 January 2016].

Natali, Denise. 2015c. Is Iraqi Kurdistan Splitting Apart … Again. *Al Monitor* [Online, 25 September 2015]. Available at: www.al-monitor.com/pulse/originals/2015/09/iraq-kurdistan-region-splitting-apart.html [accessed: 29 September 2015].

Natali, Denise. 2015d. Counting on the Kurds: The Peshmerga's Prospects against ISIS. Foreign Affairs [Online, 22 April 2015]. Available at: www.foreignaffairs.com/articles/middle-east/2015-04-22/counting-kurds [accessed: 15 January 2016].

Natali, Denise. 2015e. Islamic State Infiltrates Iraqi Kurdistan. Al Monitor [Online, 4 June 2016]. Available at: www.al-monitor.com/pulse/originals/2015/06/is-infiltration-iraqi-kurdistan.html [accessed: 26 January 2016].

Natali, Denise. 2016a. Don't Underestimate Iraqi Nationalism. Al Monitor [Online, 20 January 2016]. Available at: www.al-monitor.com/pulse/fr/contents/articles/originals/2016/01/underestimate-iraq-nationalism.html [accessed: 14 January 2016].

Natali, Denise. 2016b. The Long Road to Mosul. [Online, 4 February 2016]. Available at: http://warontherocks.com/2016/02/the-long-road-to-mosul [accessed: 12 February 2016].

Owtram, Francis. 2011. The Foreign Policies of Unrecognized States. In Nina Caspersen and Gareth Stansfield (eds), *Unrecognized States in the International System.* London: Routledge.

Owtram, Francis. 2014. The Federalization of Natural Resources. In Alex Danilovich, *Iraqi Federalism and the Kurds: Learning Live Together.* Farnham: Ashgate.

Owtram, Francis. 2012. The Kurdistan Region of Iraq: Ethnic Conflict and the Survival of Dynastic Republicanism in a De Facto State. In Hannes Artens (ed), *De Facto States and Ethnic Conflicts*, P@X online bulletin, No. 21, September 2012, Centre for Social Studies – University of Coimbra.

Sadiki Larbi. 2009. Like Father, Like Son: Dynastic Republicanism in the Middle East. Carnegie Middle East Centre [Online, 14 Feburary 2016]. Available at: http://carnegie-mec.org/2009/11/25/like-father-like-son-dynastic-republicanism-in-middle-east/ [accessed: 12 February 2016].

Salt, Jeremy. 2015. A Vacuum Waiting For a Leader. *Palestine Chronicle.* [Online, 15 February 2016]. Available at: www.palestinechronicle.com/a-vacuum-waiting-for-a-leader/ [accessed: 13 February 2016].

Stansfield, Gareth. 2013. The Unravelling of the Post World War One State System? The Kurdistan Region of Iraq and the Transformation of the Middle East. *International Affairs* 89: 2 (2013) 259–282

Stansfield, Gareth. 2015. The Struggle for the Presidency in the Kurdistan Region of Iraq. *Commentary*, 2 June 2015. Royal United Services Institute.
Tripp, Charles. 2002. The Foreign Policy of Iraq. In Hinnebush, R. and Ehteshami, A. (eds). *The Foreign Policies of Middle East States*. Boulder: Lynne Rienner.
Voller, Yaniv. 2013. Kurdish Oil Politics in Iraq: Contested Sovereignty and Unilateralism. *Middle East Policy* Vol. XX, No 1.
Wearden, Graham. 2011, Tony Hayward in line for multimillion windfall after Iraq oil deal. *The Guardian* [Online]. Available at: www.theguardian.com/business/2011/sep/07/tony-hayward-windfall-kurdistan [accessed: 13 February 2016].
Yergin, Daniel. 2009. *The Prize: The Epic Quest for Oil, Money and Power*. London. Simon and Schuster.

6 Kurdistan's independence and the international system of sovereign states

Ryan D. Griffiths

Iraqi Kurdistan has been in the spotlight of late. In a February 2015 issue *The Economist* endorsed Kurdistan's independence, arguing that a "country should be able to gain independence if it can stand on its own feet, has democratic credentials and respects its own minorities." At the moment, Kurdistan exists as an effectively *de facto* state within a severely fractured and war-torn Iraq, a troubled state within a troubled region. The recent rise of the Islamic State of Iraq and al-Sham (ISIS) helped reinvigorate the idea of Kurdish independence by drawing attention to the peril of state failure. This prompted Masoud Barzani, the President of the Kurdish regional government to say to the Kurdish Parliament last July: "The time has come to decide our fate, and we should not wait for other people to decide it for us" (Filkins 2014).

How likely is it that Kurdistan will gain its independence? What factors will shape that outcome? According to one school of thought, Kurdistan's path to independence is all but assured. The declaratory theory of statehood holds that states are ontologically prior to the state system (Buzan and Little 2000, Fabry 2010, Erman 2013, Coggins 2014). A polity that functions like a state can thereby declare its independence and join the club of sovereign states as an equal. Article 1 of the Montevideo Declaration on the Rights and Duties of States lists four criteria for statehood: (1) a permanent population; (2) a defined territory; (3) a government; and (4) the capacity to enter into relations with other states. These criteria are not explicitly dependent on the recognition of other states and, in a sense, sovereignty is determined largely by the entity declaring it. According to this view, Kurdistan can decide its own fate.

A contrasting view known as the constitutive theory of statehood posits that sovereignty is determined by the collective judgement of the international community. It is not enough to look and function like a state; true sovereignty requires that other states perceive you as a state. An extreme wing of this school of thought sees states as entirely constructed by the international system – the system creates states.

I contend that the constitutive theory of statehood is mostly correct. In the modern, interconnected and highly globalized international system, sovereign recognition matters greatly. Without it states are relegated to a *de facto* status, existing on the margins of international society without a legal identity apart from the larger state from which the region wants to break away. This is the fate of Somaliland, an island of relative but unrecognized political order within the internationally recognized but failed state of Somalia. I conjecture that the weight of the constitutive argument is historically and system dependent, and that in earlier times, states may have simply declared their sovereignty, whatever that entailed, with little or no concern for the collective judgement of other states. But that is not the case presently, as Kurdistan's fate will be determined by the norms, principles, and politics of the international system.[1]

I make my argument in several stages. First, I describe what I term the "sovereignty club": a sovereign state system that meets the requirements of a club good (excludable and non-rival), where applicants have an incentive to join just as members have reason to exclude. Second, I provide a history of the process of sovereign recognition, locate its roots in the normative traditions of sovereignty and liberalism, discuss the dynamics of independence for the Kurds during the Ottoman period, and draw conjectures about how states may be recognized in the future. I finish by examining the consequences of these practices for Kurdistan and outlining its strategic possibilities in the contemporary international system.

The sovereignty club

The sovereign state system can be conceived of as a club good. It has value like all goods insofar as it provides its members with a legal identity and access to a range of benefits (more on that below). What sets it apart from other types of goods – private, public, and common – is that it is excludable and non-rival (Buchanan 1965). Club members establish admission criteria to filter applicants. Moreover, admission to the club does not automatically reduce the welfare of other members. The good is, however, only non-rival to a point; too many members can create crowding and reduce the benefits of membership.

To consider this argument, it is useful to break it into parts. First, there are benefits to joining the sovereignty club as a sovereign state. The most definitive sign of that achievement is a full seat at the United Nations General Assembly, giving the state in question both a right to vote and a legal identity. This has more than simple symbolic value. As the leaders of Somaliland know, the absence of an international identity creates barriers to international trade, using international post, and accessing financial aid (Fazal and Griffiths 2014). Somaliland is forced to rely on secondary financial markets and foreign bank accounts because it lacks an internationally recognized central bank. *De facto* states can exist in a more or less hermetic state if they wish, but to a large extent they will be cut off from the global economy and the various benefits of international society.

Second, the sovereign state club has reason to limit membership. The reason members would choose to exclude is that the good in question is only non-rival up to a point. In that sense, a club good sits between the two extremes of private goods (excludable and rival) and public goods (non-excludable and non-rival): "For a pure public good the addition of one more member to the club never detracts from benefits of club membership ... [for] a pure private good, say an apple, crowding begins to take place on the first unit" (Mueller 1989: 131). The issue of crowding where states are concerned is quite nuanced. Any new state will subtract territory from an existing state (or set of states), and for that state one could point to a reduction in welfare depending on the value assigned to the territory. In a larger sense there is the issue of precedent-setting and uncontrolled fragmentation. Fears of domino effects are very real, and many states deny independence demands elsewhere out of a concern that recognition may set a precedent and lead to their own territorial dismemberment or sovereign dissolution (Toft 2002, Walter 2009, Griffiths 2015). Just as aspiring nations have an incentive to join the club, existing members have the incentive to control admission.

How do the club members control admission? There are various metrics used to determine international recognition. For example, one might count the total number of other states that have bestowed recognition. Currently, Kosovo has been recognized by some 108 countries, a slight majority of the club members (Meetser 2012). Another indicator is membership in international organizations. Of these, the most important is UN membership, the defining feature of club membership and the Holy Grail for stateless nations seeking sovereignty. A full seat in the UN General Assembly gives a state an equal position in the parliament of states, and a corresponding legal identity that is useful for a range of economic and diplomatic reasons. In procedural terms, the UN membership process requires that applications must be approved by the Security Council before they are submitted to the General Assembly. Thus, the Security Council acts as the gatekeeper to the club, especially the five permanent veto-holding members: France, Russia, China, United Kingdom, and the United States. So while Kosovo has been recognized by a majority of sovereign states, it is currently blocked at the Security Council level by Russia and China, who refuse to recognize Kosovar independence out of respect for Serbian sovereignty.

Of course, the procedure for recognizing other states is always built upon the various diplomatic practices that pertain to international order. Such practices are protean. They are the product of an evolving body of international legal norms, rules, and principles (i.e. the recognition regime) that determine when an applicant nation has the right to withdraw from an existing state and join the club of sovereign states as an equal.

The evolving recognition regime

The contemporary recognition regime has its origins in the early modern European state system and regional order. Beginning in Europe sometime in the seventeenth century, if not earlier, the constituent states began to develop rules for determining not only what sovereignty implied in legal and practical terms, but also who should be granted those rights (Spruyt 1994, Osiander 2001). According to Charles Tilly there were some 500 European states in the year 1500; that number had been reduced to 25 by the early 1900s (Tilly 1975). That culling of states hints at the immense cartographical changes that have been wrought over time, but obscures the contradictory processes of political aggregation and fragmentation that have characterized the continent. Although the overall trend has been toward fewer states – at least until the early to mid-twentieth century – there was also considerable fragmentation that took place. Since all European land was effectively enclosed or legally claimed by the seventeenth century, any new state implied an exit and subtraction (i.e. a secession) from an existing state (Griffiths 2014). Controlling that process was and remains the chief aim of the recognition regime (Jackson 1990, 1993, Halperin and Scheffer, and Small 1992, Ratner 1996, Shaw 1996, Osterud 1997, Bartos 1997, Krasner 1999, Radan 2002, Buchanan 2003, Fazal and Griffiths 2014).

If the recognition regime is the product of efforts by the sovereignty club to control admission, what guides these efforts? I contend that the regime is the product of international diplomacy and the competition between two competing normative traditions: sovereignty and liberalism (Sandholtz and Stiles 2008). In the sovereign tradition, rights are given to the state or, in earlier periods, the person who embodied the state. In the liberal tradition, rights are allocated to the individual. The result of these competing traditions and the resulting normative crosswinds they create is an international order composed of various friction points. One of the most salient in the contemporary period is the Responsibility to Protect (R2P), the notion that the sovereign right of states to manage their internal affairs is forfeit when human rights are violated. The core criteria for R2P and attendant debate can be seen as the working out of a basic question in international life: which takes precedence, the state or the individual?

Norms are continuously evolving phenomena, and the character and strength of a given norm at any moment is determined through persuasion, in relation to power, and via the dialectic between sovereign and liberal rights.[2] The same can be said of the recognition regime, a constellation of several norms that controls admission to the sovereignty club. Since this dialectic between sovereignty and liberalism is driven in part by power – the rise and fall of states and hegemons and the conflicts that determine their fate – the result is a somewhat episodic nature to the recognition regime. Like much in international relations, these episodes conform to historical events.

The first episode in Europe was sovereign dominant and barely liberal. It encompassed the European-based system during the eighteenth century, and perhaps earlier, and waned with the advent of the American and French revolutions. In regard to secession and independence claims, states followed a practice that I call recognition by consent, where other states were expected to withhold recognition until the breakaway region received the blessing of its sovereign. The famous break with this practice occurred when the French recognized the American secessionists prior to British consent, an act of strategic rather than normative calculation. In doing so, they helped initiate a normative turn that brought into international politics a relatively liberal, and therefore radical, country that was willing to raise the rights of individuals above that of states in certain circumstances (Armitage 2007).

The second episode began in full after the Napoleonic wars and covered the years until the end of the First World War. The normative shift occurred because of the introduction of the norm of self-determination. Grounded in liberal theory, self-determination holds that nations should have the right to control their political fate (Mayall 1990, Beran 1998, Buchanan 2003, and Wellman 2005). Since there are many more nations than states – indeed, Gellner estimated that nations exceed states by a factor of ten! (Gellner 1983: 43–44) – it naturally followed that the principle was adopted by stateless nations and used as rhetorical ammunition against existing states.

Importantly, the application of self-determination was initially interpreted as a negative right (i.e. stateless nations were entitled to self-determination without outside interference). If they could prevail over their sovereign, or win their consent, and establish *de facto* statehood as an empirical fact, then the club of states was obliged to grant recognition. Following Fabry, I call this the age of *de facto* recognition (Fabry 2010). The leading states in this practice were the United States and United Kingdom, former adversaries who nevertheless embraced the liberal turn. Their opponents were the conservative European monarchs who objected unsuccessfully to the practice of *de facto* recognition and watched in frustration as the Anglo-Americans recognized the new Latin American states against the will of Spain. With the stirrings of nationalism across the continent they gradually, but never completely, came to accept the new rules of the game.

The two world wars transformed the recognition regime via a double normative movement. On one hand, there was "a shift in the understanding of self-determination from a negative to positive international right" (Fabry 2010: 12). This is typically pinned to the Wilsonian Moment at the end of the First World War, when President Woodrow Wilson advanced a more ambitious understanding of the self-determination of nations (Manela 2007).[3] Whereas the interpretation of self-determination as a negative right meant that nations could become free by their own hand, and third parties were expected to remain neutral, the positive right placed an obligation on the international community to assist in nationalist efforts. Self-determination as an international norm had acquired an activist dimension.

There was also a parallel evolution in sovereign thinking in which conquest was made taboo. The great destruction of the wars and the naked aggression of the Second World War, in particular, gave rise to a prohibition on territorial conquest and an emphasis on maintaining sovereign borders. Atzili calls this the "border fixity norm", saying that "conquest and annexation of one's neighbour's land, commonplace in the history of the state system, is no longer on the "menu of options" for post-Second World War leaders and states (Atzili 2012: 1).[4] According to Fazal, the norm resulted in a near disappearance of formal territorial conquest after 1945 (Fazal 2007).

The product of this double normative movement was a regime based on constitutive recognition. The central feature of the regime is a normative tension between the sovereign emphasis on treating borders as inviolable and the interpretation of self-determination as a positive right. Although the borders norm originated as a barrier to external aggression, it has been equally successful in the post-1945 era as an obstacle to secessionists who, by definition, want to change borders from within. Seeing that an unconditional emphasis on borders would invalidate self-determination efforts, and that an unfettered access for stateless nations to independence would trump sovereignty, the international community of states and legal scholars has aimed for a middle path that specifies the conditions under which one norm takes precedence. In other words, they have had to determine who counts for self-determination and who does not. However, as Fabry argues, determining who counts for independence is a difficult task given the diverse interests of international politics, not to mention the simple challenge of identifying and sorting nations (Fabry 2010).

Answering the question of who counts has resulted in an evolving set of criteria. The first criterion or ticket to independence is both unstartling and uncontroversial: secession is seen as legitimate when the nation in question has the consent of its sovereign, as Montenegro did when it parted ways with Serbia a decade ago. The second path is far more dramatic, responsible for a sweeping political and cartographical transformation of international relations. This was decolonization, the application of self-determination to colonized peoples. In more precise times, one might say this was self-determination applied to overseas, first order administrative units, rightly noting that the path to independence was denied to: (1) colonial relations of continental empires, such as the peripheral and indigenous nations of the United States, Russia, and China; and (2) colonized nations of saltwater empires that lacked administrative status, such as the Baganda and the Karens.[5] This sorting of the fortunate from the unfortunate was one solution to determining who counts in a constitutive recognition regime.

A third and more recent path to the sovereignty club was for members of dissolved states, a solution that was arrived at during the Soviet and Yugoslav collapse. Not unlike decolonization, this was a legal solution meant to put daylight between legal paths to independence and other unsavoury forms of secession. Bartos argues: "the [Badinter] Commission preferred to view the Yugoslavian situation as one of dissolution, refusing to set a precedent for the secession of national groups within existing States." (Bartos 1997: 75) The final path, somewhat conjecturally, centres on Kosovo. The United States and other powers recognized Kosovar independence citing the conflict and human rights abuses that had occurred during the civil war with Serbia.

Although some saw this as the acceptance of a remedial right to secession, the United States and the related legal decision on Kosovo shied away from that move and instead determined that the case is *sui generis*. Of course, other states such as Russia and China have demurred from this position and have supported Serbian sovereignty instead. Kosovo's present status of semi-sovereignty exists because the international community cannot agree on who should count.

This brief coverage identifies three different recognition regimes. The first was recognition by consent, a sovereign-dominant solution that existed in the Eurocentric system of the eighteenth century. The second was *de facto* recognition, a curious mix of sovereignty and liberalism that existed roughly from 1815–1918. The third is the post-1945 constitutive recognition regime, arguably the first regime to have truly global reach. Of course, not all regimes are global or even Western, and it is useful to consider how these processes played out in different regions, especially the area surrounding Kurdistan.

What we think of as the international system was only really consolidated in the first years of the twentieth century (Griffiths and Butcher 2013). Prior to that there was no truly global system in the sense that all parts of the Earth were connected on a formal legal basis. Instead there existed separate systems or sub-systems that the ever-expanding European-based system gradually came to include. The disconnected systems – either partially or wholly – stretched from Africa through the Middle East and South Asia into Southeast Asia and the Pacific. Political order in those regions varied considerably with respect to patterns of recognition and sovereign diplomacy (Butcher and Griffiths 2015).

The history of Kurdistan and the politics of independence are the product of geography and demographics. Kurdistan has to some extent been a border region between the empires of Western Anatolia, the Iranian plateau, and the Mesopotamian basin. It is no surprise that these three regions would be associated in modern times with three large ethnic blocs: the Turks, the Persians, and the Arabs. Kurdistan was historically a rugged frontier zone existing at the intersection of these regions, one where numerous tribes assimilated, to varying degrees, to become the Kurds. Not unlike the many hill tribes of Southeast Asia, the Balkans, the Carpathians, or even the steppe on which Ukrainian culture gradually coalesced, Kurdish culture existed on the edge of empire (Scott 2010). This was a shatter zone subject to the push and pull of imperial ambition.

Regions such as these display a common pattern with respect to independence, autonomy, and what we might call sovereignty in a stripped-down, culturally neutral way. Imperial frontiers were quite often zones of diminishing control and it was not uncommon for a smaller polity or tribe to engage in feudal relations with distant metropoles, and the strength of that relationship was partly a function of the simple reach of the empire (Butcher and Griffiths 2015). Kurdish politics from the early Ottoman period onward was composed of a collection of emirates, or principalities, whose independence varied by degree (Ciment 1996, Bengio 2005, Ozogglu 2007, Charountaki 2011). Like other shatter zones, patterns of vassalage emerged where local rulers were supported but expected to secure the frontier. In these environments a polity can become truly independent in an empirical and declaratory manner. Sovereignty is more or less self-established and much less dependent on the bestowal of a foreign government. Relatively autarkic polities in a thinly globalized environment can declare their independence and it remains true as long as they can defend it. This is an historical example of the declaratory theory of statehood, independence by declaration, and it characterized the Kurdish region during the Ottoman period, as well as numerous other pre-modern and early modern political systems (Butcher and Griffiths 2015).

What does this survey of past regimes and patterns of independence suggest about the future? Put another way, what are the most likely future designs for the international recognition regime? A useful apparatus for considering this question is to revisit the tension between sovereign and liberal norms that have undergirded the international system for some time. If the locus of norms that comprise international order at any given moment are worked out dialectically, what can we forecast for the future with respect to secession and sovereign recognition?

One possibility is the advancement of a remedial right to secession. Remedial rights theory, or Just Cause theory, posits that groups have a right to secede when other rights have been violated (Norman 1998, Buchanan 2003). Sovereignty is conditional on upholding the social contract. When a state fails to honour the contract and, indeed, engages in predatory or perhaps genocidal behaviour, and human rights are violated, the nation in question is granted the right to secede. This was the future that the Kosovar decision hinted at, and the one that conservative sovereign states like China and Russia rejected. The consolidation of this right would extend the constitutive regime in the direction of greater liberal rights, a development that seems desirable and perhaps inevitable from the liberal perspective. It does, however, have its critics who naturally highlight the merits of defending sovereignty as well as the potential for moral hazard that arises with a remedial right – wouldn't minority groups now have incentive to provoke the state into behaving badly as a means to activate the right? (Kuperman 2008)

A second, somewhat related possibility is the entrenchment of a primary right to secession. Primary rights theory, also called "choice theory," posits that individuals and groups should be able to choose their sovereignty via a democratic process (Beran 1998, Wellman 2005). The 2014 Scottish independence referendum was to some extent an example of choice theory in action. It is a common demand among contemporary secessionist movements, especially in advanced democracies, but critics worry about the fragmentary pressures and potential for instability that it portends. Like the first possibility – the establishment of a remedial right – this future constitutes an extension of the current constitutive recognition regime.

Should, however, the normative currents of international life shift in the other direction, then we might see a return to a consent-based recognition regime. This turn toward sovereignty would occur if the border fixity norm was strengthened and the norm of self-determination was watered down to the point where it was only activated in the case of sovereign consent. Such a development is not so unlikely given the rise of states like India, China, and Indonesia, fissiparous countries that are relatively less committed to liberal values but quite concerned about fragmentation.

The other regimes and historical periods discussed above appear less likely to recur. The age of *de facto* statehood depended on the interpretation of self-determination as a negative right, and the willingness of supporting powers to both remain on the sidelines during a civil war and overrule the sovereignty of the home state once the secessionists had prevailed. That disposition runs against both the spirit of contemporary humanitarianism and the emphasis on preserving sovereign borders. Whatever its merits, it should find few supporters outside of intellectual circles. Similarly, the practice of declaratory statehood that characterized the greater Kurdish region during the Ottoman period is also unlikely to return. The declaratory theory that states can simply will themselves into existence and that they are ontologically prior to systems is a notion that seems ill-suited for modern times when the collective benefits of sovereignty are largely dependent on the recognition of others.

Iraqi Kurdistan and independence

Returning to the original query: How likely is it that Kurdistan will gain its independence and what factors will shape that outcome? My approach to answering this question is to consider the likelihood that Kurdistan would gain independence across the set of recognition regimes outlined above, and to consider the likelihood that such a regime would determine Kurdistan's fate in the future. Figure 6.1 displays the six regimes and orders that have been discussed. These include: (1) declaratory independence, where polities can more or less declare themselves a state; (2) recognition by consent, where sovereign recognition depends on the blessing of the larger state; (3) *de facto* recognition, where self-determination was regarded as a negative right; (4) constitutive recognition, where self-determination is perceived as a positive right and the sovereignty club is forced to determine who counts; (5) constitutive recognition plus a remedial right to secession; and (6) constitutive recognition augmented by a primary right to independence.

The declaratory mode of independence existed in various pre-modern and early modern regions, including the Middle East during the Ottoman period. To some extent it bears witness to the declaratory theory of statehood given that the recognition of others matters little and a polity can truly become a state by its own hand. The challenge in such an environment is both establishing and defending independence, especially against other more powerful neighbors. How Kurdistan would fare in such a system is difficult to say given the presumption of violence and the increased need for self-defense. Whatever the case, a return to such a practice seems highly unlikely in the modern and highly globalized international system.

A return to a consent-based regime is relatively more likely. This existed in Europe prior to the rise of liberalism and its corresponding challenge to sovereignty from below. I suspect on a rather conjectural basis that this set-up accurately describes other historical systems that were sufficiently dense to develop rules for recognition, such as Greece or India during their city-state periods. I submit, however, that consent-based recognition could once again become dominant should sovereign norms wax while liberalism wanes. The implication for Kurdistan is that independence would depend entirely on Baghdad. Whether the Iraqi state would consent to an independent Kurdistan is difficult to say, an issue I return to below.

The tragedy of the *de facto* regime, at least for the Kurds, is that it is unlikely to recur. By the standards of nineteenth-century Anglo-American diplomacy, Kurdistan should be recognized. It ticks all the boxes that mattered to Lord Castlereigh, George Canning, and John Quincy Adams. It is a nation that has made manifest its self-determination against the background of a failed state. However, the peculiar balance that made that pattern of recognition possible seems outdated and anachronistic since it obliges third parties to remain on the sidelines during a civil war, however violent, and recognize victorious rebels if they prevail, thereby trumping the sovereignty of the larger state. There may be a measure of justice to it, but the mutual evolution of sovereignty and liberalism has rendered it unlikely.

The remaining three regimes represent variations in constitutive order, which is essentially the encounter between sovereign territoriality and the rise of liberalism. The first describes the contemporary system and the latter two are basically liberal extensions of it. They are all solutions for how to balance the territorial integrity of sovereign states with the rights of human beings. The advancement of liberal rights would be good for Kurdistan. The inculcation of a remedial right to independence would likely open the door to sovereign recognition given the history of conflict, human rights abuses, and the current failure of the Iraqi state. Similarly, the consolidation of a primary right to independence would almost certainly pave the way to sovereignty. After all, Kurdistan is an administratively defined area where the majority appears to favour independence. The likelihood of Kurdish independence is quite high in either scenario. Whether or not either will come to pass is a different question, fascinating to speculate upon but difficult to forecast. Much will depend on the greater global contest between the sovereign and liberal traditions. In the modern era, the system makes the state.

The current constitutive order is best viewed as a frame within a motion picture (Sandholtz and Stiles 2008). At the moment, Kurdistan's path to independence would be secure if it won the consent of Baghdad, qualified for decolonization, came to be regarded as a constituent part of a dissolving state, or, like Kosovo, was treated as a *sui generis* case. Meeting the criteria

	Likelihood of Kurdish Independence	Likelihood of Regime
Declaratory Independence	medium	low
Consent-based Regime	low	medium
De Facto Regime	high	low
Constitutive Regime	medium	high
Constitutive Regime + Remedial Right	high	medium
Constitutive Regime + Primary Right	high	medium

Figure 6.1 Kurdistan and Independence

for decolonization is not a possibility given the emphasis on colonial units of saltwater empires. However, the other options are all possible and quite political. The path of consent would be best because it is the least controversial. What would it take to persuade the Iraqi Government to permit Kurdish sovereign independence? The state would have to conclude that it had little to lose (and perhaps something to gain), and moreover rest assured that the Kurdish secession would not unleash a further unravelling of the country by, for example, motivating the western Sunni-dominated region to also seek independence. Whether or not Baghdad will come to that decision on its own is unclear, but research shows that such decisions are easier when the region in question is administratively defined and distinct (Griffiths 2015). Taking the long view, Kurdish nationalists should aim to acquire as much autonomy as possible because it could gradually make it easier for Baghdad to permit independence.

However, such consent-based decisions are often shaped by the hand of other more powerful states. For example, Khartoum was set against the secession of South Sudan, but international pressure, among other factors, gradually brought the government around to the idea. Assessing this possibility for Kurdistan requires that the key players and their interests are identified (Gunter and Ahmed 2013; Kirmanj 2013; Romano and Gurses 2014). For a period after the 2003 Iraqi invasion the United States had the power to pressure Baghdad into recognizing Kurdish independence, but of course that contradicted the American one-state policy (Bengio 2013; Shareef 2014). If the US has quietly warmed to the idea in recent times, it may now lack the leverage over Baghdad to make it happen. Iran and Turkey are also vital players on account of their influence in the region and their own concerns over Kurdish separatism; neither seems keen on an independent Kurdistan, at least for the moment. The consent-based approach is quite strategic in nature, and Kurdish independence via this path will require the right configuration of interests.

The so-called path of dissolution, along with the Kosovar example of a *sui generis* case are different in kind because they carry the possibility of circumventing the home state veto. At their core they are legal renderings designed to create a conceptual distinction between the recognition of independence in specific cases and secession elsewhere. Two factors make these paths more likely. The first is an environment of state instability and failure where conflict is occurring (or likely to occur) and there is a perceived need by at least some international actors that something needs to be done. The second factor is powerful support (Coggins 2014). Kosovo and the former Yugoslav republics had friends in high places, and even the Soviet republics had the support of Moscow. Kurdistan, it seems, satisfies the first condition considering the general instability and warfare in Syria and Iraq. The second factor is more problematic for the simple reason that too many players are currently against Kurdish independence. This could, of course, change for a number of reasons, but until then the Kurds will have to bide their time.

Conclusion

The international system is dominated by the sovereignty club. There are other important non-state actors to be sure, but sovereign states still play a central role, particularly for aspiring nations who aim to join the club. Despite the arguments of declaratory theorists and the precepts of the Montevideo Declaration, stateless nations cannot simply will themselves into existence, as least not where sovereignty is concerned. It depends on the recognition of others and should continue as such as long as international relations take place in a highly interconnected and territorially enclosed environment that privileges the sovereign state. It is for this reason that Kurdistan cannot decide its own fate. It can shape it by playing at politics and increasing its chances, but others will also decide.

Kurdistan's chances over the long run will be shaped by the push and pull of the sovereign and liberal traditions. A turn toward a greater emphasis on sovereignty would eliminate the paths to independence that circumvent the home state, and reinforce the need to gain Baghdad's consent. A conservative recognition regime of this type would reinforce the existing sovereign territorial grid and reduce the likelihood that numerous secessionist regions, not just Kurdistan, would be able to gain independence. Conversely, a move in the direction of liberalism would benefit Kurdistan and many other nationalist movements by deepening the positive right to self-determination, perhaps opening the gate to independence via a remedial or primary right. The Kurds and other stateless nations have reason to hope for a more liberal world order.

In the short run, Kurdistan's chances are constrained by the current recognition regime and the corresponding importance placed on sovereign consent and power politics. The Iraqi government may yet decide that it can permit the secession of Kurdistan, especially if it comes to see the Kurds as a nation apart and not one whose independence would start a deluge of fragmentation. Of course, independence can be won without consent, particularly when aspiring nations have powerful friends and make their bid in the context of broader state failure and regional instability. Somewhat ironically, the current unrest in Iraq and Syria could open the path to Kurdish independence. Overall, Kurdistan's best move is to gain as much autonomy as possible,[6] for as long as possible, and wait to see how conditions change, for better or for worse, at both the regional and international levels.

Notes

1 See O'Leary et al (2005) for a more general discussion on Kurdistan's future.
2 When discussing norms I adopt the following definition: norms are "standards of appropriate behavior for actors with a given identity" (Finnemore and Sikkink 1998). Also see Mueller (1989), Wendt (1999), and Sandholtz and Stiles (2008).
3 Of course, Lenin simultaneously introduced similarly radical notions regarding self-determination.
4 Others refer to this as the territorial integrity norm. See Zacher (2001) and Fazal (2007).
5 Decolonization was governed by the principle of *uti posseditis* (as you possess) a legal emphasis on sovereign recognition according to administrative lines and categories. See Jackson (1990), Ratner (1996), Shaw (1996), Bartos (1997), Fabry (2010), and Griffiths (2015).
6 One recent book argues for the many merits of associated statehood (Rezvani 2014).

References

Atzilli, B. 2012. *Good Fences, Bad Neighbors: Border Fixity and International Conflict*. Chicago: University of Chicago Press.
Armitage, D. 2007. *The Declaration of Independence*. Cambridge, MA: Harvard University Press.
Bartos, T. 1997. Uti Possidetis. Quo Vadis? *Australian Year Book of International Law* 18, 37–96.
Bengio, O. 2005. Autonomy in Kurdistan in Historical Perspective in *The Future of Kurdistan*, edited by O'Leary McGarry, and Salih. Philadelphia: University of Pennsylvania Press.
Bengio, O. 2013. The Kurdish Question: The Elephant in the Room. *The American Interest* (December).
Beran, H. 1998. A Democratic Theory of Political Self-Determination for a New World Order, in *Theories of Secession*, edited by Lehning. New York: Routledge.
Buchanan, J. 1965. An Economic Theory of Clubs. *Economica* 32(125), 1–14.
Buchanan, A. 2003. The Making and Unmaking of Boundaries: What Liberalism Has to Say, in *States, Nations, and Borders*, edited by Buchanan and Moore. Cambridge: Cambridge University Press.
Butcher, C., and R. Griffiths. 2015. Alternative International Systems? System Structure and Violent Conflict in Nineteenth-century West Africa, Southeast Asia, and South Asia. *Review of International Studies* 41(4), 715–737.

Buzan, B., and R. Little. 2000. *International Systems in World History: Remaking the Study of International Relations.* Oxford: Oxford University Press.

Charountaki, M. 2011. *The Kurds and US Foreign Policy: International Relations in the Middle East since 1945.* London: Routledge.

Ciment, J. 1996. *The Kurds: State and Minority in Turkey, Iraq, and Iran.* New York: Facts on File, Inc.

Coggins, B. 2014. *Power Politics and State Formation in the Twentieth Century: The Dynamics of Recognition.* Cambridge: Cambridge University Press.

The Economist. Set the Kurds Free. February 21, 2015.

Erman, E. 2013. The Recognitive Practices of Declaring and Constituting Statehood. *International Theory* 5(1), 129–150.

Fazal, T. 2007. *State Death: The Politics and Geography of Conquest, Occupation, and Annexation.* Princeton: Princeton University Press.

Fazal, T., and R. Griffiths. 2014. Membership Has its Privileges: The Changing Benefits of Statehood. *International Studies Review* 16(1), 79–106.

Fabry, M. 2010, *Recognizing States: International Society and the Establishment of New States since 1776.* Oxford: Oxford University Press.

Filkins, D. 2014. The Fight of Their Lives. *The New Yorker*, September 29.

Finnemore, M., and K. Sikkink. 1998. International Norm Dynamics and Political Change. *International Organization* 52(4), 887–917.

Gellner, E. 1983. *Nations and Nationalism.* Ithaca: Cornell University Press.

Griffiths, R., and C. Butcher. 2013. Introducing the International System(s) Dataset (ISD), 1816–2011. *International Interactions* 35(5), 748–768.

Griffiths, R. 2014. Secession and the Invisible Hand of the International System. *Review of International Studies* 40(3), 559–581.

Griffiths, R. 2015. Between Dissolution and Blood: How Administrative Lines and Categories Shape Secessionist Outcomes. *International Organization*, 69(3).

Gunter, M., and M. Ahmed (eds). 2013. *The Kurdish Spring: Geopolitical Changes and the Kurds.* Santa Ana, Ca: Mazda.

Halperin, M., D. Scheffer, and P. Small. 1992. *Self-Determination in the New World Order.* Washington D.C.: Carnegie Endowment for International Peace.

Jackson, R. 1990. *Quasi-States: Sovereignty, International Relations, and the Third World.* Cambridge: Cambridge University Press.

Jackson, R. 1993. The Weight of Ideas in Decolonization: Normative Change in International Relations, in *Ideas and Foreign Policy: Beliefs, Institutions, and Political Change*, edited by Goldstein and Keohane. Ithaca: Cornell University Press.

Kirmanj, S. 2013. *Identity and Nation in Iraq.* Boulder: Lynne Rienner.

Krasner, S. 1999. *Sovereignty: Organized Hypocrisy.* Princeton: Princeton University Press.

Kuperman, A. 2008. The Moral Hazard of Humanitarian Intervention: Lessons from the Balkans. *International Studies Quarterly* 52(1), 49–80.

Manela, E. 2007. *The Wilsonian Moment: Self-Determination and the International Origins of Anticolonial Nationalism.* Oxford: Oxford University Press.

Mayall, J. 1990. *Nationalism and International Society.* Cambridge: Cambridge University Press.

Meetser, D. 2012. Remedial Secession: A Positive or Negative Force for the Prevention and Reduction of Armed Conflict. *Canadian Foreign Policy Journal* 18(2), 151–163.

Mueller, D. 1989. *Public Choice II.* Cambridge: Cambridge University Press.

Mueller, J. 1989. *Retreat From Doomsday: The Obsolescence of Major War.* New York: Basic Books.
Norman, W. 1998. The Ethics of Secession as the Regulation of Secessionist Politics, in *National Self-Determination and Secession*, edited by Moore. Oxford: Oxford University Press.
O'Leary, B, J. McGarry, and K. Salih (eds). 2005. *The Future of Kurdistan.* Philadelphia: University of Pennsylvania Press.
Osiander, A. 2001. Sovereignty, International Relations, and the Westphalian Myth. *International Organization* 55(2), 251–287.
Osterud, O. 1997. The Narrow Gate: Entry to the Club of Sovereign States. *Review of International Studies* 23, 167–84.
Ozogglu, H. 2007. State-Tribe Relations: Kurdish Tribalism in the 16th and 17th Century Ottoman Empire. *British Journal of Middle Eastern Studies* 23(1), 5–27.
Radan, P. 2002. *The Break-up of Yugoslavia in International Law.* London: Routledge.
Ratner, S. 1996. Drawing a Better Line: Uti Possidetis and the Borders of New States. *The American Journal of International Law* 94(4), 590–624.
Risse, T., S. Ropp, and K. Sikkink (eds). 1999. *The Power of Human Rights: International Norms and Domestic Change*, Cambridge: Cambridge University Press.
Rezvani, D. 2014. *Surpassing the Sovereign State: The Wealth, Self-Rule, and Security Advantages of Partially Independent Territories.* Oxford: Oxford University Press.
Romano, D., and M. Gurses (eds). 2014. *Conflict, Democratization, and the Kurds in the Middle East.* New York: Palgrave Macmillan.
Sandholtz, W., and K. Stiles. 2008. *International Norms and Cycles of Change.* Oxford: Oxford University Press.
Scott, J. 2010. *The Art of Not Being Governed: An Anarchist History of Upland Southeast Asia.* New Haven: Yale University Press.
Shareef, M. 2014. *The United States, Iraq and the Kurds.* New York: Routledge.
Shaw, M. 1996. The Heritage of States: The Principle of Uti Possidetis Juris Today. *British Yearbook of International Law* 67, 75–154.
Spruyt, H. 1994. *The Sovereign State and its Competitors.* Princeton: Princeton University Press.
Tilly, C. 1975. *The Formation of National States in Western Europe.* Princeton: Princeton University Press.
Toft, M. 2002. Indivisible Territory, Geographic Concentration, and Ethnic War. *Security Studies* 12(2), 82–119.
Walter, B. 2009. *Reputation and Civil War.* Cambridge: Cambridge University Press.
Wellman, C. 2005. *A Theory of Secession.* Cambridge: Cambridge University Press.
Wendt, A. 1999. *Social Theory of International Politics*, Cambridge: Cambridge University Press.
Zacher, M. 2001. The Territorial Integrity Norm: International Boundaries and the Use of Force. *International Organization* 55(20), 215–250

7 Turkey and the Iraqi Kurdistan Federal Region
Bonds of friendship

Sara Salahaddin Mustafa and Sardar Aziz

In this chapter, we attempt to explain how the relationship between Turkey and the Kurdistan Regional Government (KRG) has affected each partner. One can say that there has been a paradigm shift away from decades of Turkey's mistreatment of Kurds. The official Turkish position on Iraqi Kurdistan has undergone a radical change during the last decade. In 2003 Turkey's foreign minister stated that Turkey would intervene militarily to "guarantee Iraq's territorial integrity" in order to prevent Kurds from breaking away or getting too much autonomy. Today, Turkey has established a cordial bilateral relationship with Iraqi Kurdistan, which contrasts sharply with the way Turkey treats Kurds in Syria and at home. As for the Iraqi Kurds, Turkey seems to have become the single most significant contributor to the idea of Iraqi Kurdistan's independence by strengthening the region's economy through heavy investment and trade.

The Kurdistan Regional Government (KRG) is almost a quarter of a century old, while its territory has been part of Iraq since the country's creation in the early 1920s. Iraq as a state has suffered from many structural problems and identity issues that have prevented the country from becoming a strong, stable, and functioning state. In addition to many other small ethno-religious minorities, the country contains three main distinct groups: the Kurds, Shia Arabs and Sunni Arabs, who have never managed to create a shared common identity. As a result, Iraq has remained fragile throughout its history. The different peoples within Iraq, who lived together for almost a century, failed to create a state that would belong to all and to which all would belong. In addition, Iraq has always been governed in an undemocratic way by elites mired in corruption.

In the process of state building, Iraqi governments have hurt the Kurds in many ways in their relentless attempts to create a single Iraqi identity. This commenced with Arabisation and finished with full marginalization, forced displacement and genocide. Baghdad's efforts and successive campaigns failed, however, to turn Kurds into Arabs or even to achieve their milder assimilation.

The 1991 Gulf War marked a watershed in modern Iraq's history. It was the moment when the country failed to recover as a unitary state and was no longer able to hold its territory together. The weak and embargoed central government allowed some space for the emergence of the KRG in the periphery. The region was labeled as a *de facto* state (Gunter 1993:295). After the invasion of Iraq in 2003, the United States introduced federalism in order to restructure the governing model of the country. The aim of this form of decentralization was to grant the various Iraqi ethno-religious groups some autonomy and also to allow them to participate in the governance of the country. The new political system was also meant to "preserve the unity, integrity, independence, and sovereignty of Iraq" (Article 109 of the Constitution). As a result, the KRG became the recognized and legitimate government of the federal region. But even before, since the no-fly zone was introduced by the United Nations in the early 1990s, the KRG has gradually proved to be a significant player in the Middle East. Several factors contributed to this: the general pro-western attitude among the Kurdish people, the demise of Saddam's Iraq, the market economy, a strategic geopolitical location, and the region's wealth of energy resources and relative stability. As the Iraqi federal system allows for significant economic autonomy, the KRG has been very active in promoting economic ties with international partners, particularly in the oil sector. A business-attractive legal framework has been developed in Kurdistan through local legislation. Big foreign companies like Chevron, Shell, Schlmerger, Exxon and Total have come to the region. The prominent role in the economic development of the KRG has been played by Turkey, the regional economic powerhouse.

As Turks and Kurds seem quite unnatural partners, given their long history of antagonism and the way Turkey has treated Kurds at home and now in Syria, we contend that this novel relationship comes mostly from the similarity of the politico-economic systems both in Turkey and Kurdistan, which is characterized by a merger of business and politics. In other words, oligarchic capitalism in Turkey and Kurdistan has significantly facilitated the rapprochement and close cooperation between these two culturally, ideologically and historically antagonistic actors. After the demise of Saddam's regime, the most dangerous threat to the region, Iraqi Kurds grew more confident and the Kurdistan region became a valid partner to the central government in Baghdad, sharing the national revenue. However, a lack of separation between politics and economy, the absence of a viable and sound economic system in general, and the weakness of the political institutions in place resulted in an increasingly close symbiotic relationship between business and politics.

Literature on oligarchy capitalism

Since its inception, the KRG has been ruled by two main political parties: the KDP and the PUK. The two parties have different histories and constituencies but overlap in many areas. One area of commonality is their politburo domination. As post-dictator ruling parties, they resemble post-dictator political parties elsewhere in many ways, exhibiting a lack of experience and the domination of corrupt elites, what Ivan Szelenyi describes as swinging between the two Weberian notions of prebendal and patrimonial.

To maintain their position and have influence over the people, the politbureau elites, require money. In an underdeveloped economy like Kurdistan's, state or government is the main source of money, thus the government's control over the economy is inevitable. Against this backdrop, the politico-economic approach to the analysis of our case is particularly appropriate, as it is concerned with the "interaction of political and economic processes in a society: the distribution of power and wealth between different groups and individuals, and the processes that create, sustain and transform these relationships over time" (Collinson 2003:3).

This approach allows us to highlight what constitutes an unhealthy symbiosis and a questionable relationship between politicians and business. More importantly, it shows how the link between politics and the economy can be used by politicians to maintain both their income and their political positions. In this case, oligarchs do not influence politics but are politicians themselves. The result is a struggle for resources between the elites played out in the arena of policy-making. Under such circumstances, elites can find more commonality amongst themselves, despite their differences, than with the wider population. When politics, (i.e. force) is required to manipulate the economy, the majority of people become more dependent on the government. As Le Billon (2000) and Keen (1994) have observed, people are deliberately made vulnerable during this process. It goes without saying that a person who relies heavily on the government cannot have much influence in a democratic system.

Accordingly, examining our case through the politico-economic lens can explain "why the relative power and vulnerability of different groups changes over time," and "how the fortunes and activities of one group in society affect others" (Collinson 2003:3).

In post-Saddam Kurdistan, the symbiotic relationship between economy and politics hampered the emergence of a competitive capitalism based on a free market. The political elite captured the main regional resource – oil money – and the construction business followed suit, consolidating conditions propitious for the development of oligarchic capitalism. The KRG's weak institutions were already under the control of the political groups PDK and PUK. Politics took priority over social demands for the benefit of politicians, while politicians turned into businessmen and vice versa. As pointed out by Stiglitz and others, oligarchic control is not good for either the economy, or for democracy, as: "enterprises captured by oligarchs tend to perform poorly" (Stiglitz 1999, Black and Tarassova 2002, Goldman 2004 in Gorodnichenko and Grygorenko 2008). The domination of oligarchs also corrupts the political system: the concentration of wealth and interference in political processes negatively affects democracy, particularly when the majority of the population deems the property rights illegitimate. Under oligarchic control there is little room for competition, the free market and eventually for the emergence of the middle class, ingredients required for any healthy democracy. As Guriev and Rachinsky (2005) showed in the case of Russia, the domination of oligarchs delays the development of democracy: "A real competition between strong political parties is more likely to emerge when financial development, competition policies and openness lower entry barriers and promote the rise of the middle class."

According to Karl Polabyi's view spelled out in *The Great Transformation* (2001:317), the development of market societies is twofold. On one hand, it is the *laissez faire* part – the efforts by a variety of groups to expand the scope and influence of self-regulating markets. On the other hand, there are protectionist efforts – the initiatives by a wide range of social actors to insulate the fabric of social life from the destructive impact of market pressures. It looks like the second movement within the Kurdistan region to offset the first movement from total predominance is missing. This has prepared the ground for the merger of the oligarchs and political elites. Similar developments have taken place in Turkey in the last decade. The country has gone through a major shift not only in political identity and geopolitical ambitions, but also in its economy. Turkey departed from the highly fragmented policies of the 1990s, when it was ruled by coalitions, into a single-party government. This was associated with the renewed rise of the religiously based counter-elite (Karadag 2010; Bank and Karadag 2012:5).

These changes have created "self-reinforcing dynamics" between domestic politics, political-economy and regional developments. The AKP's domestic consolidation resulted in the country's gradual foreign policy shifts and increased activism in the Middle East. The domestic shift was mainly exemplified through the peace process which was the start of a new era of negotiations with the PKK starting from 2012, and regionally through the process of Middle Easternization which was Turkey's new approach towards its neighboring countries. Turkey reconsidered its EU bid and decided to become a regional power. Both processes affected the Kurds on a variety of levels.

Turkey-KRG relations: Origins and recent developments

For Henri J. Barkey (2010) Turkey's relationship with the KRG is a form of new engagement in Iraq and a tremendous opportunity for Iraqi Kurdistan. Prior to the current level of cooperation, the relationship went through several stages. The journey began with bitter enmity and has only recently reached the level of brotherly relations. In 2007, Erdogan described Barzani as a "tribe leader" and accused him of supporting the PKK. This is the common process of othering and orientalizing as shown by Demir and Welat (2010). However, such rhetoric is characteristic of Erdogan who is eager to use different languages for domestic and international audience, referring to Kurds as both backward terrorists and proud highlanders; this is rather typical of the Turkish nationalist rhetoric as well (Demir and Welat 2010).

In the last decade the political dynamic in the region has been changing rapidly, as the United States, the powerbroker, encouraged the KRG "to improve its relationship and coordination with Turkey" (WikiLeaks 2008). The Turkish-KRG rapprochement was also regarded by some as "oil diplomacy" (O'Byrne 2012). In spite of this, the PKK always loomed large in their relationship. If the PKK was seen by Turkey as a threat, the KRG was also initially regarded as part of that threat.

Ultimately the relationship improved and brought about significant attitudinal changes. For Turkey "Barzani became Ankara's favorite Kurd" (Park 2012:116), and later a reliable partner (Yinanç 2012). Romano (2015) raises the question of a partnership between Ankara and Erbil, and the answer for him is clear: "For a variety of reasons, the relationship between the two likely represents an emergent strategic alliance more than a temporary marriage." Still others emphasize the inequality of the relationship: "Instead of statehood or enhanced autonomy, however, the KRG has become more dependent on Turkey while remaining tied to Iraq" (Natali 2012).

Turkey's new thinking

Over the last decade Turkish elites have developed a new mindset with regard to the geopolitics of the country. A paradigm shift seems to have happened – the neighbors stopped being seen as enemies. As Akyol (2013) puts it, "in the past decade, one of the greatest achievements of the successive Justice and Development Party (AKP) governments was to save Turkey from its decades-old fear about the outside world." This fear was rooted not just in the Cold War but also in the dull minds in Ankara, used to considering all our neighbors as threats. Even Turkish children are taught in school that "Turkey is a country surrounded by seas on three sides, and by enemies on four sides" (Ibid). This change in mindset is best exemplified in the policy "zero problems with neighbors." For Davutoglu, the founder of the "zero problem policy," Turkey was different from other countries because of its culture and geography, but despite all these differences, should attempt to reach the neighboring countries through soft power, the market, and shared history.

It is clear that Turkey is positioned in a strategic location in the region. Brzezinski writes that "Turkey and Iran are not only important geostrategic players but are also geopolitical pivots, whose own internal condition is of critical importance to the fate of the region. Both are middle-sized powers, with strong regional aspirations and a sense of historical significance" (1997:124). This supports Turkey's self-vision today.

Turkey's important position was not fully recognized or utilized to deduce a foreign policy doctrine. On the contrary, Turkey has regarded itself throughout its modern history as an isolated fragile state, cognizant of the need to combine the Ottoman legacy with modernity. Davutoglu writes:

> Turkey's geography gives it a specific central country status, which differs from other central countries…. Taking a broader, global view, Turkey

holds an optimal place in the sense that it is both an Asian and European country and is also close to Africa through the Eastern Mediterranean. A central country with such an optimal geographic location cannot define itself in a defensive manner. It should be seen neither as a bridge country which only connects two points, nor a frontier country, nor indeed as an ordinary country, which sits at the edge of the Muslim world or the West (Davutoglu 2008:78).

This shift in Turkey's foreign policy has had a positive impact on Kurds both within Turkey and in Iraq. It also clearly shows that Turkey has the desire to reengage with the Middle East region. However, the improvement of the Turkey-KRG relationship was not a direct result of this mind change, but an indirect byproduct of it. In the past two decades, Turkey has emerged as a strong regional power. It has enjoyed dramatic economic growth that has propelled it into the G20, the exclusive club of major economies. The country has been run almost solely by the Justice and Development Party (AKP) with Recep Tayyip Erdoğan at its helm. In the early days of their rule, the new Islamic-oriented elites were regarded as the panaceas for the many malaises of the region. They were seen to have the capacity to combine both Islam and modernity, West and East, and become a bridge between several civilizations. This is especially evident in how Turkey has struggled throughout its modern history to become a democratic state. Meanwhile on the economic front, the area of AKP's strength, Turkey has become a manufacturing country that needs more market and raw materials. Accordingly, Turkey was not thinking of the KRG as a significant partner, and it was obvious that Turkey's aim was to engage with the whole country of Iraq. Thus, until 2003, Turkey was dealing with Baghdad only. Turkey and Iraq signed 48 various bilateral agreements and memoranda of understandings in November 2009 pertaining to energy and other economic sectors.

The Turkey and Iraq relationship did not go as planned, however, as Turkey wanted Iraq to be a unitary and centralized country ruled by the Sunni minority as during the last four centuries. This was driven by a geopolitical competition with Iran and Turkey's aim was, among other things, to contain "Kurdish nationalism in Iraq" (Weitz, 2012) and keep Iraq strong and centralized. The sectarian motive in the Turkey-Iraq relationship was exacerbated by two factors, namely the Arab Spring and Iraqi Prime Minister al Maliki's polices which alienated the Iraqi Sunnis. The relationship between Turkey and Iraq became more personalized – Al-Malki and Erdogan – and the overall bilateral political and economic interaction weakened.

The KRG, an active non-state actor

The KRG is a regional government within federal Iraq, a sub-state entity that often acts as a *de facto* state. This has had "a significant impact on the development of the KRG, its state-building, its interaction with the international community, and its policies" (Voller 2012). This happens now in a wider environment where the "traditional state system in Syria and Iraq is collapsing, due to their civil wars, and the resulting absence of institutional legitimacy" (Gunter 2015:103). As a result of the erosion of the traditional nation state, many regional and local actors have emerged and increasingly influenced the reshaping of the security map of the region. Non-state actors are increasingly setting the agenda across the Middle East.

The delicate context of the Turkey-KRG relationship

Turkey's relationship with the KRG has unfolded within a delicate context, as it directly touches on Turkey's internal stability and national security because of the Kurdish question at home. Moreover, the growing cooperation with Iraq's federal region has a serious impact on Turkey-Iraq bilateral relations. Baghdad is increasingly unhappy and opposes some deals, especially when it comes to the energy sector. As Cagaptay and Evans (2012:3) pointed out, "default support for Baghdad and a structural suspicion of the Iraqi Kurds had been hallmarks of Turkish foreign policy for decades." Due to the souring of relations between Shias and Sunni, Baghdad and Ankara drifted even further apart. This was exacerbated after the Syrian uprising and the emergence of Kurds as an important factor in Syria and the wider region. These factors affected Turkey's relationship with the KRG. Kurds in northern Iraq got much closer to the Turkish government.

Turkey is not a security partner to the KRG, as was seen during the ISIS attack on Erbil in August 2014 when the KRG's appeal for help was not heard in Ankara. On the contrary, Turkey remains a security threat to the KRG for the foreseeable future. This is especially true with the Kurdish question remaining unsolved both within Turkey and in Syria. According to Stratfor's intelligence forecast for 2016, "This is the year when Turkey, nervous but more politically coherent than it was last year, will likely make a military move into northern Syria while trying to enlarge its footprint in northern Iraq" (Stratfor 2015).

KRG benefits of friendship with Turkey

Turkey and KRG interact through many channels. Some are static, such as geography and ethnicity, while others are variable, exemplified through politics and economy.

The KRG has several characteristics conducive to its high profile in the Middle Eastern region beyond the national borders of Iraq, characteristics which help it become an active and recognized regional player: (1) stability; an expensive commodity in the Middle East, yet the KRG has been a relatively peaceful and stable place; (2) economic development – the KRG has purposefully provided for a friendly business environment in the region; and finally (3) recognition and acceptance by other countries; Turkey engaged in economic activities in Iraqi Kurdistan while having limited relations with Iraq, which shows, in some sense, a recognition of the KRG as an independent and trustworthy partner in the international arena.

Turkey was, and remains, the principal gateway for Iraqi Kurdistan's foreign trade since 1991. The Kurdistan region has been an important market for Turkish companies, with $12 billion (USD) of annual trade between the Kurdistan Region and Turkey rising in 2011 compared to $10 billion (USD) in trade with Iran. Moreover, 70 percent of the annual trade between Turkey and Iraq takes place in the Kurdistan region; in fact, Turkey's exchanges with the region exceed that of its annual trade with Syria, Lebanon, and Jordan combined (Independent Kurdish Journalism 2011).

In the area of security and the Kurdish issue, "in 2008, Turkey, Iraq, KRG, and the U.S. also established a Trilateral Mechanism to develop cooperation with a view of eradicating the PKK in Iraqi territories" (Charountaki 2013:193). The presence of the PKK in the equation poses many problems. First, Turkey is concerned about the Kurdish situation both within the country and beyond its borders. Thus, the PKK remains an important item on Turkey's security and foreign policy agenda. Linking the PKK to the Kurds in Iraq indicates that the more Turkey moves toward solving the Kurdish issues at home, the better its relationship will become with the KRG. Likewise, the worse the situation is in Turkey, the worse the security dilemma will be regarding any leap forward by the Kurds elsewhere. Based on that, we can surmise that Turkey will be likely to support the independence of KRG when the Kurdish issue is solved at home.

Kurdistan became even more attractive to Turkish interests after the discovery of giant oil fields in the region: "Shaikan fields, as calculated by Dynamic Global Advisors (DGA), independent, Houston-based exploration consultants, are a P90 value of 12.4 billion barrels to a P10 (Lowest Uncertainty Quantification) value of 15 billion barrels of oil-in-place, with a mean value of 13.7 billion barrels" (Gulf Keystone Petroleum Ltd, 2012). If Turkey is an energy-thirsty country, the KRG has many reasons to aim at a robust relationship. New Turkey under the AKP party classifies itself as "holding a special position" on the world energy map. Kurdistan contributes to Turkey's energy security, especially for gas, and this, combined with the geopolitical status of the Kurdistan Region, points to its future potential for being a good energy security source for Turkey.

An asymmetric relationship

The relationship between Turkey and the KRG is asymmetrical; the KRG is not an equal partner, due to its sub-national status and many other circumstances that make the region vulnerable to Turkey, the regional economic powerhouse. Kurdistan is landlocked, which is a geographical curse that poses serious economic and security challenges. As pointed out by Faye (Faye et al. 2015:31), "in spite of technological improvements in transportation, landlocked developing countries continue to face structural challenges in accessing world markets. As a result, landlocked countries often lag behind their maritime neighbors in overall development and external trade." If that is true for other established countries accepted by the world community, the situation is harsher for the KRG, which is yet to become a country.

Another weakness stems from the KRG's internal situation in particular from the fact that the region has to overcome the consequences of both colonialism and civil war. One can argue that Kurds in Iraq were colonized by the Iraqi government throughout Iraqi history. This status has made Iraqi Kurdistan an undeveloped peripheral agricultural region that lacks advanced forms of development and industrialization.

Moreover, the region is undergoing deep transformations: the transition from traditional to modern, from authoritarianism to democracy, from feudal economic and social relations to a capitalist market economy. These transitions are not going smoothly, primarily because of the weakness of modern institutions against the backdrop of archaic relations and traditional values. The weakness of modern institutions has blurred the differences between the public and private spheres, allowing public utilities to be exploited for private gain and creating a fertile ground for corruption. Widespread systematic corruption has disenchanted the constituencies of traditional political parties and ruling elites in general. On top of these problems, the region seems to lack a clearly defined economic system. This has made the region vulnerable to political and economic changes. This is more crystalized in the Baghdad-Erbil relationship and the vulnerability of the KRG to oil prices in international markets. There is no single economic model that would fit the KRG economy: the region's economic system has elements of free-market, rentier and socialism.

An anonymous friendship: Introducing the main players

The engines of the Turkey-KRG relationship are the KDP and the AKP. In the KRG, the Kurdish Democratic Party (KDP) promotes and steers the relationship with Turkey both for reasons of geography and solidifying its position within the KRG's political system. On the Turkish side, the Justice and Development Party (AKP) has cultivated an unprecedented relationship in Turkish history with Kurds in Northern Iraq. Turkey prefers Erbil to remain closer to Ankara than to a Tehran-aligned government in Baghdad. Other political parties within Turkey are either willing to change the relationship (such as CHP, the Republican People's Party) or totally oppose it (such as MHP, the Nationalist Movement Party). "Turkey has, therefore, been actively enmeshed in this imbroglio, having appreciated the level of danger that a departure of Barzani might pose for Turkey," one close observer from the AKP stated (Dalay 2015). We can conclude that Turkey sees other political parties in the KRG as being aloof towards Turkey; the KRG regards Turkish political parties as being aloof to the KRG.

The AKP

The exceptional role of personality in Turkish politics is well known. Turkish history is replete with parties who have been banned only to reemerge almost immediately under other names because of the strong personality of their leader. In addition to this, Turkey is a unique example in the Middle East where radical ideological changes have occurred: from Islamist (Ottoman) to secular (Ataturk) back to Islamist (AKP). These ideological re-orientations have dramatically affected the nature of the governing elites.

Contemporary Islamist movements in Turkey emerged after the 1950s and grew during the post-1980 period. During that period, peripheral political groups moved to urban centers and gained access to secular education and the opportunity for upward mobility and better economic conditions. The Islamic-oriented political parties, like the secular political parties, combined both charisma and ideology in the figure of their leader. Thus, the new Turkey, like the old, is ruled by strong personalities. For Mümtaz'er Türköne (2007), Recep Tayyip Erdoğan's success in elections was the work of these new Islamist elites. According to him, Turkey's ruling elites identified as "a new class of educated people who understand the world, have internalized the mentality of the market and have an entrepreneurial spirit. This class defends both conservative and indispensable democratic freedoms. They are far from any radical tendency and strive for a peaceful world. They comprise the main bones of the AKP. The AKP militants are newly urban, educated, market oriented yet quite conservative. The genie of this elite dates back to Özal's time. The latter played a crucial role in commencing the neoliberal era in the country. Özal was a "staunch believer and supporter of liberalism, yet his style of governance was characterized by a weak commitment to democracy, institutions and the rule of law" (Onis 2004:12). The elements of religion, militarism and capitalism are all the hallmarks of Turkish capitalism. Springing from Friedrich Hayek's view (The Principles of a Liberal Social Order 1966), the relationship between neoliberals and democracy is at best problematic. It is argued that Hayek's "ideas justify the erosion of democracy under capitalism in defense of private property" (Selwyn 2015). After the military coup in 1980, "the winner of the elections was the newly formed Motherland Party (MP), headed by Turgut Özal, the architect of the January 1980 stabilization package. This package was the most decisive attempt of the dominant groups in society and polity – the military and business circles – to launch the neoliberal agenda" (Cosar and Yegenoglu 2009). This new liberal economic atmosphere created better economic conditions for small business owners who had newly moved to the city.

The new elite also had a new vision for the country and the region; its aim was to drive Turkey towards becoming a regional power. That could be achieved "only if it brings added value to its Muslim neighbors" (Cagaptay 2015). Here lays the seed of the image of Turkey as a model. This was embraced by the majority of the Middle Easterners, especially when Turkey was a successful neighbor, a role model exercising political ambitions in the region. When Turkey pushed too far in its political activism, its positive image vanished. Soon the much-celebrated "zero problems with neighbors" policy gradually deteriorated into open hostility and even virtual undeclared warfare with some of its neighbors. Practically all the gains achieved with respect to visa liberalization and economic integration have been lost. The free trade agreement with Syria was suspended in December 2011; that with Lebanon failed to be finalized, while relations with the Nouri al-Maliki government in Iraq have reached an impasse. Most recently, the new Egyptian regime is also inclined to reassess Egypt's relations with Turkey in light of Erdoğan's bitter criticisms of the military overthrow of the democratically elected Muslim Brotherhood government. As a result, many commentators have wittily characterized this dramatic transformation in the Turkish "zero problems with neighbors" policy as a policy of "zero neighbors without problems" (Kirişci 2009). One relationship remained intact, however: that with the KRG.

Quite logically, the sharp deterioration of relations with their neighbors has brought the KRG and Turkey even closer. The dismal failure of the zero-problems policy has added a new dimension and additional value to the relationship with the KRG, which could be used as a handy tool in the regional balance of power; for instance, in Turkish policy towards Iran and Baghdad. It is not common for Turkey to internalize its regional and foreign policy, and some even argue that "the AKP has used foreign policy to frame an identity for itself, to construct party identification amongst its voter base" (Kirdiş, 2015:178). This has been particularly evident during the Syrian war. Erdogan stated: "We do not see Syria as a foreign problem, but as a domestic problem. Because we have 850 kilometers of common border, we are linked through lineage, history, and culture. Therefore, what goes on there would not permit us just to be a spectator. On the contrary, we need to hear those voices, and naturally do what is necessary" (Kalaycıoglu 2014).

Statements like this show the mindset of the ruling political class in Turkey, their vision of the region and mode of mobilization. If neighbors are not foreign, then Turkey is not foreign to its neighbors. This policy has been dubbed the "policy of erasing borders." "Our prime minister's vision is full economic integration. One day you won't notice the frontier between Turkey and Iraq," stated Aydin Selcen, Turkish Consul General in Erbil (Fielding-Smith 2010).

The KDP

After the first election in 1992, a unique form of governance emerged in the KRG. It is commonly known as 50:50, which means that each of the two main political parties (KDP and PUK) controlled half of the administration and budget of the region. From the early days when the seeds of party dominance were sown, neither Jalal Talabani nor Massoud Barzani became part of the official structures of the government. Hence the political party remained stronger than the government. The KDP dates back to after the Second World War. Today it represents the conservative tribal structure of the society. In general Kurdish society is not modern; the modern elites are few and unable to mobilize the population. Therefore, modern elites seek alliances with the traditional elites, namely clerics and Sheiks and other remnants of the feudal era, but the latter has command over the language, mythology and grand narratives both religious and traditional, and Kurdish politics suffers from the elite dichotomy. The domination of traditional norms and values, which are based more on hierarchy rather than merit, negatively affects the structure within the political parties. This hampers economic and political modernization, let alone societal. The domination of traditional elites in politics is aggravated by Kurdistan's oil-based economy. The strong presence of tradition and the civil war are the two main factors behind the domination of traditional elites: the KDP and the PUK are excellent examples.

Against this backdrop, every Kurdish political party suffers from a personalist and narrow echelon. This phenomenon was strengthened when rent money became the main source of income in the region, especially in the post-Saddam era. A sizable portion of the country's income goes directly into the hands of the ruling elites. Much of Kurdistan's politics is based on oil revenue distribution, a phenomenon well-captured by Ross: "… distribution of resource revenues to particular groups of the population is a way for incumbent political leaders to ensure support, and to credibly commit to future policy" (Ross 2001; 2008). This form of buying allegiance through the windfall depends primarily on the incentives of ruling elites to distort the rules of the political game in their favor. In addition to providing revenues, a natural resource economy also provides international support for the ruling elites. The role of the international community becomes antidemocratic when the security of supply is regarded as more significant than democratic processes. The KDP has utilized natural resources in order to maintain its traditional structure with modern tools.

Turkey eyes Iraqi Kurdistan

In the past, Turkey had a rather predictable foreign policy characterized by clear orientations toward the West through its EU membership aspirations, remaining relatively passive in the Middle Eastern region. As a result of the current shift, namely the emergence of pro-Islamic parties and a Middle Eastern reorientation, the Middle East has become a priority for Turkish foreign policy. "Such reorientation has been described as the end of the Kemalist era in Turkish foreign policy" (Edelman et al. 2013:12).

Many factors should be taken into account when explaining this overall reorientation. Turkey's turning to the East was a natural move that fits neatly within the frame of Islamic or Ottoman culture. These frames allowed, in addition to the state-based intergovernmental relations, for the development of a whole set of interactions with non-state entities, some of which were done on a personal and family level. A few examples include the cordial relations with the Assad family in the early period of the Turkey-Syria friendship, a common religious and ideological discourse, the shared attitude toward Israel, and abandoning Kemalist secularism, all of which directly contributed to this reorientation.

Opening up to the Kurds in Iraq has been an integral part of this foreign policy shift, yet the emergence of a cordial relationship with the KRG was the most unexpected move in Turkey's foreign policy. Why the KRG? This has both domestic and regional dimensions. It was the result of two overlapping processes: opening up toward the Kurds and the de-securitisation of the Kurds both internally and externally (Aras and Polat 2008).

With the rise of the AKP, the Kurds were suddenly rediscovered in Turkey and in the region, as their existence had been denied in the past. The AKP Government from the very beginning conducted a twofold foreign policy: "First, Turkey is increasingly relying on multilateralism in order to pursue key national interests, thereby taking a more active role in international relations. Second, Turkey is opening up to new areas where Turkish contacts have been rather limited in the past" (Adam 2012:141). The KRG appears to be one of those new areas. In spite of this general frame, however, the Turkey-KRG relationship is quite different from Turkey's other bilateral relationships in many ways, one among them being elite domination. In other words, the relationship between the two sides is yet to be institutionalized and solidified in a formal manner. For instance, Turkey is yet to officially recognize the KRG, and the latter has no office in Ankara, so public opinion and attitude toward the Kurds remain rather negative in Turkey. The cordiality in the relationship is primarily elite-based.

Turkey's relationship with the KRG differs significantly from a typical state-non-state interaction. The KRG politicians are received at the highest level, the region's relationship with Turkey exists despite the central government, and finally Turkey is willing to go against international norms in dealing with KRG oil exports. Turkey's relationship with the KRG contradicts Baghdad's will, especially in the energy sector, as KRG is still officially part of Iraq. Turkey's particular interest in the Kurdistan region is caused first by its energy dependence and second by the nature of Turkish capitalism that emphasises an elite-to-elite framework. The KRG, a federal region within the state of Iraq in a difficult relationship with the central government, is eager to enter into Turkey's orbit. Obviously, Turkey is in a significantly stronger position and takes advantage of the situation as a whole.

In order to overcome the difficulties associated with this asymmetric relation, the KRG aims at statehood. There are only two scenarios for Iraqi Kurdistan to constitutionally become an independent state: the disintegration of Iraq or a change of the current constitutional system, since the current Iraqi constitution does not allow for secession.

In addition, the ruling elites in the region have no awareness of the significance and knowhow of formal institutions, or they abhor institutions as an antithesis to their personal power. "The rule of a narrow elite that organizes the society for its own rent-extracting interest is a common trajectory every nation followed on its road to poverty" as Acemoglu and Robinson argue (2012). In other words, when institutions are weak, elites are strong.

Another reason why the elites play a very important role to the detriment of institutions is the economic system that is in place in Kurdistan. The wealth of energy resources makes the prevailing economic system of the KRG a rentier economy. This was partly due to the continuity of the old Iraqi rentier system and partly to the clear desire of the Kurdish major political parties to take advantage of the rent income and buy followers' allegiance. Rent economy is characterized by the domination of the political elites over economic activities, in particular revenue distribution. Turkey has significantly contributed to the establishment of a rent-based economy in the KRG and takes advantage of it. Thanks to the KRG's favoring production-sharing contracts with international firms, Turkish companies have obtained significant shares in the KRG energy sector and are greatly involved in production, transportation and refining.

On the Turkish side, the elites also prevail over institutions and have been instrumental in engaging with the KRG and in maintaining close cooperation. One of the various post-1980 transformations resulted in the emergence of what is labeled 'oligarchic capitalism.' For Roy Karadag (2010:6), "the fragmentation of the political arena, the end of corporatist social control, and the establishment of new, closed elite political business cartels that capture the state represent the crucial elements of oligarchic dynamics that have undermined state power and institutional trust." This trend in the politics-business relationship has been lingering on and flourishing in the AKP era. One can argue that it is this precise aspect of the business-politics mixture that can explain the emergence of a rather unnatural Turkey-KRG relationship. Geo-economy became the center for foreign policy making, which accounts for the "increased volumes of capital expenditures and trade that have occurred under the AKP government, as well as by the diversity of Turkish business partners in the region" (Furtig 2014:109).

Entangling economy with foreign policy significantly changes a country's behavior in the international arena, makes foreign policy driven by commercial interest, and modifies other important aspects of foreign policy making like ideology or culture: "This interweaving of foreign and trade policy also explains why the Turkish government is so eager to collaborate with the Kurds despite differing ideological orientations" (Bank and Karadag 2012:14). When energy and economy became part of the relationship, the two sides developed more and more mutual interests. To illustrate, the transport company Power-Trans, "a Turkish-controlled company with links to the administration of Turkey's Prime Minister Recep Tayyip Erdogan, markets the crude from Shaikan and manages the transportation" (Osgood and Tahir 2014).

In addition to politico-economic considerations within the neoliberal paradigm, there is also some cultural communality between the elites in Turkey and the KRG. This is represented primarily through the domination of the strong figure over the political system and people. The post-Kemalist euphoria lasted about ten years before Turkish democracy sprang back, like an overextended rubber band, to a familiar defensive posture in which the group in power focuses on defending its networks against rivals. White (2015) states that "today it is the AKP that has doubled down on disciplining and defending its lucrative networks. Independent institutions, like the courts, are being pressed to the party's breast; its leader has developed an extreme cult of personality in which he is presented as the heroic savior of his people; and critics are savaged and scapegoats cultivated and attacked as traitors" (Ibid).

The domination of powerful figures is the norm within the Turkish political culture. This political culture prepares the ground for the emergence of charismatic figures and populisms, in this case the "fusion of state and nation into a single entity, with Erdoğan himself, as both representative of the state and tribune of the people. Where a man and his vision become a program there is no room for consultation, not even for discussion" (Gunter 2014:4). The phenomenon of a single person, a man embodying the ideology of the party and imposing it on the nation, is not unfamiliar to the KRG either. Therefore, it is not surprising that the political elites in Turkey and Iraqi Kurdistan are on the same wavelength and can get along pretty well with each other.

The Turkey–KRG–Iran triangle

Turkey, as we have argued, plays a more significant role in the KRG compared with other regional powers, even with the central government in Bagdad and the rest of Iraq, chiefly in the KDP-dominated areas. In order to better understand this particular friendship, we need to put the Turkey-KRG relationship in a wider regional context. Turkey and Iran, the two regional powers, have been battling to become a hegemonic power in the region for many centuries. This competition has renewed in the last decade but the idea has proved impossible, as no regional power could achieve hegemony over the entire Middle East. Looking back at Turkey's policy towards the Middle East, in particular towards its old rival Iran, its efforts to boost its role in the region have been extremely significant. Although both Turkey and Iran have been staunch enemies of the Kurds through history, Turkey's policy has undergone dramatic changes in the last decade, while Iran's policy toward the KRG remains part of its policy toward the Middle East in general.

The best framework for understanding the complicated and violent regional politics of the Middle East is a cold war style standoff among a number of regional players, including sub-state actors, in which Iran and Saudi Arabia play the leading roles. These two main powers are not confronting and, most probably, will not confront each other militarily; rather, their contest for influence plays out in the domestic political systems of the region's weak states. It is a struggle over the direction of the Middle Eastern countries' domestic politics more than a purely military contest. The military and political strength of parties and the influence that outsiders can bring to bear to that strength seem more important than the military balance between Riyadh and Tehran. This standoff predates the Arab uprisings, but the Arab Spring has opened up new arenas and new participants in the Middle Eastern cold war.

Based on history and religion, Iran views Iraq as part of its sphere of interest. Indeed, at some point in history Iraq was the only regional power that balanced Iran in the Middle East. With the fall of Saddam Hussein, Iran has lost no opportunity to regain control over Iraq and make it part of its sphere of influence, or at least to prevent the emergence of an anti-Iranian regime in Iraq as well as to have an ally in the competition with its regional challenger, Saudi Arabia.

Thus Iran's policy towards Iraq is to maintain the Shia government, to offset Sunnis and their regional backers Saudis and Turkey, to distance Iraq from the United States, and to keep Iraq's unity. That would mean putting down Kurdish aspirations for independence. In doing so, Iran takes advantage of cultural affinity, geographical proximity, common history, shared security concerns and close links with the current ruling elites in the KRG, especially the PUK, many of whom are Persian-speaking and have lived in Iran.

Iran, the current strongest ally of Iraq in the region, is interested in preserving Iraq's unity and maintaining its dominance over the whole country. The KRG's policies that diverge from those of the central government in Baghdad are not welcomed by Tehran. A strong unified Iraq would serve Iran's interest better in the region. The KRG's attempts toward economic and political independence would pose a threat to both their ally Iraq and themselves; what is more, Tehran fears that the successes of Iraqi Kurds would inspire and encourage their brethren Kurds living on the other side of the Zagros mountains to attempt to do the same.

Interestingly enough, the KRG acts quite independently when dealing with Turkey but seems more connected to the rest of Iraq when dealing with Iran: "For Iraqi Kurds, relations with Iran must be seen through the prism of relations between Iraq as a whole and its eastern neighbor" (*The Guardian* 2013). Therefore, Iran has to catch up with its regional rivals, first Turkey and then the Gulf States, to bring the KRG closer to Iran, to balance the seesaw for its interest against Turkey, and to sustain its control over a unified Iraq.

Iranian-KRG relations significantly improved in August 2014, when the Iranian army helped to defend Erbil against ISIS advances in the region. Later the KRG Prime Minister's visit to Tehran increased prospects of economic ties and energy contracts. "Indeed, for the KRG, Iran has the potential to become an important trading partner and a source of foreign direct investment that would reduce its dependence on Turkey; especially following July's P5+1 nuclear agreement [...]. These new developments, however, are likely to reduce the prospects of an independent Kurdistan in the three-year outlook as Iran would use its increased leverage over the KRG to arbitrate in disputes between Erbil and Baghdad" (Ingram 2015).

As a result of dramatic changes in the Middle East and more confrontations among the regional powers, Turkey is becoming increasingly isolated. The coming of the Russians sends a signal of a clear attempt to seal Turkey from the rest of the region, as we have witnessed in Syria. This makes the KRG even more important for Turkey: it is the only corridor through which it can reach out to the Arab world.

Turkey and the idea of KRG independence

The more Turkey feels isolated, the more it leans on the KRG in various aspects – political, economic and, in particular, energy. The recent crisis has proved that Turkey is vulnerable compared to other regional powers when it comes to energy security. Because of the domination of particular elites on both sides of the border and shared concerns about their survival, both the AKP and the KDP are eager to rescue each other in a variety of ways. How far can that go and how may the oligarch-based bilateral relationship contribute to the KRG's independence?

The idea of having a sovereign Kurdistan is so popular that it is hard to find a single Kurd who would oppose it, but many wonder how and who will implement it. For Kurdistan independence to materialize, many changes, both in the region and in the country as a whole, need to take place. A preferable way of becoming independent would be the collapse of the Iraqi state. In current circumstances, even if the KRG breaks away from Iraq, its will be entirely dependent on support from Turkey to survive. For a long time, Turkey was the most anti-Kurdish country both at home and everywhere else in the world. Today the situation is quite different under the rule of the new Turkish elites. The modern secular Turkey was unable to become multicultural but hoped to be a melting pot.

The current elite has a new frame of thinking which is namely Islamic or Ottoman. Both Islamic and Ottoman are identifications that predate the nation-state era. When Turkey moved from an empire to a state, it not only abandoned this so-called multiculturalism but strictly opposed it. The new Islamic elites are aiming to return to the former Ottoman ideology, but in a postmodern style. The new policy is meant to attract strength from everywhere in order to boost the country's influence in the region. Islamic identity is also useful in order to mobilize and lead others. In the past, the states in the Middle East succumbed to challenges and collapsed, and new forces, such as the Kurds, emerged invisible from the point of view of the Westphalian state system. When Turkey realized the futility of its efforts to join the European Union and turned back to the East, the elites came to the realization that Islam as a unifying ideology does not always work because there are other identities that had become stronger and Islam is not sufficient. Beside, not all have good memories of when they lived together with Turks, or are now willing to submit to Turkish hegemony.

Until recently, the AKP hoped that Islam as an identity could encompass Kurds within Turkey. This process currently faces serious challenges and possible failures since the overture to Kurds increased their awareness of their ethnic identity. This seriously bothers the Turkish elites but the genie is out of the bottle. On the one hand, the crisis within Turkey delays its support for Iraqi Kurds' independence; on the other hand, Turkey is at a crossroads and cannot deal with the Kurdish issue through violence and suppression alone. Thus, considering Iraqi Kurdistan as a partner in the Middle East is a way to overcome its crisis with the Kurds.

Conclusion

In this chapter we have attempted to explain the unusually close relationship between Turkey and the Kurdistan Regional Government and shed light on the effects this relationship has on both sides, especially on the Kurdistan Region. Turkey's attitude to the Kurds outside its borders has witnessed a dramatic alteration never before seen in its history. The friendly bonds between Turkish authorities and the Kurds from Northern Iraq have changed both the security and energy maps of the Middle East. The Turkey-KRG relationship remains most advanced and integrated for the KRG, comparing to its bilateral relations with other regional powers, based on mutual needs and shared interests.

In this chapter, we demonstrated that both sides went through internal changes before they engaged in this relationship. Neither old Turkey nor Kurds before the emergence of the KRG were able to cement such a relationship. Turkey's internal shift was radical and had clear sociopolitical roots. The shift had many layers: from a military-security-oriented state to a trading state, from secular urban elite to rural and urban religious conservative elites.

The new Turkey relied more on economy and soft power in conducting its regional and foreign policy. Thus, it attempted to marginalize the army and open up toward a different identity within the country and, simultaneously, the world. Internally, this was exemplified by the Kurdish question. During this era, the country saw unprecedented improvement in this regard. This new development was a cornerstone in forming the current Turkey-KRG relationship. For reasons of geography, emerging cross-border nationalism, and the media, it is hard or even impossible to establish a stable lasting relationship with the KRG without solving the Kurdish question within Turkey. The chapter has traced the emergence of the KRG within Iraq and the historically troubled Kurdish–Iraqi relationship, showing that Iraq has been unable to become a strong centralized state by imposing a particular identity on the country. This manufactured status of the country resulted in its near collapse after the American invasion. The current Iraqi federation is more a name than a reality. Iraq has lost most of its state structures such as territorial integrity, shared identity, a unified army, and the ability to serve the population and protect the country. For the KRG to survive they have to overcome their landlocked geography and be able to reach the world market. Turkey was the obvious and only choice in this regard. In spite of this, the relationship between the two sides is still anomalous in many ways. The weakness that might harm the relationship more than anything else is its elite structure. As the chapter demonstrated, the relationship between the two sides is rather a relationship between two party echelons. On both sides a sort of oligarchy emerged. The oligarchs, as experience in other countries shows, usually weaken democracy and poorly manage their economy. While the oligarchs are internally weak, they are also poor at managing long-lasting relationships. These factors might put the Turkey-KRG relationship in jeopardy. In addition, there are other external factors shaping the relationship, such as the regional sectarian conflicts, the collapse of central states, and the competition of regional and global powers in reshaping the region. While Turkey has an opportunity to maintain the close cooperation at the same level, the relationship has been increasingly under duress. This opens up the relationship to many different scenarios. One of these scenarios is Iraqi Kurdistan's independence. If Turkey faces the hegemony of the other regional powers and is unable to protect its interests, it might be forced to take up other options, supporting the independence of the KRG being one of them.

References

Acemoglu D. and Robinson J. 2012. *Why nations fail*. New York: Crown Publishers.

Adam L. 2012. *Turkey's Foreign Policy in the AKP Era: Has There Been a Shift in the Axis?* [Online] Turkishpolicy. Available at: http://turkishpolicy.com/pdf/vol_11-no_3-adam.pdf [Accessed: July 15 2015].

Akyol M. 2013. Again, a Country Surrounded by Enemies, *Hurriyet daily news*, [Online]. Available at: http://www.hurriyetdailynews.com/again-a-country-surrounded-by-enemies.aspx?pageID=238&nid=51257%20 [Accessed: July 15 2015].

Aras B. and Polat K. 2008. From Conflict to Cooperation: Desecuritization of Turkey's Relations with Syria and Iran. *Security Dialogue*, 39(5), 495–515.

Bank A. and Karadag R. 2012. The Political Economy of Regional Power: Turkey under the AKP, GIGA Research Unit: *Institute of Middle East Studies* No 204 September 2012.

Barkey H.J. 2010. Turkey's New Engagement in Iraq: Embracing Iraqi Kurdistan, *United States Institute of Peace*, Special Reports 237, [Online] Available at: http://www.usip.org/sites/default/files/SR237_Turkey's%20New%20Engagement%20in%20Iraq.pdf [Accessed: June 12 2015].

Barkey H. (2010). *Turkey's New Engagement in Iraq*. Special Report. [Online] Washington, DC: United States Institute of Peace. Available at: http://carnegieendowment.org/files/USIP_SR_Turkey_Iraq.pdf.

Black B.S. and Tarassova A.S. 2002. "Institutional Reform in Transition: A Case Study of Russia" Stanford Law School Working Paper.

Brzezinski Z. 1997. *The Grand Chessboard: American Primacy and its Geostrategic Imperatives*, New York, Basic Books.
Cagaptay S. 2015. *The Rise of Turkey*. Nebraska: University of Nebraska.
Cagaptay S. and Evans T. 2012. Turkey Changing Relation with Iraq Kurdistan Up, *Baghdad Policy Focus* 122 October 2012.
Charountaki M. 2013. Turkish Foreign Policy and the Kurdistan Regional Government, *Perceptions*, Winter 2012, Vol XVII (4), 185–208.
Collinson S. 2003. Power, Livelihoods and Conflict: Case Studies in Political Economy Analysis for Humanitarian Action, *Humanitarian Policy Group*, Overseas Development Institute, 2003, 10–18.
Cosar S. and Yegenoglu M. 2009. *The Neoliberal Restructuring of Turkey's Social Security System*. [Online] Monthly Review. Available at: http://monthlyreview.org/2009/04/01/the-neoliberal-restructuring-of-turkeys-social-security-system/ [Accessed July 15 2015].
Daily News, H. 2015. *TURKEY – PM: Barzani is a tribe leader, supports PKK*. [Online] Hurriyetdailynews.com. Available at: www.hurriyetdailynews.com/default.aspx?pageid=438&n=pm-barzani-is-a-tribe-leader-supports-pkk-2007-06-08 [Accessed July 15 2015].
Dalay G. 2015. Regional implications of Iraqi KRG's presidency row, *Middle East Eye*. Available at: www.middleeasteye.net/columns/regional-implications-iraqi-krgs-presidency-row-1521167001#sthash.CWg9mf2G.dpuf.
Davutoglu A. 2008. Turkey's Foreign Policy Vision: An Assessment of 2007. *Insight Turkey*, [Online] 10(1). Available at: http://arsiv.setav.org/ups/dosya/9595.pdf.
Davutoglu A. 2001. The "Strategic Depth" that Turkey Needs', *The Turkish Daily News*, 15 September 200.
Demir I. and Welat Z. 2010, On the Representation of 'Others' at Europe's Borders: The Case of Iraqi Kurds, *Journal of Contemporary European Studies*, Vol 18 (1) 7–23.
Edelman E. S. Svante E. C. Aaron L. and Michael M. 2013. The Roots of Turkish Conduct: Understanding the Evolution of Turkish Policy in the Middle East. *Washington D.C.: Bipartisan Policy Center*. Available at: www.silkroadstudies.org/new/docs/publications/1312BPC.pdf [Accessed: February 22 2015].
Faye M. McArthur J. Sachs J. and Snow T. 2015. The Challenges Facing Landlocked Developing Countries. *Journal of Human Development*, [Online] 5(1). Available at: http://unmillenniumproject.org/documents/JHD051P003TP.pdf [Accessed: October 14 2015].
Fielding-Smith A. 2010. *Turkey finds a gateway to Iraq – FT.com*. [Online] *Financial Times*. Available at: www.ft.com/intl/cms/s/4e027bc0-47e6-11df-b99800144feab49a,Authorised=false.html?_i_location=http%3A%2F%2Fwww.ft.com%2Fcms%2Fs%2F0%2F4e027bc0.html%3Fsiteedition%3Dintl&siteedition=intl&_i_referer=http%3A%2F%2Fsearch.ft.com%2Fsearch%3FqueryText%3DTurkey%2BFinds%2Ba%2BGateway%2Bto%2BIraq#axzz3ffDl999A [Accessed April 14 2014].
Furtig H. 2014. *Regional Powers in the Middle East: New Constellations after the Arab Revolts*, New York, Palgrave MacMillan.
Goldman M. 2004. "The Rule of Outlaws is Over!" *Transition Newsletter* 14/15, 23–25.
Gorodnichenko Y. 2007. "Using Firm Optimization to Evaluate and Estimate Returns to Scale" NBER Working Paper.
Gorodnichenko Y. and Grygorenko Y. 2008. Are Oligarchs Productive? Theory and Evidence, *Forschungsinstitut zur Zukunft der Arbeit Institute for the Study*

of Labor *(The Institute for the Study of Labor (IZA))*, Discussion Paper No. 3282, 6–12, University of California, Berkeley, USA. Available at: http://ftp.iza.org/dp3282.pdf.

Gunter M. 2015. Iraq, Syria, ISIS and the Kurds: Geostrategic Concerns for the U.S. and Turkey, *Middle East Policy* Vol 22(1) 102–111.

Gunter M. 1993. A De-facto Kurdish Region in Northern Iraq, *Third World Quarterly* 14(2), 295–319.

Gunter S. 2014. *Erdoğan's "New Turkey": Restoring the Authoritarian State in the Name of Democracy*. [Online] SWP Comments. Available at: www.swp-berlin.org/fileadmin/contents/products/comments/2014C44_srt.pdf [Accessed July 15 2015].

Guriev S. and Rachinsky A. 2005. The Role of Oligarchs in Russian Capitalism, *Journal of Economic Perspectives*, Vol 19(1) 131–150.

Independent Kurdish Journalism, (2011) "Open for Business: Turkey's bankers tap into Kurdish boom," IJK News, June 21 2011. Available at: http://ikjnews.com/?p=881.

Ingram J. 2015. Iranian support for Iraqi Kurdistan president strengthens political stability and improves prospects for investment in energy, telecoms, construction, *IHS Jane's Intelligence Review*. Available at: www.janes.com/article/53488/iranian-support-for-iraqi-kurdistan-president-strengthens-political-stability-and-improves-prospects-for-investment-in-energy-telecoms-construction [Accessed: August 21 2015].

Kalaycıoglu E. 2014. *Turkish Foreign Relations and Public Opinion*. [Online] The German Marshall Fund of the United States. Available at: www.gmfus.org/galleries/ct_publication_attachments/Kalaycioglu_ForeignRelations_Sept11.pdf [Accessed: June 7 2015].

Karadag R. (2010). *Neoliberal Restructuring in Turkey*. 2nd edn [pdf] Köln: Max Planck Institute for the Study of Societies. Available at: www.mpifg.de/pu/mpifg_dp/dp10-7.pdf.

Keen D. 1994. *The Benefits of Famine: A Political Economy of Famine and Relief in Southwestern Sudan, 1983–1989*. Princeton, NJ: Princeton University Press.

Kirdiş E. 2015. The Role of Foreign Policy in Constructing the Party Identity of the Turkish Justice and Development Party (AKP). *Turkish Studies*, 16(2), 178–194.

Kirişci K. 2009. The transformation of Turkish foreign policy: The rise of the trading state. New Perspectives on Turkey, [Online] 40, pp. 29–57. Available at: www.esiweb.org/pdf/news_id_412_5%20%20Article%20Kemal%20Kirisci.pdf.

Le Billon P. (with Macrae, J., Leader, N. and East, R.). 2000 The Political Economy of War: What Relief Agencies Need To Know. *Network Paper* 33. London: ODI.

Natali D. 2012. *The Limits of Turkey's Kurdish Efforts in Iraq*. [Online] Al-Monitor. Available at: www.al-monitor.com/pulse/originals/2012/al-monitor/turkeys-tactics-in-iraq.html [Accessed: October 18 2014].

O'Byrne D. 2012. *Turkey's Oil Diplomacy with Iraqi Kurds*. [Online] *Financial Times*. Available at: http://blogs.ft.com/beyond-brics/2012/07/30/turkeys-oil-diplomacy-with-iraqs-kurds/?Authorised=false.

Olson R. 2005. *The Goat and the Butcher*. Costa Mesa, CA: Mazda Publishers.

Onis Z. 2004. *Turgut Ozal and His Economic Legacy: Turkish Neo-Liberalism in Critical Perspective*. [Online] Istanbul: Koc Uuniversity, p. 12. Available at: www.yarbis1.yildiz.edu.tr/web/userCourseMaterials/gonel_8bf768c04cebd234db948c0d2899f8ac.pdf [Accessed July 15 2015].

Online.hemscottir.com 2015. Gulf Keystone Petroleum Ltd. – Shaikan Oil-in-Place Upgrade. [Online] Available at: http://online.hemscottir.com/ir/gkp/ir.jsp?page=newsitem&item=1024407682300269.

Osgood P. and Tahir R. 2014. *Gulf Keystone to continue trucked oil exports from Kurdistan*. [Online] Iraq Oil Report. Available at: www.iraqoilreport.com/energy/production-exports/gulf-keystone-continue-trucked-oil-exports-kurdistan-11713/ [Accessed January 2014].

Park B. 2012. Turkey, the US and the KRG: Moving Parts and the Geopolitical Realities. *Insight Turkey*, 14(3), 109–125.

Romano D. 2015. Iraqi Kurdistan and Turkey: Temporary Marriage? *Middle East Policy Journal*, Vol 22(1) Available at: www.mepc.org/journal/middle-east-policy-archives/iraqi-kurdistan-and-turkey-temporary-marriage [Accessed: October 11 2015].

Ross M. 2001. Does Oil Hinder Democracy? *World Politics* Vol 53 (April), 325–361.

Ross M. 2008. Oil, Islam, and Women *American Political Science Review* Vol 102(1) February.

Ross M. 2015. *Oil and Democracy Revisited*. [Online] UCLA Department of Political Science. Available at: www.sscnet.ucla.edu/polisci/faculty/ross/Oil%20and%20Democracy%20Revisited.pdf [Accessed July 13 2015].

Selwyn B. 2015. *Friedrich Hayek: In Defence of Dictatorship*. [Online] openDemocracy. Available at: www.opendemocracy.net/benjamin-selwyn/friedrich-hayek-dictatorship [Accessed: July 15 2015].

Stansfield G. 2013. The Unravelling of the Post-First World War State System? The Kurdistan Region of Iraq and the Transformation of the Middle East. *International Affairs*, 89(2), 259–282.

Stiglitz J. 1999. "Wither Reforms? Ten Years of the Transition," ABCDE conference, Washington, DC: World Bank.

Stratfor 2015. *Annual Forecast* 2016. Available at: www.stratfor.com/forecast/annual-forecast-2016 [Accessed: June 13 2015].

Szelenyi I. 2015 Capitalism after Communism, *New Left Review* 96 Nov.Dec

The Guardian 2013. *Across the Zagros: Iranian influence in Iraqi Kurdistan: The complicated relationship between Iran and Iraqi Kurdistan has eased in recent weeks.* Available at: www.theguardian.com/world/2013/nov/21/iran-influence-iraqi-kurdistan [Accessed: June 18 2015].

Tol G. 2014. Untangling the Turkey-KRG Energy Partnership. Istituto affari internazionali. [Online] Available at: www.iai.it/sites/default/files/GTE_PB_14.pdf.

Turkone M. 2015. Turkey's new elites. [Online] *Today's Zaman*. Available at: www.todayszaman.com/op-ed/columnist/mumtazer-turkone/turkeys-new-elites_118478.html [Accessed: July 13 2015].

Voller Y. 2012. From Rebellion to De facto statehood: International and transnational sources of the transformation of the Kurdish national liberation movement in Iraq into the Kurdistan Regional Government. *A Thesis Submitted to the Department of International Relations of the London School of Economics for the degree of Doctor of Philosophy*, London, June.

Weitz R. 2012. Turkey-Iraq Relations: From Bad to Worse. [Online] Turkeyanalyst.org. Available at: www.turkeyanalyst.org/publications/turkey-analyst-articles/item/307-turkey-iraq-relations-from-bad-to-worse.html.

White J. 2015. The Turkish Complex, *The American Interest*, Vol 10(4). Available at: www.the-american-interest.com/2015/02/02/the-turkish-complex/ [Accessed: May 12 2015].

Wikileaks.org, (n.d.). *Cable Viewer*. [Online] Available at: https://wikileaks.org/cable/2008/05/08BAGHDAD1526.html [Accessed July 12 2015].

Yinanc B. 2015. *Seeing in Barzani a reliable partner for Turkey*. [Online] Hurriyetdailynews.com. Available at: www.hurriyetdailynews.com/seeing-inbarzaniareliablepartnerforturkey.aspx?pageID=449&nID=26702&NewsCatID=412.

Zeydanlıoğlu W. 2009 "Torture and Turkification in the Diyarbakır Military Prison" in *Rights, Citizenship and Torture: Perspectives on Evil, Law and the State*, Welat Zeydanlıoğlu and John T. Parry (eds). Oxford: Inter-Disciplinary Press, 73–92.

8 The Kurdish issue on the USA foreign policy agenda

Paula Pineda

The Kurds have no friends but the mountains.[1]

Introduction

In August 2015, a popular editorial titled "US Betrayal of the Kurds" opened with: "President Obama's betrayal of the Kurds is possibly the most grotesque."[2] This declaration highlights the increasingly salient issues surrounding US policy towards the Kurds, including past policy, Kurdish expectations, and the nature of US foreign policy.

This chapter analyzes the evolution of US foreign policy towards the Kurds in Iraq. As Iraq's largest ethnic minority, the Kurds have a history of grievances and rebellion against the Iraqi government beginning with Kurdish resistance to becoming a part of Iraq and continuing under oppression from the Ba'ath regime. Currently, the Kurdistan Region (KR) and Baghdad are engaged in disputes regarding the present federal arrangement of Iraq (Ahmed 2012; Danilovich 2014; Natali 2010). Throughout these tensions, the Kurds have consistently turned to the US as an ally. US policy towards the Kurds, however, is often perceived as inconsistent (Romano and Gurses 2014). For example, the US helped the Kurds after the invasion of Iraq in 2003 by supporting the current federal system,[3] which granted the Kurds significant autonomy (Romano and Gurses 2014; Danilovich 2014). On the other hand, the Kurds currently seem disillusioned by a lack of US support for an independent Kurdistan. US attention is instead focused on the Kurds' role in the fight against the self-proclaimed Islamic State (ISIS). Yet, in August 2014, the US came to the Kurds' aid when it engaged in emergency airstrikes against advancing ISIS troops and prevented the fall of Erbil, the capital of the Kurdistan Region (U.S. Department of Defense 2014).

We seek to understand these shifting dynamics via the underlying decision-making mechanism of US policy. As will be demonstrated, there is little literature that specifically addresses US decision-making towards the Kurds of Iraq. The prevailing views on this dynamic, either echo conventional perceptions about the US as a Kurdish ally, or argue that US policy towards the Kurds is a function of US strategy, but they lack specified causal theory and analysis.

Drawing from the IR literature, we use an intervention framework to shed light on the factors that influence US decision-making towards the Kurds. We argue that in past US policy, affective motivations such as the notion of a US-Kurdish alliance were eclipsed by the US' instrumental considerations regarding the Kurds and its regional aims. We assert that the same dynamic is shaping current US policy towards the Kurds in relation to the protection of the KR, the role of the Kurds in the counter-ISIS agenda, Kurdish independence, and the possible disintegration of Iraq. By transcending pattern-tracing of US policy and addressing its decision-making mechanism, we contribute not only a richer understanding of US relations with the Kurds of Iraq, but also a means to more accurately assess present and future US policy.

This chapter first highlights the "Kurdish Issue" on the US policy agenda, followed by a brief literature review and the analytical framework. We analyze the past trajectory of US policy towards the Kurds of Iraq in terms of the framework's instrumental and affective considerations. The primacy of these factors is then applied to the current US policy aims of protecting the KR and countering ISIS in Iraq. Then, possible future policy paths in light of recent increases in Kurdish mobilization and the impending possible reality of a disintegrated Iraq are set forth.

The US and the Kurds

The increasingly salient "Kurdish Issue" often refers to a wide scope of identity, mobilization, and conflict dynamics regarding the Kurds in Turkey, Iraq, Syria, and Iran.[4] Pinpointing what the "Kurdish Issue" on the US policy agenda entails, therefore, is difficult. Some scholars uphold a cohesive "Kurdish Issue" based on the similarities underlying Kurdish claims across territories (Charountaki 2011:29). We conceptualize the "Kurdish Issue" in relation to the host states and specifically examine US policy towards the Kurds of Iraq. The analytical framework corresponds to foreign state intervention, and the factors that influence intervention are primarily derived from the interaction of a foreign state's aims and the host-state context.

In the case of the US and the Kurds of Iraq, relations were largely absent until the end of the 1960s due to the US stance of non-interference towards the Iraqi-Kurdish conflict, which was viewed as an internal problem. Additionally, the US was preoccupied with its aims regarding Iraq and Iran (2011:132–146). By the 1970s, however, an "interactive relationship" arose between the US and the Kurds, who were "seen as a central component of regional and international politics" (2011:31). Specifically, the US focused on the Kurds' utility for its aim of containing regional Soviet influence (2011:132). US-Kurdish relations continued to solidify throughout the 1990s culminating in an individualized policy in the post-Saddam era, which Charountaki labels the "fifth-stage" of US-Kurdish policy in Iraq. This interaction between the US and the Kurds of Iraq contrasts with the limited

US contact with counterpart movements in Iran, Syria, and Turkey (2011). The unique position of the Kurds of Iraq on the US foreign policy agenda renders classifying the "Kurdish Issue" in relation to host states optimal for policy analysis.

Analytical framework

This study examines US policy towards the Kurds via the framework of foreign intervention in internal conflict, which classifies instrumental and affective motivations as influences on decision-making (Carment 1993; Carment et al. 2009; Chazan 1991; Davis et al. 1997; Heraclides 1990; Regan 1998, 2000; Saideman 1997, 2001; Suhrke and Noble 1977).[5] Instrumental motivations incorporate gains that states can achieve from policy decisions from the international system or the domestic sphere, including economic and strategic gains (Heraclides 1990; Suhrke and Noble 1977, cited in Carment 1993). State decision-making can also be a factor of affective motivations, including humanitarian considerations and cultural or religious affinity. Both types of motivations can simultaneously influence state behavior, at times in a complementary manner, but also in a "contradictory" manner (Carment 1993:139). We assert that multiple motivations may "compete" in the decision-making arena, and that those considerations with the most weight ultimately shape foreign policy. Thus, policy is the result of the configuration of a state's motivations at critical junctures. The next section demonstrates the intervention framework incorporates various elements from both traditional and recent foreign policy and IR literature, rendering it an inclusive approach for this research. For example, the framework accounts for both internal and external contexts, which are normally exclusive in the literature. The inclusion of both instrumental and affective factors captures the influence of interests and norms, which are both essential (Nau 2002). Importantly, this framework allows analysis of the US decision-making process, which is important in the comparative sense, as a process mechanism can be applied over time. We follow the call in Brown (1994) to understand policy beyond tracing documents and by seeking "the *operational* premises ... the considerations prevailing at crucial junctures." Accordingly, we offer not only a review of this US policy, but also an understanding of how and why it has evolved.

In the case of US policy towards the Kurds of Iraq, this framework is first utilized to define which motivations dominated past US policy, which we then apply to current and future US policy aims. This section begins with the emergent literature on US policy towards the Kurds, which usually features the non-state actor (NSA) framework. We then present the limitations of the NSA framework, the components of foreign policy decision-making included in our approach, and the literature on intervention in internal conflict. The intervention framework's instrumental and affective factors are then defined and applied to past US policy towards the Kurds of Iraq.

Recent literature

Recent literature by Charountaki (2011) and Shareef (2014) analyzes US foreign policy towards the Kurds as NSAs. Charountaki notes the "dearth of literature" devoted to this agenda, and Shareef (2014) asserts that the bulk of Kurdish literature lies within the scope of nationalism.[6] Charountaki (2011: 1-2) argues:

> The main body of scholarly references to the Kurds and their issue (pinpointed mainly since the 1970s) has either been limited to a socio-political identification and anthropology of the Kurds, or else has referred to the issue within an analysis of aspects of Middle Eastern regional and domestic politics.

Moreover, Charountaki notes that IR as a conceptual resource lacks applicable literature because little is devoted to the comparative mechanism of foreign policy towards NSAs. We seek to contribute to this foreign policy niche, but deviate from other studies by rejecting the NSA framework.

Rejection of the NSA framework

Briefly, NSAs are entities other than nation-states involved in the international political system (Taylor 2002, cited in Charountaki 2011:10). Globalization has catalyzed studies on the impact of NSAs on foreign policy, including Charountaki's classification of the Kurds as a political NSA. We reject this framework, for two reasons. First, as noted by Charountaki (2011:9), NSA literature focuses on NGOs, international organizations, and economic corporations, and fails to include religious and political groups, such as the Kurds. The bulk of this literature is dedicated to NSA "global governance" that pressures governments to address concerns such as global warming and nuclear proliferation,[7] and even if internal conflict is explored, it still features the organizations and corporations as NSAs (e.g. Voltolini 2012). Not surprisingly, the Kurds have been defined as an "exceptional" NSA in this context (Halliday 2006, cited in Charountaki 2011:30). It is not ideal, however, for generalizations from the NSA literature to be assumed to be directly applicable to a subgroup, such as the Kurds of Iraq, that differs from the typical sample. Second, this literature mostly focuses on the impact of NSAs on the *domestic* policy sphere (Baumann and Stengel 2013:2). Our focus, however, is not the impact of the Kurds on domestic Iraqi policy. Instead, the aim is to understand the development of the foreign policy of an external state, the US, in relation to the Kurds. As the two major thrusts of the NSA literature do not directly apply to the case of an external state's policy towards a political, ethnic group within an internal conflict context, we reject the NSA framework. Instead, we conceptualize the Kurds of Iraq as a sub-state ethnic-minority.

Internal and external contexts

An important element is the context that shapes foreign policy decision-making. The classic IR approach is a structure-oriented, macropolitical study of interactions among international systems (Walker, Malici and Schafer 2011:6). Accordingly, the factors that influence foreign policy in this body of work emanate from the global context. Importantly, this approach captures geostrategic arguments that uphold the influence of global dynamics on policy.[8] On the other hand, IR's subfield, Foreign Policy Analysis (FPA), is generally an agent-centered, micropolitical study of leaders (Walker, Malici and Schafer 2011; Hudson 2005). This literature dismisses systemic theories and focuses solely on the domestic sphere: bargaining between government agencies, interests groups, and policy makers (see Gourevitch 2002 and Neack 2008, cited in Hook and Spanier 2010).[9] Recently, scholars have attempted to bridge both approaches, assuming that the "world" in the minds of actors and the larger "world" of external events that the actors inhabit are intertwined (Walker, Malici and Schafer 2011:5–6).

We follow the combined approach and conceptualize US policy towards the Kurds as a function of both the domestic and global contexts.

Policy-making process

This study analyzes the *process* by which US foreign policy decisions are made. As argued by Mintz and DeRouen (2010:4), understanding how decisions are made enables predictions of future decisions. In turn, who partakes in the process must be considered. The literature is divided; the realist IR framework upholds the rational actor assumption, in which states are unitary actors that maximize gains and minimize losses as they navigate the international system (Walt 1979; Mearsheimer 1995, cited in Mintz and DeRouen 2010:7). On the other hand, the Foreign Policy Decision Making (FPDM) literature accounts for diffuse participants because it refers to the choices made by individual leaders, groups, and coalitions that shape a nation's policy.[10] We combine both approaches by examining the participation of multiple actors assumed to be rationally motivated, including the US president, legislators, analysts, and military members. The decision rules used by these actors are the affective and instrumental motivations from the literature on intervention in internal conflict.

State intervention in internal conflict[11]

The literature on state intervention in internal conflict is not substantial (Heraclides 1990; Gurr 1992; Saideman 1998, 2012; Tenorio 2001; Carment and James 2004).[12] Yet, this is the most applicable literature to this case due to the legacy of conflict between the Iraqi state and its Kurdish minority.[13] In other words, this framework captures the political characteristic of the Kurds and the conflict context in Iraq that the NSA approach lacks. In this framework, two classifications exist regarding the determinants of intervention in ethnic conflict: instrumental motivations and affective motivations (Gurr 1992:16–17; Wieland 2001:209, cited in Carment and James 2004; Suhrke and Noble 1977; Heraclides 1990, cited in Carment 1993).

Instrumental motivations

The instrumental motivations theory asserts that states are motivated to intervene in terms of associated costs and benefits; this approach complements the IR literature's rational-actor assumption, in which leaders are expected to respond in order to "maximize their security, wealth, and power" (Meadwell 1991, 1993, cited in Carment and James 2004:15). Instrumental motivations include international considerations, economic gains, domestic politics, and military (strategic) considerations (Heraclides 1990; Carment and James 2004; Carment et al. 2009).

International considerations stem from the international system's reaction to the internal conflict (Heraclides 1990; Carment 1993). There are three reactions that the international system can have to internal war: diffusion, reconciliation, and isolation or suppression (Heraclides 1990:345).[14] The conventional wisdom assumes an isolationist reaction, which restrains against intervention (Heraclides 1990; Jackson and Rosberg 1982). This restraint occurs due to the presence of the international regime, a global norm against secession and intervention (Heraclides 1990).[15] The international regime restrains US intervention in support for the Kurds because the Iraqi-Kurdish internal conflict context renders aid as support for a potential secession, a costly norm violation.[16] The next section demonstrates that this restraint has strongly influenced the US in its past policy towards the Kurds.

Additionally, strategic considerations are activated when involvement can provide long- or short-term gains for a state (Ibid.). This dynamic can occur if the intervening state is not allied to the state in conflict, the host state. For example, involvement can catalyze secessionists to divert an enemy host state, reduce a host state's resources, or provide the intervening state with bargaining power against a host state (Ibid.:370). This strategic factor is congruent with geopolitical arguments, which examine the influence of a state's geographical, economic, socio-cultural, and political features and resources in its patterns of connections (Cohen 2003:3).

The dominance of instrumental considerations in past US policy

The beginning of US relations with the Kurds

In the late 1960s, the US was allied with Iran and Saudi Arabia in order to contain hostile Iraqi behavior threatening US oil interests in the area (Romano 2006:192). Additionally, the US was increasingly concerned about

Soviet penetration of Iraq and Iran (Charountaki 2011:136–137). Official relations between the US and the Kurds of Iraq began with a secret meeting between Kurdish, Iranian, and US officials in the summer of 1972 (Ibid.). In this meeting, the Kurds framed themselves as an effective ally for reversing Soviet expansion in the area; soon after, the CIA (along with allies Iran and Israel) provided the Kurds with arms, funds, and pledges of support with the aim of bolstering the Kurdish rebellion against Baghdad and weakening Iraq as the USSR's ally (Chaliand 1980:7, cited in Charountaki 2011:88; Romano 2006:193). After Iran and Iraq settled a border dispute in early 1975, Iran agreed to withdraw its support for Kurdish rebels in Iraq, and the Shah ordered the CIA and Mossad to withdraw from Iraq, cutting off the Kurds' supplies (Romano 2006:196). The sudden US policy shift away from aid to the Kurds revealed the weight of its strategic considerations; a US attaché later stated that:

> [Henry] Kissinger was asked about the morality of a policy that encouraged the people to revolt against their central government in order to obtain a minor political gain for us-and then when we achieved other goals, we would betray the people and allow them to be slaughtered. And Kissinger replied that covert military activity is not to be confused with missionary work.[17]

This revelation highlights the absence of affective motivations for Kurdish grievances in US policy; instead, the US capitalized on Kurdish grievances for its aims. The irrelevance of affective motivations is also observable in the US' repeated previous rejection of Kurdish requests for aid; the US denied Mustafa Barzani asylum in the 1940s, rejected the Kurds' request for assistance in their fight for autonomy in the 1960s, and cancelled its Title II program designed to provide relief to the Kurds after 1967 (Charountaki 2011:136). Clearly, the US' establishment of relations with the Kurds and the temporary provision of aid that followed was purely strategic to counter Iraqi strength (Ibid.:138).

The Gulf War

The priority of instrumental over affective considerations in US decision-making continues into the Gulf War period; the US' strategic motivations stemmed from concern over Saddam's increasingly aggressive politics and the implications for the stability of the oil-rich region. In 1991, President Bush publicly called for a revolt against Saddam (US Executive Office of the President 1991). The Kurds, encouraged by what they perceived to be US support, mobilized against the regime (Romano 2006:204). When the Kurdish uprising almost succeeded, however, the US administration became concerned that Kurdish autonomy in Iraq could catalyze problems with Iran, Turkey, and Syria in relation to their Kurdish populations, thus destabilizing the region (Charountaki 2011:142). The US thus refrained from supporting the Kurds, who then faced Saddam's brutal retaliation (Romano 2006:206). The US shift away from its support for Kurdish mobilization against Saddam clearly followed the reshuffling of its strategic considerations; its initial support was never motivated by an affective motivation for Kurdish independence.

US invasion of Iraq

US support for the Kurds after the invasion of Iraq in 2003 was also instrumental; amidst the turmoil, the Kurds presented themselves as the only dependable ally that the US had (Romano 2006:212; Charountaki 2011:200). The Kurds became "a major part of the liberation of Iraq and a front against terror." (Ibid.:222). The Kurds' utility translated to favorable US policy, such as US involvement in the negotiation of the Transitional Administrative Law (TAL). The TAL rendered significant support to the Kurds because it established the "Kurdish Veto," guaranteeing the Kurds power over constitutional developments (Ibid.:214). It also stipulated a federal structure, which greatly increased the Kurds' autonomy by allocating them a region and various political and administrative rights (O'Leary et al. 2005:48). These US involvements reflect an overarching policy of intervention in favor of the Kurds again stemming from their utility for the US' strategic considerations.

Strategic considerations outweigh the international regime

We previously noted the presence of the international regime, and its constraint on intervention. Here, we argue that the Kurds' value outweighed the regime constraint against intervention in their favor. Support for such malleability of the international regime can be drawn from Saideman's (2002:42) finding that states in "hostile neighborhoods" may support each other's separatists because strategic considerations (weakening an enemy state) outweigh the international regime constraint.

Affective motivations

Affective motivations involve ideologies and norms such as ethnic allegiances and humanitarianism (Carment et al. 2009; Carment and James 2004; Heraclides 1990, cited in Carment 1993:138). The literature indicates that affective motivations are relatively weaker than instrumental motivations; for example, cross-border ethnic ties do not consistently influence intervention (see Carment and James 2004:12–13). And, while liberal theory has usually asserted that states intervene in ethnic conflicts in reaction to human rights violations (see Esman 1995:21 and Brown 1996:592, cited in Carment and James 2004), recent findings demonstrate that aid is strategically given (Bueno de Mesquita and Smith 2007, 2009, cited in Heinrich 2013). In other words, humanitarian motivations are conditioned by underlying instrumental motivations, and the following reveals this is the case in US policy to the Kurds.

Humanitarian vs economic motivations

Economic considerations are an instrumental constraint to humanitarian agendas in internal conflict because aid drains finances. Additionally, aid can harm commerce and investments with the state in question (Mitchell 1970:172, cited in Heraclides 1990:353). We cite the strength of economic considerations in US policy towards Saddam's deadly Anfal campaign against the Kurds.[18] At first, humanitarian concern generated support for the Kurds and the US Senate voted to impose sanctions on Iraq. However, this soon threatened US-Iraq relations and the US shifted its stance towards a condemnation of chemical weapons only (Charountaki 2011:148). The Reagan administration stopped the motion for sanctions and instead approved $1 billion in financial credit for Baghdad (Entessar 1992:139). The aim behind this shift was the preservation of US financial interests, including benefits to the US from Iraq's oil pipelines and lucrative business contracts and weapons sales to Iraq (Entessar 1992:139; Charountaki 2011:148; Everest 2004:104, cited in Charountaki 2011:90). Economic considerations constrained intervention as the US sought to avoid angering Baghdad and jeopardizing these interests;[19] a US congressman lamented:

> Iraq is a booming market for almost everything – consumer goods, technology, manufacturing plants, manpower training, and support. English is the second language taught in schools, and the United States, with its great resources, logically should fill most of Iraq's shopping list. But the outlook is bleak. Even the billion dollar market US farmers enjoyed last year is in jeopardy. Unappreciated for its historic victory over Iran, offended by America's unfounded charges of genocide and our close collaboration with Israel, Iraq is turning elsewhere. On Baghdad's busy streets, US cars will likely remain scarce, and US firms will be screened out as Iraq buys the tools, supplies, and training its development requires. Still worse, the United States will retain few avenues of influence in an important capital (Findley 1988, quoted in Entessar 1992).

It may be argued that the primacy of these instrumental considerations appears to give way soon after to affective motivations. This is because in 1991 the US helped to establish a "free zone" for the safe return of the thousands of displaced Kurds (Romano 2006:208; Charountaki 2011:168–171). We argue, however, that this policy shift back towards aid for the Kurds does not reflect more influence of affective motivation. Instead, this intervention can be traced to various changes in the surrounding context, and a closer look at these changes reveals that instrumental motivations still dominated US decision-making.

The first change was the surrounding political climate; relations with Saddam, previously warmer, had become hostile as he became increasingly unreliable as an ally in the region (Byman 2000; Charountaki 2011:151). As a result, US strategy shifted away from protecting its relations with Baghdad and towards "regime change" (Charountaki 2011:151); economic considerations gave way to the strategic consideration of removing Saddam. In turn, this shift made the US more amenable to humanitarian considerations involving intervention on behalf of the Kurds for two reasons. First, the constraint of avoiding displeasing Baghdad, which had previously halted the implementation of US sanctions against Baghdad in response to the Kurds' plight, was no longer present. Second, the Kurds could be a strategic asset for toppling the regime, evidenced by the $40 million US dollars given to the Kurds after establishing the "free zone" to bolster their opposition to Saddam (Ibid.:171).

Additionally, the international community had been shocked by the plight of the Kurdish refugees and was demanding action (Romano 2006:207). The international concern for the Kurds eliminated the international regime restraint. Also, geostrategic considerations surfaced because Turkey, the regional ally of the US, did not want the Kurdish refugees to stay within its territory (Romano 2006:207–8; Charountaki 2011: 147). Together, all of these different instrumental motivations generated a different context at the time of the US establishment of the "free zone" than the context during the earlier attempt to sanction Iraq. We argue that these shifts in the US economic, international, and strategic motivations were conducive to aiding the Kurds at this juncture, instead of blocking aid as before. In other words, the US intervention in favor of the Kurds via the establishment of a "free zone" was a function of the instrumental considerations that arose in the rapidly changing context, and was not a policy primarily motivated by humanitarian considerations. The humanitarian considerations influenced this policy because they did not negate – and even served – the overhead instrumental agenda; humanitarian motivations alone did not shape US policy at this critical juncture. Ultimately, this section reveals that the dominance of instrumental considerations remained an underlying constant in the US' past policy trajectory towards the Kurds and that humanitarian motivations influence policy via their interaction with instrumental configurations. The next section reviews current US policy towards the Kurds in light of this dynamic.

Current US protection of the Kurdistan region

Recent events indicate that a US aim is the stability of the KR in the surrounding context of Iraq's rising civil unrest fueled by sectarianism (Cordesman and Khazai 2012). The US willingness to intervene for this aim is exemplified by its emergency military action in the summer of 2014 to prevent the fall of Erbil, the capital of the KR, to the oncoming advancement of ISIS.[20] US President Barack Obama cited strategic considerations for the administration's decision to intervene, including the need to defend American interests, particularly the security of American diplomats and military personnel (US White House 2014). Additionally, Obama cited the affective motivation of humanitarian aid for the Yezidi religious minority threatened by ISIS (Ibid.). A counter, however, stems from the domestic sphere. Domestic politics are commonly an instrumental consideration against involvement; pressure against intervention can stem from ethnic, religious, or ideological links with the dominant group of the state involved in the secessionist war, or from public opinion (Heraclides 1990:354). In this case, public opinion is a constraint because the American public opposes additional involvement in the Middle East following the reduction in support for the War in Iraq.[21] Obama noted this constraint:

> I know that many of you are rightly concerned about any American military action in Iraq, even limited strikes like these. I understand that. I ran for this office in part to end our war in Iraq and welcome our troops home, and that's what we've done. As Commander-in-Chief, I will not allow the United States to be dragged into fighting another war in Iraq. And so even as we support Iraqis as they take the fight to these terrorists, American combat troops will not be returning to fight in Iraq, because there's no American military solution to the larger crisis in Iraq. The only lasting solution is reconciliation among Iraqi communities and stronger Iraqi security forces.
> (US White House 2014)

Along with the lack of public support for intervention, another constraint is the international regime, which stresses states' sovereignty and unity. In this case, intervention violates the US' strategic aim of maintaining Iraqi unity, an entrenched US goal; the administration's attachment to a unified Iraq has been cited in the complete reversal of Joe Biden's support for a division of Iraq before he became part of the Obama administration to support for a unified Iraq since becoming a part of the administration (Alamiri 2015).

Yet, despite these instrumental constraints from the international regime and the domestic sphere, the US decided to intervene to defend Kurdistan. Was this due to the strength of humanitarian motivations? We revealed that such affective factors are secondary to instrumental ones, particularly economic interests; accordingly, we consider the current US economic interests.

The US is dependent on Iraq's oil wealth (Pollack 2014:14). Kurdistan's large share of this wealth has led to the entrenchment of American economic interests in the region; significant production stems from Kurdistan, and ExxonMobil and Chevron are among the various US companies drilling there.[22] Given the primacy of economic interests over humanitarian considerations, it follows that the preservation of these interests spurred intervention in light of the advance of ISIS in 2014.[23] The humanitarian rhetoric surrounding the policy, therefore, does not fully reflect the underlying considerations. Instead, the humanitarian component may indicate a presence of instrumental aid, as previously noted, where aid to the at-risk minority group served the US' economic interests and justified intervention to protect the region. Given these economic interests, it can be expected that a future threat to the KR will again elicit intervention from the US, whereas humanitarian concerns unrelated to these economic interests cannot be expected to do so.

Perception of Kurds as integral to aims in Iraq

Currently, US policy towards the Kurds relates to the US' present challenges in Iraq following the 2012 withdrawal of its military presence and the embankment of its low-key involvement as the head of a "country team" dedicated to the transition of Iraq (Cordesman and Khazai 2012). The fall of Ramadi to ISIS in May 2015 greatly undermined this policy (Clary 2015). US General Keane argued that the current policy is "fundamentally flawed," and that the US is "not only failing ... [but is] in fact, losing this war ... this strategy will not defeat ISIS" (Committee on Armed Services 2015a). This dissatisfaction with the current Iraq strategy is relevant for US policy towards the Kurds because it impacts the US' strategic considerations. The military strength of the Kurdish armed forces, the Peshmerga, is also becoming increasingly attractive as the US strives to improve its policy to counter ISIS in Iraq. The Peshmerga are capable and willing, and they are reliable US allies, yielding two potential US policy paths: officially incorporating the Kurds into the US-led coalition against ISIS, or directly arming the Peshmerga so that they may effectively counter ISIS in Iraq. Support for the Kurds' reliability as US allies and for US support to the Kurds is observable in recent advocacy by Senator Ernst:

> The Kurdish people have been vital in supporting our coalition efforts to defeat ISIS and in providing support to around the 1.6 million displaced persons from Iraq and Syria. And also, for the past quarter century, Iraqi Kurds have proven to be reliable partners by supporting U.S. interests every time that we have sought their assistance. And I have spoken with many of the men that have served up in that region, and they always state what great allies the Kurds have been to them in our fight. So, they are proven to be great allies of ours. Earlier this week, former CIA and NSA Director, Michael Hayden, once again spoke for the need to increase U.S. support to the Kurds in the fight against ISIS. And, on Tuesday, General Hayden said, 'I would double down on the Kurds. Their military has the virtue of showing up when it comes to a fight, and they've been our friends in the area for decades'.
> (Committee on Armed Services 2015a:50)

However, while some praise the Kurds' capability and call for US support for the Peshmerga, others argue that the Kurds have no desire to assist in any efforts beyond their region and therefore cannot be relied on to recover Iraqi territories which are vital to US interests but are beyond the borders of the KR, such as Ramadi or Mosul. General Keane expressed this concern:

> As good as the Kurds are, they have, also, a limited interest in what they're willing to fight for inside Iraq. And they certainly are not going to participate in reclaiming Anbar Province and other parts of Iraq. So, yes, we have to do what we should for the Kurds, but we also need to recognize that a lot more needs to be done with others, as well.
> (Committee on Armed Services 2015a:51–52)

These statements reveal that whether or not the Kurds are strategic assets for the US is at issue in decision-making. Moreover, the international regime constraint is invoked because directly arming the Peshmerga forces would render tacit US aid for Kurdish independence. The Obama administration is strongly restrained by this factor and is unwaveringly committed to the unity of Iraq; this commitment has even permeated the arguments for arming the Kurds. For example, Senior Fellow for the Center for American Progress Katulis stated:

> A second thing I think we need to start to entertain – and I know people are discussing this – is the notion of greater decentralization inside of Iraq, decentralization of authority, in some of the proposals that people have discussed about mechanisms for giving arms directly to Sunni tribes or to Kurdish forces. Again, I think we should consider that and balance it against the overall objective of trying to keep Iraq together.
> (Ibid.:37)

Katulis also cautions:

> The more that the United States or other actors within the region invest in subnational actors or nonstate actors for the benefit of trying to defeat terrorist organizations like ISIS, there's ... a potential long-term disadvantage to it [... which is that] we could further inadvertently accelerate the fragmentation of these state entities.
> (Ibid.)

This rhetoric demonstrates not only the awareness among policy-makers of the connection between directly arming the Kurds and supporting their independence aspirations, but also the dominant disinterest in doing so. This policy juncture, therefore, is characterized by competing instrumental considerations: the Kurds' strategic value for combat versus violating the unity of Iraq. The decision to directly arm the Kurds is not likely to gain enough support as long as the Obama administration supports the unity of Iraq. However, an increase in the perception of the Kurds' strategic value could override the international regime constraint. This could occur if the

Kurds quell concerns about their lack of commitment to combat beyond their borders, increasing their strategic value for defeating ISIS enough to override the international regime restraint and echoing the dominance of strategic considerations over the regime in past US policy.

Kurdish mobilization in Iraq and US policy

Growing calls for independence

While US policymakers remain committed to the unity of Iraq, direct allusions to Kurdish independence are increasing in media and political platforms in and beyond Kurdistan, especially after the Peshmerga captured Kirkuk (Hawramy 2014). Kurds assert that oil-rich Kirkuk is their historical capital, and its control increased perceptions of Kurdish "readiness" for independence. Consequently, talk of impending independence has been surging throughout Kurdish media, especially after Kurdistan's president, Massoud Barzani, pledged to hold an independence referendum (e.g. Amos 2014).

As independence appears increasingly possible, we incorporate it into the intervention framework as a potential factor of US decision-making. We consider whether an increase in Kurdish mobilization affects the US' considerations relating to the Kurds, and therefore indirectly impacts policy. We argue that an increase in mobilization could affect US considerations in two ways. First, it can enable Kurdish independence to transcend its position as a component of the counter-ISIS agenda and become a stand-alone issue for US policy-makers to confront. Second, the strength of Kurdish mobilization can affect how US decision-makers perceive the Iraqi-Kurdish conflict.[24] However, we note a caveat: despite what appears to be an increase in public support for independence, the Kurds' mobilization movement in Iraq is not a secessionist movement.[25] This characteristic, and its implications for US policy, are presented in the following section.

The nature of Kurdish mobilization in Iraq

Beginning in the 1940s, Kurdish leaders continuously asserted that they did not want to separate from Iraq, but instead desired Kurdish autonomy within Iraq (Charountaki 2011; McDowall 1996; Romano 2006). After Saddam's fall in 2003, the Kurds stressed their desire to be a part of the new Iraq (Romano 2006:212).[26] In more recent years, however, it appears that Kurdish officials' rhetoric has been inching towards secessionism. For example, in 2014, Kurdish officials spoke of a "new reality" in Iraq and of the possibility of an independence referendum in the region (Solomon 2014). In June 2015, Massoud Barzani alluded to the independence referendum, for many the "strongest-ever indication ... [that the Kurds] would seek formal independence from the rest of Iraq" (Krever 2015).

This type of rhetoric has given the impression that the time for Kurdistan's independence has come. Yet, while the presence of such assertions and a collective desire for independence is not denied, we conceptualize Kurdish mobilization via the movements of political elites, because they interact with US officials as representatives of the Kurdish people. From this perspective, the statements of the Kurdistan Regional Government (KRG) and Kurdish party officials do not indicate that Kurdish leadership is directly advocating for secession. Barzani's last statement in DC above, for example, defers to the will of the Kurdish people towards independence, instead of asserting the people's right to independence in more classical secessionist terms.[27] Moreover, the lack of clarity about the logistics, including a specified timeframe for independence and institutional, economic, and political transitional objectives, does not establish an active secessionist agenda. Finally, the continued lack of an actual assertion of independence from any Kurdish official in any platform demonstrates that the Kurdish leadership is still refraining from full secessionism.[28]

Impact of Kurdish mobilization on US policy

We highlight the importance of properly identifying the degree of mobilization in Kurdistan in order to avoid conflating public perceptions with the agenda of Kurdish officials because only the latter are a factor in US decision-making. Additionally, some may argue that a relevant aspect of Kurdish mobilization in Iraq is that Kurdish elites may not declare independence as a strategic move (Le Billon 2015:73). However, the motives behind the Kurdish mobilization are not at issue because we theorize that policy considerations are potentially invoked by the presence or expectation of secessionism, and not by its underlying motives. For example, the international regime against intervention is a global reaction to the presence of internal conflict and mobilization, and not primarily the reasoning behind secessionism. Underlying motivations aside, then, we argue that whether or not the Kurds' mobilization is significant depends on whether or not an increase in mobilization affects the US' most influential considerations, such as its economic interests.

The US' current economic interests in the KR are a function of Iraq's 2005 federal arrangement. Kurdistan asserted autonomy over its oil resources and passed its own hydrocarbons law (Natali 2010).[29] This enabled the KRG to enter into contracts with international oil companies, including various US oil companies. Because of this decentralized context, the lack of full autonomy did not preclude the US as an external actor from establishing its independent economic interests in the KR. Because these interests are already entrenched, greater Kurdish mobilization for independence does not pose a heightened economic opportunity for the US that would, in turn, affect the economic considerations of the US and invite policy change.

However, a factor that could have more impact on these considerations is the increasing tension over oil production and revenues between the KRG and Baghdad since 2013.[30] One of the KRG's grievances is that it has not consistently received its (constitutionally) allotted oil revenue transfers from Baghdad (Faucon 2015). In turn, the increasingly cash-strapped KRG has been unable to make timely payments to the companies drilling in the region. Yet, despite these complications, US companies have remained because the region's "vast oil riches could make it worth the risk in the long term" (Williams and Kent 2015). However, as time and owed debt accrues, an independent Kurdistan with full autonomy over its energy sector may become more appealing to US economic interests. At this point, greater mobilization could have more impact on US decision-making as the potential benefits of an independent Kurdistan for these economic interests become more prominent in decision-making.[31] Importantly, US interest in an independent Kurdistan is not likely to be proximate until US economic interests are negatively impacted more strongly, and over more time. Ironically, a recent manifestation of greater Kurdish autonomy can delay this dynamic: the KRG's independent sale of oil. The KRG began bold steps in this direction in midsummer 2015 (Al-Ansary, Stanley and DiPaola 2015). In turn, this enables the KRG to make payments on its debts (Ashcroft 2015). Such intermittent payments can prevent the accrual of negative impact on the US interests that could spur a policy shift.

In terms of strategic considerations, a greater push for independence could affect the perception of the Kurds' role in the aims of the US to counter ISIS in Iraq. The Kurds' strategic appeal is their military ability, a unique characteristic of Kurdistan's relatively high level of regional autonomy (Danilovich 2014:67).[32] A shift to independence, then, would not enhance the already institutionalized Kurdish military capacity. In fact, there is concern about problematic internal divisions in the Peshmerga administration that could worsen in a more autonomous context (Fantappie 2015). Assuming Kurdish disinterest in efforts beyond their borders, securing independence is not likely to render the Kurds more amenable to fighting the battles they perceive as belonging to the Arabs, on Arab territory. Thus, independence could increase US concern about the reliability of the Kurds for countering ISIS aims, preventing perceptions of an independent Kurdistan as more conducive to US strategic aims. Consequently, a shift to a more pro-independence US policy towards the Kurds is not foreseeable, a reality likely to contrast with Kurdish expectations.

Kurdish disappointment with US policy

A conventional belief among Kurds, premised on US and Kurdish alliance, is that greater mobilization can engender greater US support for Kurdish independence. In terms of the intervention framework, this expectation translates to the argument that mobilization could impact the US' affective considerations via the humanitarian appeal of providing support to Kurds as US allies; stronger mobilization could be a "louder" demand that more effectively elicits public sympathy. We have shown that affective considerations alone do not affect the US' considerations.[33] Instead, aid to the Kurds has been a function of strategy or economic interests. Therefore, even if a stronger independence movement evokes these affective considerations, they will not have weight enough to impact US policy.

In fact, a stronger secessionist stance could be to the Kurds' detriment because it may provoke a firmer constraint from the international regime. Heraclides (1990) finds that international considerations ranked first among all constraints, but the cases used in the analysis include only strong secessionist movements seeking independence.[34] In contrast, the Kurds' abstention from secessionism has perhaps invoked softer international regime constraints up to this point that could be countered. Research supports the expectation of different global reaction levels to different mobilization levels; for example, Saideman (2002:30) finds that secessionist groups "are *greater* [italics added] threats to other states and to existing international norms because they seek to revise existing boundaries." It follows, then, that non-secessionist movements may be perceived as less threatening, and may trigger a smaller reaction from the international community. To this end, it may behoove the Kurds to continue to refrain from demanding full independence – an ironic indicator of the leverage that the US has in this relation.

The US' leverage in the Kurdish independence sphere

As the central sphere in Baghdad, regional neighbors, and the international regime are all opposed to independence, the Kurds are rendered desperate for US support. Yet, we posit that as long as the US supports a unified Iraq, direct US support for independence is not viable. An alternative is a more tacit US support via the direct arming of the Kurds, but this option is still not receiving enough backing from policy makers. For example, in late June 2015, the United States Senate voted to block an amendment to the 2016 National Defense Authorization Act that would allow the US to directly arm Kurdish forces fighting against ISIS (Klimas 2015). While the House of Representatives version had already passed earlier in May, the initiative received a harsh condemnation from Baghdad, which halted further support (Ibid.).

To tip the scales in favor of directly arming the Kurds despite the international regime constraint, strategic considerations in favor of arming the Kurds must be bolstered. To this end, the Kurds' perceived strategic value should increase, and concern about their motivation to fight beyond their borders decrease. The latter is possible if the US induces the Kurds to commit to assist with military operations beyond their borders – possible as the Kurds' fervor for independence increases and the US secures more leverage against them with which to pressure them to cooperate. Contributing to this pressure is the Kurds' need for more arms to continue protecting their region from ISIS. The ability to offer the Kurds arms, therefore, gives the

US significant leverage, which becomes an endogenous influence on US decision-making because it can pressure the Kurds to collaborate with the US against ISIS, which can assuage concerns about Kurdish reticence to collaborate.

Possibility of Iraq's disintegration

The Obama administration's support for Iraq's unity may appear ironic in light of an increasingly unstable country; some argue dissolution "is so likely that American strategists should be thinking about how to respond" (Metz 2015). What are the relevant considerations involved in US decision-making towards the Kurds in this chaotic context? Naturally, a dissolved Iraq would eliminate the conceptualization of US foreign policy towards the Kurds within the intervention framework. Yet, as is often the case, the disintegration of Iraq, should it occur, is not likely to be an immediate occurrence but instead would involve a protracted conflict (McGarry and O'Leary 1993). In this context, we argue that before actual dissolution, *impending* dissolution will become a unique factor as considerations involving the Kurds will stem from the assumption of a dissolved state. By accounting for impending dissolution, it is possible to capture strategic factors that are unique to conflict cases with greater likelihoods of disintegration.

The relevance of impending dissolution is its potential impact on the US' perception of the Kurds' willingness to contribute to the anti-ISIS effort beyond its borders as well as the US leverage. The reliance on the Peshmerga to counter ISIS, combined with the fact that in a dissolved Iraq the Kurds would no longer need the US to secure independence, would reduce US leverage. Moreover, autonomy can be expected to lower the Kurds' willingness to collaborate beyond their borders as it cannot be assumed that they would engage in combat out of a sense of loyalty to any of the successor configurations. At this point, a power shift would yield less US leverage and increase Kurdish leverage. The Kurds' leverage would increase as a result of their value to the US for combat against ISIS, and as the only reliable successor ally that the US would have in a dissolved Iraq, as the Shiite area is "Tehran's client" and the Sunni Arab area likely to see "protracted conflict"(Metz 2015). As a result, US foreign policy decision-making could begin to prioritize fostering a strategic relationship with the Kurds, perhaps via the provision of security guarantees, or "a military presence to deter Kurdistan's enemies and execute raids and strikes" against ISIS (Ibid.). The US could capitalize on the fact that the concept of Kurdish independence has been continuously met with hostility from neighboring states, and strategically cultivate itself as a potential ally of Kurdistan in the region. The possibility of more equitable leverage between the US and the Kurds that could arise from a dissolving Iraq could usher in a new era of US policy that instead of continuously disappointing the Kurds, might favor the interests of both.

Conclusion

In this chapter we set out to explain the evolution of US policy towards the Kurds using the intervention theoretical framework and its conceptualization of instrumental and affective considerations. This approach contrasts with previous studies on US foreign policy towards the Kurds, which tends to use an NSA framework. In relation to the increasingly salient "Kurdish Issue," this study demonstrates the intervention framework's capacity to yield nuanced observations of US policy in relation to the context of the host states of Kurdish populations.

For the case of the Kurds of Iraq, this study demonstrates not only that multiple motivations influence US decision-making towards the Kurds, but that their respective influences vary in magnitude. Importantly, instrumental motivations, especially strategic and economic considerations, have consistently shaped US policy towards the Kurds of Iraq. Specifically, this analysis of critical political-time junctures reveals which of these instrumental considerations predominates in US decision-making over time. Moreover, while we demonstrate that humanitarian motivations do at times factor into US policy decision-making, we make the important distinction that the impact of these affective considerations hinges on their interaction with the surrounding instrumental context. Thus, we show that the instrumental character of US decision-making towards the Kurds is more than a simple broad label, but a complex mechanism with varying context-dependent impact. While the instrumental nature of US policy has been previously noted, we identify *which* instrumental considerations have the most weight in this case, as well as *how* these considerations shape the influence of humanitarian considerations.

In this study we find that the very establishment of US relations with the Kurds of Iraq in the early 1970s was not due to US consideration of the Kurds' ongoing fight for autonomy, but reflects the starting point of the US perception of the Kurds' utility for its regional aims. This motivated the temporary aid for the Kurdish rebellion in Iraq, which abruptly ceased as US regional relations shifted, marking the first US "betrayal" of the Kurds. The strategic motivation behind US support for Kurdish autonomy is again invoked in the Gulf War period, but is shown, once again, to cease in light of the US' surrounding regional agenda, in this case the priority of its relations with Iran, Turkey, and Syria.

Some continue to cite US support for the Kurds following the US invasion of Iraq as evidence of a refreshed alliance with the Kurds. Ironically, we demonstrate that it is the utility of this alliance, the Kurds' position as the US' only dependable ally amidst the turmoil in Iraq that spurred favorable US intervention towards the Kurds in this context. Thus, while the factors that appeal to the US agenda in relation to the Kurds shifts over time, the US pursues a consistent pattern of responding favorably to the Kurds only when they become a strategic factor, and never in light of their plight or cause per se.

These strategic considerations in US policy towards the Kurds continue into the present context of an Iraq riddled with sectarian conflict and the threat of ISIS. We demonstrate that the relevant factor for this policy towards the Kurds becomes the protection of the KR, shaped by the US regional economic interests. However, strategic considerations regarding the Kurds' value for combating ISIS aims may influence the possible provision of arms to the Kurds. The provision of arms to the Kurds again invokes the issue of Kurdish independence; given the US-revealed nonchalance to this notion up to this point in relation to its considerations, we examine this salient dynamic in light of its potential appeal to the current instrumental agenda of the US. We argue that affective motivations of loyalty or justice arising out of the US-Kurdish alliance, which dominate the rhetoric surrounding independence, are insignificant influences on US decision-making. Similarly, we contend that increases in Kurdish mobilization will not significantly impact US policy per se because it will not substantially affect strategic and economic considerations. Moreover, we argue that increased Kurdish secessionism may be to the Kurds' detriment in relation to US policy as it will undermine the weight of their current strategic value to the US strategy in Iraq.

We also utilize the framework to examine the potential US-Kurdish dynamic given the possibility of a disintegrated Iraq. To this end, we argue that the Kurds' interests may be more favorably served by US policy as Iraq's disintegration becomes more imminent and US-Kurdish relations could enter a new phase characterized by a more equal distribution of leverage. In this possible future context, we show that US strategic considerations regarding the Kurds may finally begin to shift US policy in a direction that would result in less Kurdish disappointment instead of the currently increasing expressions of US "betrayal." Whether or not this shift takes place, however, remains to be seen as the realities of the KR and Iraq continue to interact with the US policy-making agenda.

Notes

1 A Kurdish saying.
2 "US Betrayal of the Kurds," *The Pasewan*. August 15, 2015.
3 For a review of the official US arguments in support of an Iraqi federal state, see Makiya (2003).
4 Also referred to as the "Kurdish Question," the bulk of this literature addresses the Kurdish dynamic in Turkey (e.g., Bozarslan 1996; Gunes and Zeydanlioglu 2013; Roach 2005; Robins 1993; Updegraff 2012).
5 For more on the motivations classification, see Carment (1993), "Theoretical Considerations," 138.
6 This literature generally focuses on the causes of Kurdish mobilization, whereas mobilization in this chapter is included as a potential causal factor.
7 Especially organizations such as Green Peace and Amnesty International (e.g., Slaughter 2004).
8 These arguments include the traditional, territorial-based realist account of the impact of a nation's geographic position and resources relative to other powers, and the post-modern interpretation of geopolitics based on deteritorrialization (see Brzesinki 2007; Cohen 2003, cited in Hook and Spanier 2010).

9 Alternatively, more recent IR literature, such as the "neobehavioral" approach set forth by Walker et al. (2011) captures cognitive factors that influence leader's decision-making, but the emphasis on psychological processes does not take into consideration the independent influence of external, global factors beyond the cognitive filter. We note, however, the utility of the psychological approach for incorporation into more nuanced future research; for example, international norms may have varying impact on actors, which can alter the aggregate direction of decision-making.
10 Participating units include the US Department of Defense and the CIA (Minz and DeRouen Jr, 2010:3–7). In relation to this study, Charountaki (2011) notes that the CIA has been especially influential in US-Kurdish relations, including the overthrow of Saddam.
11 A larger body of work on intervention focuses on the characteristics of the conflict's host-state, such as ethnic cleavages, institutional breakdowns, and security dilemmas, that draw in external actors (see Lake and Rothchild 1998; Kaufman 2001; Suhrke and Noble 1977; cited in Carment and James 2004:13). Future cross-national research in this direction can benefit from controlling for these components.
12 Heraclides (1990:341) notes that general external involvement is "ubiquitous" in the literature, but external involvement in secessionist conflict is rarely studied, and if it is, it is within the scope of ethnicity studies. Thus, ethnic conflict is virtually absent from international relations theory (Carment 1993:128).
13 The research on international democratic assistance may come to mind, but this body of work largely focuses on the efforts of sub-state or coalition institutions, such as USAID or the UN, whereas the actors of interest in this study are states who may or not engage in assistance or other forms of intervention. For example, Milner and Tingley (2013) present a principal-agent model on US support and opposition to multilateralism in aid. This study reflects the humanitarian intervention agenda of institutions but does not shed light on the decision-making of state actors. Similarly, the recent research on KRG paradiplomacy is also not an analysis of the decision-making process of foreign states, such as the US, towards the Kurds, but instead examines the assertions of the Kurdistan Region of Iraq within a federal context.
14 This includes the postures of both external states and (IGOs) international governmental organizations (Heraclides 1990). Briefly, a diffusion and encouragement reaction is characterized by either high international involvement in the conflict where the internal war is internationalized or dominant support for the incumbent government. This is in contrast to the settlement-oriented aims of a reconciliation reaction and the noninterventionist stance of the isolation reaction (Hassner 1971; Suhrke and Noble 1977, cited in Heraclides 1990:345).
15 The international regime is premised on both legal principles as well as political principles such as the "fundamental norm" of territorial integrity and the unity of sovereign independent states. Intervention is only condoned if the state itself requests it, or has given its consent, or if intervention is based on the decision of an IGO (Heraclides 1990:351).
16 Heraclides (1990:344–45) defines supportive intervention as a state's "partisan involvement" on the side of the secessionist minority, including: (1) an act that is deliberately aimed to help the substate group; (2) an act that actually helped the substate group; and (3) an act that was defined by the secessionists themselves as helpful. The third is most relevant to this chapter because it is found that affective motivations arising from altruism are never the main US motive in decision-making towards the Kurds.
17 James Akins, "The Survival of Saddam," interview. *PBS Frontline*, January 2000, quoted in Romano (2006:196).

18 The Anfal campaign was a series of attacks on the Kurdish population that began in 1987 and includes the infamous attack on Halabja, where about 5,000 Kurds died after Iraqi war planes dropped mustard gas onto the city (Romano 2006).
19 For more about how policy makers characterize problems overseas to advance priorities, see Widmaier (2007).
20 ISIS seized territories in Iraq's Sunni heartland in the summer of 2014 (Laub and Masters 2015).
21 Levels of support for pulling out of Iraq reached 75% in 2011 (PEW 2011).
22 Others include: Aspect Energy, Marathon Oil Corporation, Hillwood International Energy, Hunt Oil, Prime Oil, Murphy Oil, Hess Corporation, HKN Energy, and Viking International. The International Energy Agency (IEA) estimated that the KR contains 4 billion barrels of proved reserves (U.S. Energy Information Administration 2015).
23 Admittedly, it can be argued that the intervention in Erbil does not constitute an intervention in an internal conflict because ISIS is an external actor, and the defense of Erbil is not economically-driven US policy towards the Kurds but is instead part of the counter-ISIS policy. Yet, the counter-ISIS agenda itself is a function of US economic interests because of the threat an ISIS encroachment on Iraqi territory – especially oil-producing territory – poses for US oil interests in Iraq. Thus, economic motivations are not negated. The context of interventionism applies still because, as mentioned in the chapter introduction, supportive interventionist policy also includes actions which are deemed helpful by the sub-state group, such as the US rescue of Erbil, and not just actions intended to help a sub-state group.
24 Carment et al. (2009:70) discuss how conflict expansion draws more attention from the international system, and intervention levels, in turn, are affected by the "importance" of the conflict to the system.
25 Secessionism is defined as "a demand for formal withdrawal from a central political authority by a member unit or units on the basis of a claim to independent sovereign status (Hechter 1992).
26 We note that more public support for independence was strongly voiced at the local level, and expressed though initiatives such as the Kurdistan Referendum Movement (Halkawt 2006). This incongruence between Kurdish leadership and the Kurdish public, and its implications, is addressed later in this section.
27 See Hechter (1992).
28 The lack of a full mobilization movement by the Kurds in Iraq can be better appreciated by contrasting it to the modern mobilization movement of the Kurds in Turkey. See Romano (2006:25–66).
29 Petroleum Law of the Kurdistan Region-Iraq 2007. According to the Baghdad's interpretation of the Iraqi Constitution, however, oil resources are under the jurisdiction of the central government (Natali 2010).
30 See "Issues between the Kurdistan Regional Government and Baghdad," in "US Energy Information Administration Information Country Analysis Brief: Iraq," (U.S. Energy Information Administration, last updated January 30, 2015), 7.
31 One source of actors in this context is the group of individuals leading the US companies in the region, many are retired US military officials. These "ex-military men have become strong advocates for the Kurdish cause, calling for expanding US airstrikes and providing more sophisticated weapons to Kurdish Peshmerga forces. They also back what they say may well emerge as an independent, pro-American, pro-business Kurdish state" (Erlich 2014).
32 The Iraqi Constitution lends support to the presence of the forces by outlining that the regional government is responsible for all administrative requirements of the region, including internal security forces (Danilovich 2014).

33 This might differ were the affective considerations of "kinship" present; research shows that a state might have more aggressive foreign policy towards a state where its ethnic "kin" is disadvantaged (Davis and Moore 1997).
34 The groups in the analysis endorsed independence or other forms of self-rule with armed violence as the means to achieve these goals (Heraclides 1990:344).

References

Abdullah, Goran. 2015. "Liberating Mosul: Why should the Kurds care?" *The Kurdistan Tribune*, February 25. Accessed: December 12, 2015. Available at: http://kurdistantribune.com/2015/liberating-mosul-why-should-the-kurds-care/.

Ahmed, Mohammed. 2012. *Iraqi Kurds and Nation Building*. New York: Palgrave Macmillan.

Akins, James. "The Survival of Saddam," interview. *PBS Frontline*, January 2000. Accessed: July 1, 2015. Available at: www.pbs.org/wgbh/pages/frontline/shows/saddam/interviews/akins.html.

Alamiri, Yasmeen. 2015. "Biden's Policies on Iraq: From Separation to Unity." *Al Arabiya News*, April 12. Accessed: July 12, 2015. Available at: http://english.alarabiya.net/en/perspective/analysis/2015/04/11/Biden-s-policies-on-Iraq-from-separation-to-unity.html.

Al-Ansary, Khalid, Bruce Stanley and Anthony DiPaola, 2015. "Iraq's Kurds Bypass State for Oil Exports to Tighten Control," *Bloomberg Business*, July 15. Accessed: December 2, 2015. Available at: www.bloomberg.com/news/articles/2015-07-14/iraq-s-kurdish-region-exporting-550-600k-b-d-oil-of-own-output.

Amos, Deborah. 2014. "Kurds Put Their Independence Dreams on Hold." *National Public Radio*. December 23. Accessed: July 1, 2015. Available at: www.npr.org/sections/parallels/2014/12/23/372487690/kurds-put-their-independence-dreams-on-hold.

Ashcroft, Jamie. 2015. "Kurdistan oil payments will start in early September," *Proactiveinvestors.co.uk*, August 27. Accessed September 4, 2015. Available at: www.proactiveinvestors.co.uk/companies/news/110345/kurdistan-oil-payments-will-start-in-early-september-110345.html.

Barzani, Masrour. "Iraqi Kurds: We're Ready to Fight for Mosul." Interview. NPR, February 24, 2015. Accessed: September 6, 2015. Available at: www.npr.org/sections/parallels/2015/02/22/387744947/iraqi-kurds-were-ready-to-fight-for-mosul.

Baumann, Rainer and Frank A. Stengel. 2013. "Foreign policy analysis, globalisation and non-state actors: state-centric after all?" *Journal of International Relations and Development* 17(4): 489–521.

Berwari, Azad and Thomas Ambrosio. 2008. "The Kurdistan Referendum Movement: Political Opportunity Structures and National Identity." *Democratization* 15(5): 891–908.

Bozarslan, Hamit. 1996. "Political crisis and the Kurdish issue in Turkey." In *The Kurdish Nationalist Movement in the 1990s: Its Impact on Turkey and the Middle East*. Robert Olson, 135–153. Lexington, Ky.: University Press of Kentucky.

Brown, Michael E. 1996. "The Causes and Regional Dimensions of Internal Conflict." In *The International Dimensions of Internal Conflict*. Cambridge: MIT Press.

Brown, Seyom. 1994. *The Faces of Power: Constancy and Change in United States Foreign Policy from Truman to Clinton*. New York: Columbia University Press.

Brzezinski, Zbigniew.1997. *The Grand Chessboard: American Primacy and Its Geostrategic Imperatives.* New York: BasicBooks.
Bueno De Mesquita, Bruce, and Alastair Smith. 2007. "Foreign Aid and Policy Concessions." *The Journal of Conflict Resolution* 51(2): 251–84.
Bueno De Mesquita, Bruce, and Alastair Smith. 2009. "A Political Economy of Aid." *International Organization* 63(2): 309–40.
Byman, Daniel. 2000. "After the Storm: U.S. Policy Toward Iraq Since 1991." *Political Science Quarterly* 115(4): 493–516.
Carment, David. 1993. "The International Dimensions of Ethnic Conflict: Concepts, Indicators, and Theory." *Journal of Peace Research* 30(2): 137–50.
Carment, David and Dane Rowlands. 1998. "Three's Company: Evaluating Third-Party Intervention in Intrastate Conflict." *The Journal of Conflict Resolution* 42(5): 572–99.
Carment, David, and Patrick James. 2000. "Explaining Third-Party Intervention in Ethnic Conflict: Theory and Evidence." *Nations and Nationalism* 6(2): 173–202.
Carment, David, and Patrick James. 2004. "Third-party states in ethnic conflict: Identifying the domestic determinants of intervention." In *Ethnic Conflict and International Politics: Explaining Diffusion and Escalation.* 11–34. New York: Palgrave Macmillan.
Carment, David, Patrick James, and Zeynep Taydas. 2009. "The Internationalization of Ethnic Conflict: State, Society, and Synthesis." *International Studies Review* 11(1): 63–86.
Chaliand, Gérard. 1980. *People without a Country: The Kurds and Kurdistan.* Northampton, MA: Interlink Pub Group Inc.
Charountaki, Marianna. 2011. *The Kurds and US Foreign Policy: International Relations in the Middle East since 1945.* New York: Routledge.
Clary, Gregory. 2015. "US Calls Fall of Ramadi 'Very Serious.'" *CNN Politics.* May 22. Accessed: July 1, 2015. Available at: www.cnn.com/2015/05/20/politics/ramadi-isis-dempsey/.
Cohen, S.B. 2003. "Geopolitical Realities and United States Foreign Policy." *Political Geography* 22(1): 1–33.
Committee on Armed Services. 2015a. *Hearing To Receive Testimony on United States Policy in Iraq and Syria: Hearing before the United States Senate,* 114th Cong. Washington, D.C.
Committee on Armed Services. 2015b. *U.S. Policy and Strategy in the Middle East: Hearing before the United States Senate,* 114th Cong. Washington, D.C.
Cordesman, Anthony and Sam Khazai. 2012. "Iraq after US Withdrawal: US Policy and the Iraqi Search for Security and Stability." CSIS. Washington, D.C. Accessed July 3, 2015. Available at: http://csis.org/publication/iraq-after-us-withdrawal-us-policy-and-iraqi-search-security-and-stability.
Danilovich, Alex. 2014. *Iraqi Federalism and the Kurds.* Burlington, VT: Ashgate.
Davis, David R., Keith Jaggers, and Will H. Moore. 1997. "Ethnicity, Minorities, and International Conflict." In *Wars in the Midst of Peace: The International Politics of Ethnic Conflict* eds David W. Carment and Patrick James. Pittsburgh: University of Pittsburgh Press.
Eisenstadt, Michael. 2015. "Aligning Means and Ends, Policies and Strategy in the War on ISIL." Testimony submitted to the House Armed Services Subcommittee on Emerging Threats and Capabilities. 114th Cong. Accessed: November 19, 2015.

Available at: http://docs.house.gov/meetings/AS/AS26/20150624/103678/HHRG-114-AS26-Wstate-EisenstadtM-20150624.pdf.
Entessar, Nader. 1992. *Kurdish Ethnonationalism*. Boulder, CO: Lynn Rienner Publishers.
Erlich, Reese. 2014. "Retired U.S. officials move into oil business in Kurdistan's 'Wild West.'" *Los Angeles Daily News*. September 4, Accessed: October 4, 2015. Available at: www.dailynews.com/general-news/20140904/retired-us-officials-move-into-oil-business-in-kurdistans-wild-west.
Esman, Milton J. 1995. "A Survey of Interventions." In *International Organizations and Ethnic Conflict*, ed. Milton J. Esman and Shibley Telhami. Ithaca: Cornell University Press.
Everest, Larry. 2004. *Oil, Power and Empire: Iraq and the U.S. Global Agenda*. Monroe, Me: Common Courage Press.
Fantappie, Maria. 2015. The Peshmerga Regression. *Foreign Affairs*. June 14. Accessed: July 23, 2015. Available at: www.foreignaffairs.com/articles/iraq/2015-06-14/peshmerga-regression.
Faucon, Benoît. 2015. "Kurds Say Iraq's Oil Payments Coming up Short." *Wall Street Journal*. June 9. Accessed: November 24, 2015. Available at: www.wsj.com/articles/kurds-say-iraqs-oil-payments-coming-up-short-1433875115.
Findley, Paul. 1988. "The US State in Good Relations with Baghdad," *Washington Report on Middle East Affairs*. December 1988. Accessed: July 4, 2015. Available at: www.wrmea.org/1988-december/the-us-stake-in-good-relations-with-baghdad.html.
Flint, Colin. 2001. "The Geopolitics of Laughter and Forgetting: A World-Systems Interpretation of the Post-Modern Geopolitical Condition." *Geopolitics* 6(3): 1–16.
Gamu, Jonathan, Philippe Le Billon, and Samuel Spiegel. 2015. "Extractive Industries and Poverty: A Review of Recent Findings and Linkage Mechanisms." *The Extractive Industries and Society* 2(1): 162–176.
Gourevitch, Peter. 2002. "Foreign Policy." In *Handbook of International Relations*, edited by Walter Carlsnaes, Thomas Risse-Kappen, and Beth A. Simmons. Thousand Oaks, CA: Sage Publications.
Gunes, Cengiz, and Welat Zeydanlioglu. 2013. *The Kurdish Question in Turkey: New Perspectives on Violence, Representation and Reconciliation*. Abingdon: Routledge.
Gurr, Ted Robert.1992. "The Internationalization of Protracted Communal Conflicts since 1945: Which Groups, Where and How." In *The Internationalization of Communal Strife*, edited by Manul I. Midlarsky. London: Routledge.
Haddad, Fanar. 2011. *Sectarianism in Iraq: Antagonistic Visions of Unity*. New York: Columbia University Press.
Halliday, Fred. 2006. "Can We Write a Modernist History of Kurdish Nationalism?" In *The Kurds: Nationalism and Politics*, edited by Faleh A. Jabar and Hosham Dawod. London: Saqi.
Hassner, Pierre. 1971. "Pragmatic Conservatism in the White House." *Foreign Policy* 3: 41–61.
Hawlkat, Abdullah. 2006. "Iraqi Kurdish movement wants self-determination stipulated in constitution." *BBC Monitoring Middle East*. September 1.
Hawrami, Fazel. 2014. "Kurdish Peshmerga seize a chaotic victory in Kirkuk." *The Guardian*. June 13. Accessed: July 23, 2015. Available at: www.theguardian.com/world/2014/jun/12/kurdish-peshmerga-kirkuk-iraq-maliki.
Hechter, Michael. 1992. "The dynamics of secession." *Acta Sociologica* 35(4): 267–283.

Heinrich, Tobias. 2013. "When Is Foreign Aid Selfish, When Is It Selfless?" *The Journal of Politics* 75(2): 422–35.

Heraclides, Alexis. 1990. "Secessionist Minorities and External Involvement." *International Organization* 44(3): 341–78.

Hook, Steven W. and John W. Spanier. 2010. *American Foreign Policy since World War II*. Washington, D.C.: CQ Press.

Hudson, Valerie. 2005. "Foreign Policy Analysis: Actor-Specific Theory and the Ground of International Relations." Foreign Policy Analysis, 1(1): 1–30.

Jackson, Robert. 1987. "Quasi-states, Dual Regimes, and Neoclassical Theory: International Jurisprudence and the Third World." *International Organization* 41(4): 519–49.

Katzman, Kenneth, Christopher Blanchard, Carla Humud, Rhoda Margesson, Alex Tiersky, and Matthew Weed. 2014. "The 'Islamic State' Crisis and U.S. Policy." Congressional Research Service. Washington D.C.: Library of Congress. Accessed: July 1, 2015. Available at: https://fas.org/sgp/crs/mideast/R43612.pdf.

Kaufman, Stuart. 2001. *Modern Hatreds: The Symbolic Politics of Ethnic War*. New York: Cornell University Press.

Klimas, Jaqueline. 2015. "Senate Blocks Directly Arming Kurds in Islamic State Fight." *The Washington Times*. June 16. Accessed: July 1, 2015. Available at: www.washingtontimes.com/news/2015/jun/16/senate-blocks-directly-arming-kurds-in-islamic-sta/?page=all.

Krasner, Stephen. 1982. "Structural Causes and Regime Consequences: Regimes as Intervening Variables." *International Organization* 36(2): 185–205.

Krever, Mick. 2014. "Exclusive: Iraqi Kurdistan Leader Massoud Barzani Says 'The Time is Here' for Self-determination." *CNN*. June 23. Accessed: July 1, 2015. Available at: http://amanpour.blogs.cnn.com/2014/06/23/exclusive-iraqi-kurdish-leader-says-the time- is-here-for-self-determination/.

Kumar Sen, Ashish. 2015. "Barzani: 'An Independent Kurdistan is Coming'". *Atlantic Council*. May 6. Accessed: July 1, 2015. Available at: www.atlanticcouncil.org/blogs/new-atlanticist/barzani-an-independent-kurdistan-is-coming.

Lake, David, and Donald Rothchild. 1998. *The International Spread of Ethnic Conflict: Fear, Diffusion, and Escalation*. Princeton, N.J.: Princeton University Press.

Laub, Zachary, and Jonathan Masters. 2015. "The Islamic State." Council on Foreign Relations. Accessed: July 1, 2015. Available at: www.cfr.org/iraq/islamic-state/p14811.

Makiya, Kanan. 2003. "A Model for Post-Saddam Iraq." *Journal of Democracy* 14(3): 5–12.

McGarry, John, and Brendan O'Leary. 1993. *The Politics of Ethnic Conflict Regulation: Case Studies of Protracted Ethnic Conflicts*. London; New York: Routledge.

Meadwell, Hudson. 1991. "A Rational Choice Approach to Political Regionalism." *Comparative Politics* 23(4): 401–21.

Meadwell, Hudson. 1993. "The Politics of Nationalism in Quebec." *World Politics* 45(2): 203–41.

Mearsheimer, John. 1995. "The False Promise of International Institutions." *International Security* 19(3): 5–49.

Metz, Steven. 2015. "The US must prepare for the dissolution of Iraq." *World Politics Review*. February 20. Accessed: December 2, 2015. Available at: www.worldpoliticsreview.com/articles/15123/the-u-s-must-prepare-for-the-dissolution-of-iraq.

Milner, Helen, and Tingley, Dustin. 2013. "The Choice for Multilateralism: Foreign Aid and American Foreign Policy." *The Review of International Organizations* 8(3): 313–341.

Mintz, Alex, and Karl DeRouen Jr. 2010. *Understanding Foreign Policy Decision Making*. Cambridge; New York: Cambridge University Press.

Mitchell, C.R. 1970. "Civil Strife and the Involvement of External Parties." *International Studies Quarterly* 14(2): 166–94.

Nasr, Seyyed Vali Reza. 2013. *The Dispensable Nation: American Foreign Policy in Retreat*. New York: Doubleday.

Natali, Denise. 2010. *The Kurdish Quasi-State*. Syracuse: Syracuse University Press.

Nau, Henry. 2002. *At Home Abroad: Identity and Power in American Foreign Policy*. Ithaca: Cornell University Press.

Neack, Laura. 2008. *The New Foreign Policy: Powerseeking in a Globalized Era*. Maryland: Rowman and Littlefield Publishers, Inc.

O'Leary, Brendan, John McGarry, and Khaled Salih. 2005. *The Future of Kurdistan in Iraq*. Philadelphia: University of Philadelphia Press.

Park, Bill. 2004. "Iraq's Kurds and Turkey: Challenges for US Policy." *Parameters*. Strategic Studies Institute, U.S. Army War College. Accessed: July 1, 2015. Available at: http://strategicstudiesinstitute.army.mil/pubs/parameters/Articles/04autumn/park.pdf.

Pew Research. 2011. "Iraq and Public Opinion: The Troops Come Home." Pew Research Center. December 14. Washington, D.C. Accessed: July 3, 2015. Available at: www.pewresearch.org/2011/12/14/iraq-and-public-opinion-the-troops-come-home/.

Pollack, Kenneth. 2014. "Oil and the Iraqi Civil War: How Security Dynamics May Affect Oil Production." *Brookings*. Accessed: July 2, 2015. Available at: www.brookings.edu/blogs/up-front/posts/2014/06/23-oil-iraqi-civil-war-pollack.

Regan, Patrick. 1998. "Choosing to Intervene: Outside Interventions in Internal Conflicts." *The Journal of Politics*, 60(3), 754–779.

Regan, Patrick. 2000. "Substituting Policies during US Interventions in Internal Conflicts A Little of This, a Little of That." *Journal of Conflict Resolution* 44(1): 90–106.

Roach, Steven C. 2005. *Cultural Autonomy, Minority Rights, and Globalization*. Vol. 36. Aldershot: Ashgate.

Robins, Philip. 1993. "The Overlord State: Turkish Policy and the Kurdish Issue." *International Affairs (Royal Institute of International Affairs 1944–)*: 657–676.

Romano, David. 2006. *The Kurdish Nationalist Movement: Opportunity, Mobilization, and Identity*. Cambridge, UK; New York: Cambridge University Press.

Romano, David, and Mehmet Gurses. 2014. *Conflict, Democratization, and the Kurds in the Middle East: Turkey, Iran, Iraq, and Syria*. New York: Palgrave Macmillan.

Saideman, Stephen. 1997. "Explaining the International Relations of Secessionist Conflicts: Vulnerability of Ethnic Ties." *International Organization* 51: 721–753.

Saideman, Stephen. 1998. "Inconsistent Irredentism? Political Competition, Ethnic Ties, and the Foreign Policies of Somalia and Serbia." *Security Studies* 7: 51–93.

Saideman, Stephen. 2001. "Taking Sides: Dyadic Analyses of Involvement in Other Countries' Ethnic Conflicts." Lubbock: Working Paper, Department of Political Science, Texas Tech University.

Saideman, Stephen. 2002. "Discrimination in International Relations: Analyzing External Support for Ethnic Groups." *Journal of Peace Research* 39(1): 27–50.

Sarigil, Zeki, and Omer Fazlioglu. 2013. "Religion and Ethno-nationalism: Turkey's Kurdish Issue." *Nations and Nationalism* 19(3): 551–571.

Shapiro, Ari. 2015. "Iraqi Kurds: We're Ready to Fight For Mosul." *NPR*. February 24. Accessed: November 18, 2015. Available at: www.npr.org/sections/parallels/2015/02/22/387744947/iraqi-kurds-were-ready-to- fight-for-mosul.

Shareef, Mohammed. 2014. *The United States, Iraq and the Kurds: Shock, Awe and Aftermath*. Abingdon, Oxon: Routledge.

Slaughter, Anne-Marie. 2004. *A New World Order*. Princeton, N.J.: Princeton University Press

Solomon, Jay. 2014. "Iraqi Kurds Officials Lobbying for Independence in Washington." *Wall Street Journal*. July 3. Accessed: November 24, 2015. Available at: www.wsj.com/articles/iraqi-kurd-officials-lobbying-for-independence-in- washington-1404407746.

Suhrke, Astri and Lela Garner Noble. 1977. *Ethnic Conflict in International Relations*. New York: Praeger.

Taylor, Philip. 2002. Introduction: Non-state actors and the State-centric Model." In *Non-State Actors in World Politics*, edited by Daphne Josselin and William Wallace. New York: Palgrave Macmillan.

Tenorio, Teresa. 2001. "Why Do States Intervene? A Study into the Reasons for Intervention?" Paper Presented at the Annual Meeting of the International Studies Association (Midwest), St. Louis, Missouri. University Press.

Tyler, Patrick E. 2002. "Anti-Baghdad Talks Shunned by Top Kurd. (Foreign Desk)." *The New York Times*. August 15.

"US Betrayal of the Kurds." *The Pasewan*. August 15, 2015. Accessed: September 14, 2015. Available at: http://pasewan.com/blog/category/editorial/.

U.S. Department of Defense, Pentagon Press Secretary. *Statement by Pentagon Press Secretary Rear Admiral John Kirby on Airstrikes in Iraq*. 2014. Release No: NR-419-14. Accessed: September 4, 2015. Available at: www.defense.gov/Releases/Release.aspx?ReleaseID=16878.

U.S. Energy Information Administration. 2015. *Country Analysis Brief: Iraq*. Accessed: July 5, 2015. Available at: www.eia.gov/beta/international/analysis_includes/countries_long/Iraq/iraq.pdf.

U.S. Executive Office of the President, *White House Briefing*. 1991, No. 28/4/2549.

U.S. Office of the Special Inspector General for Iraq Reconstruction, Hard Lessons: The Iraq Reconstruction Experience, 2009, Washington, D.C.

U.S. White House. 2014. "President Obama discusses the US' military airstrikes in Erbil." August 7. Accessed: July 1, 2015. Available at: www.whitehouse.gov/the-press- office/2014/08/07/statement-president.

Updegraff, Ragan. 2012. "The Kurdish Question." *Journal of Democracy* 23(1): 119–128.

Voltolini, Benedetta. 2012. "The role of non-state actors in EU policies towards the Israeli Palestinian conflict." European Union Institute for Security Studies. Accessed: August 8, 2015. Available at: www.iss.europa.eu/uploads/media/The_role_of_non- state_actors_in_EU_policies_towards_the_Israeli-Palestinian_conflict.pdf

Walker, Stephen G., Akan Malici, and Mark Schafer. 2011. *Rethinking Foreign Policy Analysis: States, Leaders, and the Microfoundations of Behavioral International Relations*. New York: Routledge.

Waltz, Kenneth. 1979. *A Theory of International Politics*. New York: McGraw Hill.

Widmaier, Wesley. 2007 "Constructing Foreign Policy Crises: Interpretive Leadership in the Cold War and War on Terrorism." *International Studies Quarterly* 51(4): 779–794.

Wieland, Carsten. 2001. "Ethnic Conflict Undressed: Patterns of Contrast, Interest of Elites, and Clientelism of Foreign Powers in Comparative Perspective-Bosnia, India, Pakistan." *Nationalities Papers* 29: 207–241.

Williams, Selina and Sarah Kent. 2015. "Oil Earnings From Kurdistan Prove Elusive." *Wall Street Journal*. February 8. Accessed: November 6, 2015. Available at: www.wsj.com/articles/why-oil-earnings-from-kurdistan-are-so-elusive- 1423442505.

Conclusion

In this volume we attempted to determine the role Iraqi Kurdistan has been playing and has the potential to play in the Middle East. The Kurds have been involved in a prolonged and drawn out game since the First World War, in which the prize of state independence has remained elusive. This has been a game of high stakes in which the Kurds have had to deal with the genocidal regime of Saddam Hussein, segregation in their homeland in Syria, persecution by the regime of Ayatollahs in Iran, severe Turkish oppression and the fickleness of Western powers.

The *de facto* abolition by ISIS of the artificial partition of the Ottoman Empire a century ago has created a powerful new dynamic, bringing the Kurds into the center of the Middle Eastern equation. Events are unfolding at a rapid pace and it is rather difficult to come up with one comprehensive and straightforward understanding.

Chapter 1 provided a brief overview of the history of Kurdish nationalism in an attempt to understand what went wrong for this large nation in its efforts to achieve statehood. The deep political changes that have happened since the 1991 uprising in the Kurdistan region combined with dramatic transformations in the Middle East in the wake of the Arab Spring have created more favorable conditions for the establishment of an independent Kurdish state. The chapter's contributor claims that a combination of post-Arab spring geopolitical changes in the Middle East, the successful efforts the KRG has deployed in the international arena, the political and economic impact of Kurdistan's oil, and the Kurdistan region's effective fight against ISIS suggest that Kurdistan may be closer to full autonomy than any time before in its modern history.

Meanwhile, Kurdish nationalism has been both enhanced and legalized by the establishment of a federal system in Iraq. Iraqi federalism has offered broad autonomy and potential for fostering Kurdish national identity and more, as it allows this ethnic federal region to have its own military and conduct pretty independent economic and foreign policies.

In Chapter 2, I contended that federalism has done a good job of serving the Kurds of Iraq and has more potential to do so in the future despite its obvious shortcomings caused by the non-implementation of certain constitutional provisions, deep-rooted distrust and idyllic hopes for a sovereign Kurdish state. In general, federalism is considered a technological solution to deeply-rooted human problems and the introduction of a federal system in Iraq, as with the creation of the Kurdish federal region, was meant to achieve the following goals:

1. Ending the civil war between the Kurds and Arabs that at some point verged on ethnic cleansing and genocide.
2. Protecting and fostering Kurdish culture and identity.
3. Giving the Kurds significant political and economic autonomy.

The Iraqi federal constitution has indeed provided the Kurds with extraordinary opportunities and set only one precondition – the will to learn to live together. Given many new and unexpected developments, some external to Iraq, such as the emergence and rise of ISIS and other adverse regional events, it is hard to accurately forecast which way the proverbial paradox of federalism will play out.

We believe that the territorial devolution of power and polycentric governance in Iraq has brought peace between Kurds and Arabs; nascent federalism can be adjusted and fine-tuned through limited constitutional amendments, judicial interpretation, fiscal arrangements and intergovernmental collaboration. The Kurds, like the Quebecois, may eventually learn to live together with their federal partners.

Iraqi federalism is an ongoing experiment whose outcomes are rather positive, but painstaking efforts, compromises and a purposeful fine-tuning are in order. Writing in 2016, we can say that major disputes between Erbil and Baghdad are being resolved within the federal system by negotiation rather than by force. This has never been easy, as the actors also have to navigate the rocky environment of regional and international politics. The federal system remains unstable, but a solid alternative to the uncharted journey of independence in a region in turmoil.

Chapter 3 looked into the socio-economic relations in the Kurdistan region in order to evaluate its viability as a would-be independent state. A modernist transformation of society typically finds its ultimate cause in economic life, but here the author finds no evidence of any significant progress. It was argued that Kurdistan conforms in certain degree to Marx's model of the oriental society. The key element here is the conflation of economic and political power. These conditions coupled to the massive influx of oil move Kurdistan towards a rentier state system. Rentier states have many features of modern capitalist economies yet preserve their deeply premodern social structures. The economy is based predominantly on external revenue generated by foreign oil companies and little if any economic revenue is sourced domestically. The domestic economy is turned over to retail and services in a series of the sub-feudal landlord-serf relationship.

Ordinary Kurds are, and will remain, the beneficiary subjects of government, rather than developing into a participating citizenry and drivers of social and economic change.

That leads the author to conclude that Kurdistan is rooted in pre-modern conditions highly resistant to change, and the move toward an independent Kurdistan with a rentier state economy is unlikely to bring about any fundamental restructuring of Kurdish society and politics. Future independence will most probably result in business as usual domestically with few differences to the current Kurdish way of life.

In Chapter 4, the author attempted to look into Kurdish ordinary citizens' attitude towards the elites' plans to break away from the Iraqi federation and build a sovereign Kurdish state. That was done in an anthropological manner by juxtaposing the construction of luxury high-rises with state-building. While tall towers bring an image of modernity and might encourage people to think of independence, they also invoke corruption and conspiracy, and produce doubts about the potential for Kurdish statehood. Recently erected luxury buildings may generate a state effect – the state appears as an entity unto itself, at the same time creating suspicions about whether an independent state can be immune from the excessive interests of the ruling oligarchies.

The view advanced in Chapter 5 is that although oil seemingly provides economic resources for the development of an independent state, and therefore might represent 'an ace in the hole[1]', due to the vagaries of international politics, intensification of pre-existing divisions and rivalries, the erosion of human capital, that is to say, the 'curse of black gold', oil for the Kurds can more accurately be described as 'the joker in the pack'. The region's ongoing financial crisis caused by the dramatic fall of the oil price reinforces this assumption. The enactment of the controversial regional oil law by Erbil in 2007, despite Baghdad's objections, did not help to become economically self-sustainable even within the loose Iraqi federation. The current severe financial crisis demonstrates that the KRG may lead the region into a catastrophe by declaring independence. The secession will undermine the essential relations with Baghdad and make the region heavily dependent on Turkey and by the same token, even more financially vulnerable.

Chapter 6 examines the claim that despite some furtive claims of globalists, the international system remains dominated by sovereign states. True, there are important non-state actors, but sovereign states still play a central role. In spite of some theoretical precepts and the Montevideo Declaration's optimism, sub-state and stateless entities cannot become sovereign simply because they wish so. Much depends on the will of the restricted club of sovereign nations whose acceptance of newcomers is crucial as long as international relations takes place in a highly interdependent and territorially determined environment that privileges the sovereign state. It is for this particular reason that Kurdistan cannot decide its own fate. It can shape it by playing at politics and increasing its chances, but the final decision lies with others.

The overall conclusion of Chapter 6: Kurdistan's Independence and the International System of Sovereign States is that Kurdistan's chances to become a sovereign state significantly depends on which mood will prevail in the international arena – traditionalist/sovereignist or liberal. A greater emphasis on sovereignty would reduce the chances for independence and reinforce the need to gain Baghdad's consent for a civilized divorce. A conservative recognition regime would strengthen the currently robust sovereign territorial constraints and reduce the likelihood that numerous secessionist regions, not just Kurdistan, would be able to gain independence. On the other hand, a move in the direction of liberalism in world politics would benefit Kurdistan and many other nationalist movements by supporting the right to self-determination, perhaps opening the gate to independence via a remedial or primary right.

As of today, Kurdistan's chances are significantly constrained by the current recognition regime where emphasis is placed on sovereign consent and power politics in the international arena. Obviously, independence can be declared without consent from Baghdad, particularly if Kurdistan garners support from powerful friends and makes its bid in the context of broader state failure and regional instability. The current unrest in Iraq and Syria could open the path to Kurdish independence. Overall, Kurdistan's best move is to gain as much autonomy as possible, for as long as possible, and wait to see how conditions change, for better or for worse, at both the regional and international levels.

With the disarray in the Middle East, Turkey's foreign policy has undergone incredible metamorphoses in its recent reorientation of priorities from an assertive bid for EU membership to a more region-oriented policy, which has also suffered a serious blow. The recently proclaimed 'no problems with the neighbors' approach turned into a 'no neighbors without problem' outcome. Not a single friendly state remains in its neighborhood and a state of war has almost begun with Russia over Syria. Turkish foreign policy based on Turkey's grandiose view of itself in the region has been an abysmal failure.

In sharp contrast is Turkey's relationship with the Kurdish regional government in Iraq. The way the Turkish government has always treated ethnic Kurds at home and now in Syria makes this friendship bond even more paradoxical. The cordial relationship has significantly affected both the security and energy configurations in the Middle East. The Turkey-KRG relationship remains most advanced and integrated, comparing to its bilateral relations with other regional powers, based on mutual needs and shared interests. The relationship between the two sides is still anomalous in many ways. On both sides a sort of oligarchy emerged. The oligarchs, as experience in other countries shows, usually weaken democracy and poorly manage the economy. While the oligarchs are internally weak, they are also poor at managing a long-lasting relationship. These factors might put the Turkey-KRG relationship in jeopardy. In addition, external factors shape the relationship, such as the regional sectarian conflicts, the collapse of central states, and the competition of regional and global powers.

The Kurdish item on the US foreign policy agenda figures prominently in the context of Washington's strategy to remodel the greater Middle East. The Iraqi Kurdish federal region has actively engaged in Middle Eastern politics where the KRG has successfully maintained good relations with the West, particularly with the USA. Relations with the outside world have conveyed to the Kurdistan Region a certain degree of international acceptance and thereby legitimacy, but as a federal region, not a sovereign state.

US policy towards the Kurds, both in Iraq and Syria, is pretty much shaped by political expediency and by the desire to please several external players with various regional agendas, as well as its relationships with the Iraqi central government. Therefore, we witness "inconsistencies" while the Kurds see "betrayal." The interventionist explanatory framework used helped us to shed light on the inconsistencies of US policy towards Iraqi Kurdistan and its intentions to declare independence. The US has changed its attitude towards the Iraqi Kurds many times in recent history depending on the expediency of the moment and regional politics. By empowering the Kurds of Iraq, the US creates pressure in the Middle East in order to induce change of adverse behavior, leaving the Kurds to their own device when the situation changes.

These strategic considerations in US policy towards the Kurds continue into the present context of an Iraq riddled with sectarian conflict and the threat of ISIS. The relevant factor for this policy towards the Kurds becomes the protection of the Kurdistan Region, shaped by US regional interests. On the other hand, strategic considerations regarding the Kurds' value for combating ISIS may influence the possible provision of arms to the Kurds. The provision of arms to the Kurds invokes again the issue of Kurdish independence; given the US revealed indifference to this notion up to this point, we examine this salient dynamic in light of its potential appeal to the US' current instrumental agenda. Affective motivations of loyalty or justice arising out of the US-Kurdish alliance, which dominate the rhetoric surrounding independence, are insignificant influences on US decision-making. Similarly, increases in Kurdish mobilization will not significantly impact US policy per se because it will not substantially affect the US' strategic considerations. Moreover, increased Kurdish secessionism may be to their detriment in relation to US policy, as it will undermine the weight of their current strategic value to US policy in the Middle East.

Note

1 Let us recollect that in a card game, an ace in the hole is a card placed facedown which once turned over will have the certain effect of winning the game. In contrast, a "joker in the pack" is a card which could lead to different unexpected and unpredictable outcomes.

Index

abandoned buildings 88
advertisements 87–8
affective considerations 159, 164, 173–4, 176, 180
Al-Malki 140
Al-Qaeda 62
Algiers Agreement 106
Anfal campaign 107, 166, 179
Ansar al-Islam 62
Arabization campaign 35, 53
Ataturk 99, 104, 144
authoritarianism 20, 143

Baghdad 99, 105–07, 110, 114, 129–31, 136, 140–43, 145, 147, 150–51, 154, 158, 164–67, 173–74, 179
balance of power 16, 24, 145
Barzani, Masoud 3, 44, 65, 67, 76, 106, 111, 120, 146
Barzani, Mustafa 17–18, 91, 106
Barzani, Nechervan 45, 65, 67, 111
Bureaucracy 3, 14–15, 70, 72, 85, 90

Capitalism 14–15, 57, 71, 136–37, 144, 147–48
Chevron 136, 168
China 84, 122, 125–28
cleavages 5, 66
club good 121–22
Coalition Forces 36
coalition, party-political 68
conspiracy theories 85, 87
constitution 19, 23, 36–46, 48, 50–2, 93, 109, 136, 147, 188
constitutive theory of statehood 120
construction sites 87–8
corruption 67, 79, 84, 87, 91–3, 102, 104, 110–11, 136, 143, 189

Council of Representatives 41–2, 47
culture 14, 57–8, 64–5, 69, 74, 79, 80, 84, 87, 91, 93, 126, 139, 146, 149

Davutoglu 139–40
de facto statehood 124, 128
Declaratory theory of statehood 120, 127–28
devolution of power 40, 51, 188
disputed territories 48–9, 102

Electoral Law 43
elite 106, 135, 137–38, 140–44, 146–53, 172
elitism 68
enclave urbanism 82–4
Enlightenment 61
Erbil Agreement 48
Erdogan 6, 112–13, 138, 140, 145, 149
Eskandar 16–17
Ethnie 11, 14–15, 31
Ethnoscapism 60
Exxon 136, 168

federacy 40
federal government 19–20, 41–2, 45–6, 48, 51–2, 111
Federal Supreme Court of Cassation 43
federal accommodation 37
federal design 7, 36–8, 41
Federalism Law 39, 41
Federation Council 42, 46–7
Feudalism 58–9, 66, 70, 72
Fuad Masum 42, 46
Fundamentalism 29–31

gated communities 80, 82, 84
Gorran 19, 44–5, 48, 58, 65, 67–8, 74

Index

Governmentality 94
governorates 40–3, 45–7
Gramsci, Antonio 5, 59, 64, 66, 68–70
Gulf War 18, 26–7, 36, 135, 164, 176

hegemony 64, 149, 152–53
Higher Judicial Council 42
historicist 4, 57

ISIS 167–71, 173–75, 177, 188, 191
Identity 15–16, 22, 35, 37, 49–51, 60, 62, 64, 91, 102–04, 106, 114–16, 121–22, 135, 138, 145, 151–53, 159, 187–88
Ideology 14, 15, 18, 21, 31, 61–3, 70, 144, 148–49, 151
Independence 17, 21, 26, 28, 30–1, 37–9, 58–9, 65, 69, 71, 73–5, 99–100, 102, 114–16, 120–32, 135–36, 142, 150–53, 159, 165, 170–75, 177
Inequality 83, 91–2, 139
instrumental considerations 159, 163, 167, 170, 176
international regime 163, 165, 167–68, 170–72, 174
international system 6, 103, 109, 120–22, 126–27, 129, 131, 160, 162–63, 189–90
intervention framework 159–60, 171, 173, 175–76
Iran 2–3, 12–15, 18, 22, 24, 29–31, 35, 61, 65, 106–08, 114, 116, 130, 139–40, 142, 145, 149–51, 159–60, 163–64, 166, 188
Iraqi Accord Front 41
Iraqi Bill of Rights 40
Iraqi Kurdistan Parliament 43
Iraqi Presidency 42, 46, 52
Iraqi Supreme Court 39, 43, 47
Islamic Movement of Kurdistan 61
Islamic State of Iraq and al-Sham (ISIS) 61
Islamic Virtue Party 41

Jalal Talabani 42, 46, 65, 106, 111, 146
Judicial review powers 42

Kemalist 35, 146–47, 149
Kurdish issue 7, 24, 27, 101, 142, 152, 158–60, 176
Kurdish Regional Government (KRG) 61, 121, 190

Kurdish independence 120, 129–32, 159, 165, 170–71, 173–75, 177, 190–91
Kurdish rebellions 35
Kurdistan Democratic Party 17, 19, 44, 65, 106
Kurdistan Islamic Group 61
Kurdistan Islamic Union 61
Kurdistan Oil and Gas Law 46

Liberal/Liberalism 6, 63, 65, 67, 79, 107, 109, 121, 123–24, 126–31, 144, 165, 190

Marx, Karl 5, 58–9, 70, 74, 188
Materiality 92, 94
Military 1–3, 18–20, 27, 40, 99, 104, 106, 109, 112, 114, 141, 144–45, 150, 152, 162–64, 167–69, 173, 188
Modernity 5, 29, 57, 59, 61–3, 66, 69, 79, 93, 139–40, 189
Modernization 13–15, 22, 146
Mohammad Pasha 12
Motherland Party 144
multinational democracies 37
mythomoteur 60

National Defense Authorization Act, 2016
national identity 16, 35, 37, 49, 60, 64, 121, 187
national popularity 66
nationalism 2–4, 12–17, 22–23, 30–31, 37, 52, 57–8, 60–4, 73, 78, 114–15, 124, 140, 152, 161, 187
nepotism 67, 110
non-state actors (NSA) 131, 141, 189

oil, oil revenues 110–12
oil-based economy 146
oligarchy capitalism 136, 148
one-state policy 130
oriental despotism 70
orientalism 69
Ottoman Empire 1, 11, 13, 15–16, 22, 35, 99, 104–05, 110, 187
Özal, Turgut 144

paradox of federalism 38, 51–2, 108, 188
passive revolution 69, 74
Patriotic Union of Kurdistan 19, 44, 46, 65, 106, 111
Persian Gulf 71

Peshmerga 48, 61, 86, 106, 114, 169–71, 173, 175
policy-making process 162
power sharing 45
powers of the federal government 45–6
powers of the regions 40, 45
pre-modern 5, 58, 62–3, 66, 69, 71, 74, 127–28, 189
primary right 127–31, 190
public symbols 94

rational-legal society 67–8, 72
recognition regime 122–29, 131, 190
regional schism 5, 58
religion 13, 21–2, 29, 50, 58, 61–3, 67, 99, 144, 150
remedial right 126–30
rentier state 59, 71–5, 104, 106, 188–89
Republic of Mahabad 35
Responsibility to Protect (R2P) 123
Russia 2–3, 13, 21–3, 28, 112–13, 116, 122, 125–27, 138, 151, 190

Saddam Hussein 18, 61, 64, 106–08, 116, 150, 187
Sadrist movement 41
Saudi Arabia 61, 84, 100, 107, 149–50, 163
Schlmerger 136
secession 3, 38–9, 108, 123–32, 147, 163, 168, 171–74, 189
secularism 14, 22, 62, 147
Security Council 28, 122
self-determination 28, 58, 63, 124–25, 128–29, 131, 132, 190
Shell 136
Shia 1, 20, 23, 26, 29–31, 43, 107, 114, 135, 141, 150
Simko Agha 13
simulations 88
Southern Kurds 3, 7, 37
sovereignty 17, 36, 58, 69, 103, 107, 120–23, 125–31, 136, 168, 190

sovereignty club 121, 123, 125, 128, 131
sui generis 126, 129, 131
Sulaymaniyah 65–8
Sunni 1–2, 23, 26, 29, 39, 41–3, 49, 50, 52, 61, 99, 106, 109, 112, 114, 130, 135, 140–41, 150, 170, 175
symmetrical and asymmetrical federalism 37

taxation 72, 104
Tehran 18, 143, 150, 175
territorial integrity 6, 25, 36, 129, 132, 135, 153
traditional society 67
Transitional Administrative Law (TAL)
trasformismo (transformation)
tribalism 21, 59
Turkey 2–3, 6–7, 13–15, 22, 24, 30, 35, 45, 61, 65, 81, 86, 99, 104, 112–13, 130, 135, 138–40, 144–53, 159–60, 165, 167, 176, 189–90

US foreign policy 7, 158, 160–162, 175–76, 191
unitary assimilative integration 37
United Nations General Assembly 121
United States 25, 30, 37, 45, 113, 122, 124–26, 130, 136, 139, 150, 166, 168, 170, 174
uprising 4, 11, 13, 29, 35–3, 106, 141, 150, 165, 188
urbanisation 83

war of position 64
Weber, Max 59, 66–8, 73, 93, 137

Yezidis 48

Zebari, Babaker Shawkat 46
Zebari, Hoshyar 46
Zero Problem Policy 139, 145